Green Nation

The Irish Environmental Movement
from
Carnsore Point to the Rossport 5

Liam Leonard

Ecopolitics Series Vol. II
Greenhouse/Choice Publishing

*carnsore point-anti nuclear-tynagh mines-donegal
uranium-mullaghmore-burren action-cork
environmental-alliance
meath no incineration alliance-galway for a safe
environment-chase cork harbour for a safe
environment-shell to sea-rossport five-glen of the
downs-carrickmines-tara-skryne*

IBSN: 1-905451-11-3

A CIP catalogue for this book is available from the National Library.

Printed in Ireland.

This book was published by Greenhouse Press in cooperation with Choice Publishing & Book Services, Drogheda, Co. Louth, Ireland.
Tel. 041 9841551 Email : info@choicepublishing.ie
www.choicepublishing.ie

Green Nation: The Irish Environmental Movement from Carnsore Point to the Rossport Five.

Liam Leonard

Ecopolitics Series Volume II
Greenhouse/Choice Publishing

Environmental Change Institute
National University of Ireland, Galway, Ireland

Acknowledgements

The author would like to acknowledge the following people for their support and assistance: my family, Greenhouse Press, Michelle at Choice Publishing. Eileen Leonard, John Doorty; my colleagues at the Department of Political Science and Sociology at NUI Galway; the Community and Environmental Studies Association of Ireland including Brendan Flynn and Vesna Malesevic; Chris Curtin, Tony Varley, Su ming Khoo, Brian McGrath, Henrike Rau, Mark Haugaard and Ricca Edmondson and the Social Science Research Centre NUIG, Mary Cawley, Mark Garavan, Robert Allen, Gearoid Mannion, and George Taylor.

The author would like to thank the Environmental Change Institute, NUI Galway, including Development Officer Martina Prendergast and Director Emer Colleran for their support in funding this book. He would like to acknowledge the Environmental Change Institute and the National University of Ireland Galway Press Office for the cover photographs for this book.

He would also like to dedicate this work to the many people who have participated in the environmental campaigns that have made up the grassroots movement in Ireland, and acknowledge their part in providing information for this book on the websites, free-sheets or pamphlets mentioned in the work.

While many continue to debate the issues surrounding environmental disputes, communities remain committed to defending their hinterlands from risk. These actions are sometimes dismissed as 'irrational' or emotive. However, when faced with the degradation of local environments, the responses of the communities featured in this book are perhaps the most rational responses of human beings whose very lives are defined by the hinterlands they inhabit. This book purports to analyse these responses, rather than provide answers to the vexed questions of economic growth, waste and resource management and infrastructural planning in a rapidly modernising country such as the Republic of Ireland. Despite this, the responses of the communities covered in this work can be said to represent a positive aspect of pluralistic society, which should be valued for their contribution to the ongoing dialogue about the future of this *Green Nation.*

About the Author

Dr. Liam Leonard lectures in Environmental Politics and Social Movements in NUI Galway. He has written on environmental movements, including a study of the campaign against incineration in Ireland. His current research interests include collective action, environmental politics and policy, political sociology and community access to education. Future works will include a study of institutional approaches to environmentalism in Ireland.

Recent releases by this author

Ecopolitics Series Volume I:
Politics Inflamed: Galway for a Safe Environment and the Campaign against Incineration in Ireland

Ecopolitics Series Volume II:
Green Nation: The Irish Environmental Movement from Carnsore Point to the Rossport Five

Forthcoming releases from this author

Ecopolitics Volume III:
Planning a Green Future: Environmental Politics and Policy in Ireland

Contents

Preface

Although many academics, writers and commentators have grappled with the social and political responses to disputes about the introduction of industrial plants or the development of infrastructure in Ireland, few books have been written on the subject. *Green Nation* addresses this gap in the literature about the environmentally based community social movements which have emerged since the 1970s. These campaigns have been primarily rural, while disputes in the cities outside of Dublin such as Cork and Galway have retained a rural perspective as local communities came to identify themselves with the surrounding hinterlands in the face of modernisation. Throughout the years of state sponsored multinational led development and post boom infrastructural expansion, local communities have proven themselves to be adept at mobilising responses, framing arguments and establishing the networks and alliances that become possible in a populist society.

The processes of mobilisation and framing responses to perceived risks have drawn on existing reserves of what I have termed *rural sentiment*, or the commonly held understandings and beliefs which lie underneath the surface of everyday life in rural Ireland. This rural sentiment has been formed over time, emerging in response to local incidents throughout Ireland's colonial history and fermenting into a subconscious belief system which is called upon in times of collective threat. As society faces into problems created by growth, consumption and waste, traditional scepticism about mass urbanisation and industrialisation in rural communities is resurfacing and finding expression in community based opposition to the imposition of major industrial or infrastructural projects. This expression is rooted in the very landscape threatened by such expansive development, and as such is the basis for the articulation of a community based environmentalism in Ireland, born from the experiences of the past, while shaping the politics of the future.

Chapter One

Territorialism, Rural Sentiment and the Irish Environmental Movement

Introduction

In August 2005 a large crowd gathered at the Spanish Arch in Galway city in support of the "Rossport 5" who had been imprisoned because of their stance against a gas pipeline through their community. A succession of speakers lambasted the state for selling out "our" resources to the multinational sector over many decades. For some observers the rally indicated a return to the rhetoric of the past, as a form of cultural nationalism which has particular resonances in rural Ireland, was invoked by many of those addressing the supporters. As a cultural discourse this rhetoric has its roots in rural Ireland's resistance to authority which can be traced back to colonial times.

In attempting to define the sociology of the rural in 1992, Hilary Tovey surmises that Irish rural sociology has been understood as 'sociology of farming' (Tovey 1992a p. 97). This analysis equates rurality with an agricultural way of life, once deemed to have a primary significance by the state, but now under threat from political and socio-economic fixations with technologically derived modernisation. The traditional agricultural sector which spawned the 'informed institutions of municipal support provided by the local community' (ibid) have given way to the systems of globalised capitalism as new forms of production have been introduced through scientific and technological innovations. As the process of market-led efficiency favoured larger producers over the last fifty years small holdings and their traditionally rural way of life have been eroded.
At the same time, the state has attempted to inject new patterns of production and lifestyle into rural communities, through its agenda for multinational-led development (O'Hearn 1998). In

so doing, a new understanding of rurality can be identified; this extends the connotation of rural as primarily agricultural towards a new conceptualisation of rural as environmental. Moreover, the interaction of rural communities with their hinterlands takes on an integrative aspect, beyond the production based model which was derived from an emphasis on farming activity alone. It follows that the recent engagement with environmental issues in an era when agricultural production has shifted from localised practices to the multinational agribusiness section would be reflected through emergent notions about the very basis of what is meant by the rural.

While Tovey cites Curtin's maxim that rural agricultural lifestyles could be defined through 'a form of production which … is embedded in sets of non-commoditised relationships' (Curtin 1986 in Tovey 1992a p 100), contemporary concerns about the environment may have reconstituted these arrangements as a form of relationship embedded in a set of traditionalist and community centred interactions that go beyond production. Essentially, Curtin has anticipated the emergence of a predominantly consumerist commoditisation of both farming produce and community relationships in the post-economic boom era. In addition, this new set of commoditised relations involving communities as mass consumers has foisted a post-productionist crisis about waste management and infrastructural development on a rural population still in transition in recent years.

The structural transition from traditional practice to modern economic setting led to an increased sense of marginalisation in rural communities (Kelleher and O'Mahony 1984). For this reason, longstanding suspicions and hostility directed towards the authorities in Dublin or Brussels have been reinforced at a time when the imposition of environmental directives had further alienated that sector of the population (Leonard 1999). From this ferment of discord the simmering rancour inherent in much of rural fundamentalism can be found. Such malcontent cannot be assuaged by state or EU handouts, which seem to have been paid over to accelerate the demise of the small holder, in any event. The much vaunted subsidies paid out to farmers to alter or prevent traditional practices are a bitter stipend, increasing the sense of desolation amongst its recipients who have, at times, been lampooned as ungrateful cheque-grabbers at a time when their very way of life has been decimated.

The state's response to increased dissent in rural areas has been two-fold: promoting 'rural development' while increasingly broadening the extent of infrastructural and industrial growth. Subsequently a type of rural industrialisation has emerged involving the onset of 'part-time farming' which theoretically allows farmers to maintain their links to small scale agricultural practice while simultaneously becoming viable economic units working a multinational industry. The combination of a self-sufficient but otherwise unskilled and non-unionised labour force was one that many multinationals, as well as influential local interests, found attractive and easy to exploit (Tovey 1992a, p.109).   The first section of this book will examine the articulation of dissent from rural populations who felt that their people and environment has been violated by the onset of rural industrialisation. Rural opposition to large-scale infrastructural projects such as mines, nuclear plants or toxic industries formed the basis of the first wave of community opposition to what was perceived as a threat to local ways of life, community relations and values, personal health and environment in the regions.

While rural communities may not be as rooted in the type of mutual dependency represented in Arensberg and Kimball's seminal study on life in the Irish countryside, a strong sense of identity and place still characterises life in the regions, creating an 'ideology of community' (Harris, 1984 p. 171). Ultimately, 'rural community' may be defined through embodiment of a response by the periphery exploitation of the institutional core at the centre of power. The fact that 'rural' remains an important 'mobilising concept within Irish society' (Tovey 1992a, p.111) during an era when many of the grand narratives of Irish society have become diminished is testament to the crucial nature of individual, family and community relations with the surrounding hinterlands, landscape and earth in which those rural populations are embedded. The extent of this entrenchment has been characterised through the response of rural communities to the perceived threats posed by industrialisation and changing patterns of consumption and waste in an era when Irish society has been dramatically altered. Seen in that context, rural communities' opposition to the destruction of 'a sustainable, ecologically managed way of life for the short term benefit of outsiders (Varley 1991 b p. 186) is not surprising, but rather represents an articulation of defence of space, lifestyle and environment by a social group who are concerned about the degradation of all that they hold dear.

This book examines the mobilisation of environmental community campaigns over the last forty years and also gives an analysis of community mobilisation over two phases. The origin of this mobilisation brings us back to the 1970s when Irish communities began to resist state policy agendas aimed at introducing toxic or nuclear industries in rural or suburban areas. We will analyse these campaigns through the application of resource mobilisation (RM) theory and present an understanding of collective access frames and political opportunity structure (POS) to illuminate certain areas of commonality and differences successive community campaigns have shared. In so doing, the book will demonstrate the manner in which a pool of community resources and environmental consciousness fermented over the decades which encompassed the twenty first century.

In addition, the particularist nature of Irish politics, including its clientelism, populism and increased dependence on coalitional politics will be placed in the context of the comprehensive accounts of community politics (Varley 1991, Curtin and Varley 1991, 1995), which will provide us with an overview of how the Irish case presents a framework of community based environmental politics that has notable differences to existing Anglo-American or European models.

One of the most significant differences identified in this book is that the inception of environmental campaigns in Ireland is derived from the groundswell of cultural nationalism which formed the backdrop to community life in rural regions across the country. Neither can the resistance of local communities which is rooted in a colonial mistrust of both Dublin and London and which has more recently been extended to include a disdain for the officialdom of the EU or 'big shots' from US multinationals, be dismissed simply as a form of NIMBYism, as such community identity has a local basis but has been shaped by a wider and shared identity.

Moreover, community based environmental campaigns have drawn on a type of cultural nationalism that is characterised by a rural traditionalism which has, at certain times, been infused with new left radicalism, moralistic dogma, ecological consciousness and a concern for the land of generations gone or yet to come that defines rural identity and shaped the meanalities of landscape and resource contestation.

In many environmental responses to perceived threats, defence of space campaigns can be better understood as 'territorial' rather than NIMBYist. Traditionally, rural communities have formed a collective identity based on their relationship with their local landscape, particularly in the years before independence when people did not have a state or flag to demonstrate their allegiance to. Since the formation of the state the spatial divide between the rural periphery and the urban core has been replicated with the location of the core of power changing from London to Dublin and later Brussels, or even corporate headquarters in the United States. What is clear is that the dichotomy between rural communities and urban-based elites has been an ongoing feature of Irish society over the centuries and in some ways represents a type of class division within our society between an urbanised elite with links to the political or economic core and local communities that remain marginalised due to this ongoing spatial hierarchy. Therefore, we can include urban-based population in cities such as Cork and Galway in this understanding of territorial distinction within the traditional demarcation of 'the West' as represented by phrases such as 'beyond the pale', 'all points west of the Shannon' or 'the line running from Derry to Cork'. Many of the territorial based environmental disputes in Ireland have occurred west of that imaginary boundary.

Essentially we can look to writers such as David Storey (2001) for an understanding of how territorialism informs community responses to the perception of risk. We can also acknowledge that these responses involve the mobilisation of what I call a rural sentiment by advocates who wish to preserve local ways of life or environments. In the case of Irish environmentalism territory is defined by local discourse rather than boundaries except perhaps for the county allegiance which has been developed as an integral part of the ideology of the GAA which is now recognised as an important component in the formation of social capital in the regions. When it comes to environmental disputes the mobilisation of territorial responses derived from traditional rural sentiment or more recently formed local identities represents the political articulation of progressive social capital as such local responses empower communities in an era of globalised economy and culture. And it is within this understanding that new sections of the population have been assimilated with many providing wider networks and areas of expertise for campaigns which have allowed communities to challenge globalised corporate entities on a more equal footing. Without doubt, as I have indicated in my book on anti-incinerator campaigns it is the utilisation of the internet and communication technologies that has underpinned this increased flow of expertise networks for campaigns allowing them to move 'beyond NIMBY' as Szasz (1994) has stated or to emerge from their initial territorial response.

Politically this form of expansive territorialism allows environmental campaigns to challenge the spatial exclusion caused by the neo-corporatist model prevalent in Ireland. While partnership has served many sectors in society like unions and employers well, its focus on economic growth has also led to the exclusion of other sectors of the population such as women's groups, the poor and environmentalists. As local authorities have had many of their powers removed territorial campaigns have come to represent the grassroots in the regions articulating a 'bottom up' response to the neo-corporate core which prioritises multinational agendas over local concerns.   And despite the emphasis on rural development in the National Development Plans it is quite evident that multinational-led growth remains the economic priority for the state. For Storey, sub-state regional development is part of the hegemonic process of state dominance. Nonetheless, we can see that neo-corporatist exclusion provides the political opportunity for territorial campaigns to mobilise around environmental issues. Equally the inherent populism which characterises Irish politics provides leverage for campaigns, for instance, at times of elections when the coalitions formed from necessity due to the returns of PRSTV can be undermined. However as my study on the GSE campaign has shown this leverage is only temporary as the neo-corporatist core soon reasserts itself in the aftermath of post-election government formation.

While the traditional clientelism renowned in Irish politics allows territorial groups local political access the spatial dichotomy extended to rural communities can include its political representatives particularly that most isolated breed the backbencher from a rural constituency.   While the GSE campaign attempted to gain access to the power core as represented by the cabinet this led to a loss of support from their own grassroots, a fatal outcome for any territorial campaign.

As neo-corporatism comes to represent the triumph of economically based sectional interests over others territorial groups become more reliant on the input of new middle class professionals who become the entrepreneurs or advocates of environmental disputes. These advocates retain a degree of economic autonomy from the state's neo-corporatist plans despite or perhaps because they may be in the employ of the state as academics or researchers. In many cases the adversaries of the territorial advocate can be the technocratic advisor who creates a contest between competing sets of expertise, a forum which has up until recently provided equal footing for advocates who often outperform their technocratic opponents. Invariably, many territorial advocates are charismatic figures whereas the technocrat remains an untrusting, secretive figure and the media performances of advocates such as GSE's Conchuair O'Brádaigh or Shell to Sea's Mark Garavan are a testimony to this.

However, recent events have demonstrated that the advocate is coming under threat from the neo- corporatist elite who have come to view territorially-based campaigns as NIMBYist or self interested missing the significance of rural responses to environmental issues. We can say that the nature of the ruling against Robert Salafia over The M3 at Tara, and the tone of subsequent articles in the press are in keeping with a climate of intolerance which has been demonstrated in the needless and unjust imprisoning of the Rossport 5, the censure of the Centre for Public Inquiry after their reports on Trim Castle and the Shell pipeline, and the treatment of John Hanrahan. And yet, despite these events, I remain optimistic that environmental advocacy has been a significant factor in the consolidation of a nascent environmental lobby, built from a series of campaigns which began at Carnsore Point with the anti-nuclear protests and have culminated in the Shell to Sea campaign. So then, how can we define this loose coalition of disparate territorial groups?

Writing in 2002, Hilary Tovey posed the question: 'when is a campaign a movement?' We can look to the recent writings of Charles Tilly (2004), who claims that a movement emerges from interaction of 'political circuits'. Therefore, a movement occurs when a campaign moves beyond a single event or localised focus and results in the interplay of activists' planning and agitating together resonating against the seemingly impenetrable walls of the neo-corporatist elite, leading ultimately to the achievement of social or political change. And as growth and greed come to threaten the environment all the more, it is this challenge to neo-corporatism that provides the environmental sector with its greatest difficulties and opportunities.

It is not a coincidence that we as a society are searching for a way to accommodate environmental perspectives at a time when accelerating rates of growth challenge our ability to protect and conserve the nation's hinterlands. At a time when negotiations for partnership have recommenced between business the government and unions we might ask the question as to why environmentalists remain excluded from the neo-corporatist table. Surely, a state which purports to embrace the concept of sustainable development would be better served in reaching out to the environmental lobby in an inclusive manner? However, like women's groups or the economically disadvantaged environmentalists have found to their cost that participation in partnerships is the sole preserve of those involved in the generation of financial wealth.

The imperative of economic growth through multinational-led development first set out by Lemass and Whitaker in the 1950s has served the country well, as indeed has the partnership model. Nonetheless, as the Good Friday Agreement has demonstrated, it is only when those diametrically opposed to each other build consensus that progress based on social inclusiveness can be achieved. For those involved with environmental issues in Ireland inclusiveness remains elusive with competing sets of interests vying against each other in an attempt to convince the wider public that their perspective is the only way forward. Adversaries are depicted as sinister polluters or self interested 'NIMBYs' with little or no dialogue between the two. At the centre of this debate are representatives of the state, parties of government or relevant agencies such as the EPA or An Bord Pleanála. In many cases the only dialogue between both groups is provided through the courts, with environmental advocates providing the expertise, and sometimes bearing the cost, of these challenges.

There is little doubt that environmental advocates have made a significant contribution to the development of a coherent civil society in Ireland over recent decades. In *Green Nation: the Irish Environmental Movement from Carnsore Point to the Rossport 5*, I will examine the emergence of a community-based environmental movement in Ireland which has articulated the grievances of rural communities over projects perceived to carry environmental or human health risks. These projects can be divided into two phases. In the first, pre-Celtic Tiger phase communities mobilised against multinationals that had relocated from the US to escape regulation or against energy sources like nuclear power which represented the worst elements of what Ulrick Beck has called 'risk society'. The second phase, which has come in the years subsequent to economic growth, involves campaigns against infrastructural projects such as sewage treatment plants, incinerators and landfills as the state struggles to deal with the waste which is a by-product of increased rates of consumption (Leonard 2005).

Throughout both phases of community based collective action one common theme has been the importance of environmental advocates who provide leadership, mobilise responses to commonly held grievances and articulate a path for campaigns that move away from initial concerns about local issues into something that Szasz has described as going 'beyond NIMBY' into a form of environmentalism that can embrace wider issues of national or global importance.

The cases I have researched indicate that many local campaigns have taken this path and a network of national and international ecological activism has emerged which complements existing levels of mainstream environmentalism such as An Taisce or the Green Party. All of the campaigns examined in the book achieve some level of networked environmentalism where the shared knowledge and expertise of prior campaigns is drawn upon or added to, creating an important layer of civil society which is a key tenet of pluralistic democracy. The one exception is the tragic case of Tynagh mines where the local community's isolation from other environmental groups concerned about resources left the local community struggling to put up even a basic backyard campaign, never mind evolving into a more coherent ecopolitical grouping. As a result of this inability to mobilise effectively, the Tynagh hinterland and waterways were scarred and polluted with demands for reclamation going unanswered.

As we know, the campaign to prevent the mining of Croagh Patrick in Mayo, which occurred at that time, had more success thanks to a strong campaign led by the local Archbishop and links with the campaign against mining in Donegal. Moreover, some of those involved in the 'Shell to Sea' campaign took their first steps along the environmental path during the Croagh Patrick dispute, something perhaps which Shell overlooked when they planned their pipeline across the Mayo countryside. For many environmental campaigns, the existence of experienced and committed activists in a region becomes a valuable resource in the process of mobilisation.

The importance of environmental advocates was also witnessed during the Mullaghmore dispute, when Emer Colleran and others were able to combine their expertise with a locally held understanding of the ecological significance of the Burren region. Again the contribution of local advocates became more potent when engaged with international figures from the legal or environmental world who could demonstrate, with Professor Colleran, that the Burren should be protected from the impacts of tourism development. Without doubt, the actions of Emer Colleran and her colleagues at Mullaghmore represent a major contribution to the conservation of a region which is an area of special environmental value for people across Ireland and the world.

So, then how can we define these territorial campaigns as an environmental movement? We can apply Fine's 1995 definition of movement culture as one of 'public narration' as a framework for understanding the significance of environmental activism. For Fine, movements are defined by their development of group culture based on shared goals attained through shared beliefs and knowledge. By using the tools of group culture such as political activism, a social reality is constructed which challenges and redefines our cultural expectations. *Green Nation* examines the emergence of territorially derived group culture which has come to define the campaigns of socio-political and culture resistance to the modernising projects of the state or industrial sector.

Fine highlights the concept of a movement as a 'staging area' for social interaction and cultural expression. This process is undertaken through a process which encompasses three main movements:

- Group identification
- The rituals of activism
- The mobilisation of resources
            (Fine 1995)

The culmination of this process is a 'public performance' which enhances democratic values through political activism, while extending the knowledge once held by experts into the public domain, empowering society in an age of contested expertise. At this point, we can say that the 'public performance' of campaigns such as Shell to Sea has been particularly effective in the mobilisation of wider public support for its cause.   Rural territorial campaigns have opened up a socio-cultural narrative at a key point of departure in Irish society, as we move into a post-consumptionist phase, providing an integrity which is all too often lacking in the behaviour of prominent politicians and cabinet ministers. So where has this environmental territorialism with integrity emerged from?

There are many competing understandings surrounding community-based environmental disputes in Ireland with almost as many accounts as there are participants or advocates who often baulk at the sobriet of 'environmentalist'. Environmental scientists also take a different viewpoint calling for accuracy and expertise during debates about the anthropocentric development of the landscape while the technocratic advisers employed by the multinationals or the state always find enough evidence to demonstrate the safety of their technology – no matter how many complaints such technologies have raised in the past. Therefore, we can see many environmental disputes as debates about rational choice. For communities the scientific evidence which demonstrates the safety of technologies provides little comfort when prior campaigns have argued about the inherent risks posed by the same technologies. And so many disputes become contests between rational science versus community concerns with one side marshalling data and the other mobilising grievance. Set in this context it seems difficult to imagine that communities can bring themselves to accept infrastructure or technologies until after they have been proven to be safe. Such is the nature of the 'risk society' outlined by Ulrick Beck (1992).

How will we come to understand community-based environmental disputes within the context of the paradigms of consumption and choice? Using the rational underpinning consumption-based behaviour, scientists advocates and the community adopt particularistic roles within the process of accepting change within the context of modernisation. And yet the state or multinational, despite their array of technocrats scientists and consultants, often fail to recognise the unpopularity of the technology they are attempting to introduce be it nuclear power, sewage treatment plants, incinerators or gas pipelines. From the community perspective technologies or infrastructure are understood in three stages. At the 'pre-issue' stage communities come to an understanding about the pros and cons of the technology being introduced. During the 'issue-acceptance' stage communities attempt to comprehend the competing expertise provided by consultants in favour of or advocates who oppose technologies or infrastructure. At the 'post-issue' stage the functional performance of any new technology or infrastructure is assessed providing that technology or infrastructure is actually introduced. Environmental impacts are assessed at this stage and poor performance or results may lead to further mobilisation against the offending project. In this way we can see that the process whereby projects are introduced to (or imposed on) communities has become part of the culture of the modernising state. Segments of the community may then feel the need to resist modernisation at certain moments where technology or infrastructure is anticipated as too great a risk.

In the absence of the recognition of community concerns by the authorities advocates can mobilise grievance by establishing 'consensus' (Klandermans 1989) built from symbiotic understandings of local heritage with a nostalgic sentiment for an era characterised by understandings formed from local discourse. Once re-ignited this form of what I term *rural sentiment* can be mobilised through collective activity which allows communities to share the experience of communal resistance to projects, leading to enhanced integration, communication and participation. By moving beyond the single issue surrounding the technology or infrastructure being challenged local campaigns can open up networks with global movements which provide expertise and data that can be used to challenge the science of the state or multinational. And while projects are introduced to address a social need which the state has identified through its policy framework, the response of communities is based on a competing set of needs that emerge in the pre-issue stage. These community based needs are constituted from within, in what the 'Shell to Sea' advocate Mark Garavan has described as a 'visceral' response based on fear of large-scale projects. This is a fear which scientists dismiss as irrational but it is a fear which is all too natural when viewed from the perspective of members of the public who have grown up in an era where risk and toxicity have become a feature of popular culture, appearing in films, books and even cartoons with the classic 'good guy' advocate challenging the 'mad scientist' and the 'evil corporate entity'. The state, which is viewed with suspicion in an era of democratic deficit driven by successive corruption-based 'scandals' is seen as a compliant facilitator of multinational agendas.

Within this dynamic of social change community based environmental campaigns have become an integral part of the rights-based autonomous politics which spawns the new social movements. These environmentally based social movements emerge from a range of issues including social psychology and group behaviour, economics and the consumer society, demographic change within the context of urban sprawl and the cultural setting that creates an anthropologically or historically derived territorial response from within a community that feels threatened by risk-based projects. Within this understanding of collective behaviour the responses of communities in the face of risk are anything but irrational.

It follows, then, that environmental perspectives can be divided into two competing paradigms. One is dominated by a science-based positivistic rational which holds that modern technology can provide a functional answer to existing social or ecological problems. The other perspective has emerged from an age of scepticism and takes a post-modern view which questions or interprets the material assumptions and grand narratives of science. Both perspectives are embedded in current socio-cultural thought and in that context community-based interpretivist responses to large scale projects, should be seen as one form of rationality rather than being dismissed for not conforming to another. As the state continues to exclude community-based environmental groups when introducing major projects social movement mobilisation becomes part of a conditional response to neo-corporatistconstraints. It is part of a process of socialised behaviour where each subsequent campaign draws on the existing knowledge of prior disputes to formulate their challenges. In many cases a community wishes to be seen to take a strong stance in defence of their territory to be seen in keeping with the sacrifices and challenges of the past.

It is this reinforced and accumulative sentiment that provides part of the motivation for collective action responses to perceived risks. The backdrop to Irish history has encoded interpretivistic (Solomon 2002) responses into the collective folk memory of our rural communities by way of a series of key events such as the Land Wars of the late 1800s. These understandings form what Giddens has described as 'practical consciousnesses'. This form of social encoding can become part of an ongoing interpretive or 'discursive consciousness' (Haugaard 1997 p. 179) that can be drawn upon to formulate understandings based on traditional perspectives at times of accelerated change. While science-based meanings tend to be presented in a fixed manner, due in part to their technocratic presentation, the 'interpretative horizons'(ibid) which shape local discourses during territorial disputes can be a potent source in the formation of collective responses to perceived threats from outsiders, be they state or multinational. When faced with the certainty of science, the emotive responses of communities during environmental disputes can draw on encoded local understandings in the process of articulating a coherent challenge to infrastructural developments providing a degree of equality until such time as rural based sentiment is dissipated, which in the Irish case usually occurs during the ubiquitous 'oral hearing' (Peace 1997).

We can place these interpretivistic contests within the concepts of structure and agency where deterministic understandings about social responses are formulated. Of course, individuals and communities are not constrained by the collective consciousness formed over the ages. Nonetheless, the social relationships of a region shape that region's perception of what is internal or external. The commonly-held structures which form community sentiment create an institutionalised, or learned, response when faced with external risks. The flow of knowledge becomes part of the associative process by which a community defines itself and formulates responses. By forming extended linkages with communities that have previously dealt with similar technological or infrastructural risk, a network of consensus can be built, transforming disparate campaigns into a movement. One of the integral figures involved in this transformative process is the advocate or interest-led expert who provides the expertise necessary to authenticate campaigns that would otherwise decline in the face of positivistic interrogation during legal challenges. It can be said that environmental campaigns operate at two levels of rationality within the shared understandings of territorial consciousnesses as well as in the more pragmatic realm of shared knowledge which can inform challenges to technocratic science. Community responses formed from rural sentiment are triggered by advocates or 'entrepreneurs'(Della Porta and Diani 1999) who harvest the grievances held by rural communities in order to create the motivation for collective action. While some responses are more instinctively driven by the threat of whatever project is being imposed motivations for collective action are invariably driven by the advocate who manages such responses.

This shaping of community motivation is part of the agenda setting which occurs at the inception of a campaign and sets the tone for the initial phase of that action. The cognitive process where communities map out a response is a complex one and the depth of collective identity built from adversity has underpinned much of the interpretative cognisance in the Irish case. We can understand the formation of this response as part of a hierarchy of basic grievances or concerns for communities. Ranging from the need for safety from risk and protection for domestic environments at the basic level through to the fulfilment of collective capacities by association with and mobilisation of community through moral framing the process of collective action can ultimately provide communities with significant levels of esteem and accomplishment in an age of contested legitimation or democratic deficit. Ultimately, environmentally-based activism creates an important stratum of a pluralistic democracy allowing peripheral social groups to create evolutional and political interaction with the core.

Chapter Two

Meanings of Environmentalism

Introduction

"Thus even nature is not nature, but rather a concept, norm, memory, utopia, counter image" (Beck 1995, p.38).

We will explore how environmentalism has come to be understood in society and how this understanding, in turn, has shaped responses to environmental crises. Inherent in these responses has been a growing questioning of aspects of industrialised development and related patterns of consumption which have had a major impact on the environment. This questioning has led to the rise of 'green politics' which has become characterised by localised protests and disputes, but which forms the basis of the modern environmental movement.

In particular, we will outline the various forms of ecological thinking which have come to define environmental political approaches. Eckersley argues that a 'division can be identified between anthropocentric and eco-centric environmentalism'. From these distinct paradigms, new forms of environmental practices can be understood, including the separate rise of 'deep green and eco-modernist discourses'. Here, a distinction can be found in the theoretical and ideological constructions of environmentalism. At the heart of this distinction is an acceptance or rejection of human development as it has existed since the industrial revolution.

In other words, the question posed by an examination of these divides would be: Does the Western Liberal notion of humankind's 'natural' rights of freedom go so far as to allow the type of environmental destruction currently happening throughout the world? Clearly, deep green and eco-centric politics reject this. And as the rise in the politics of environmental protest show, many people have decided to question and reject current development models, in favour of an improved coexistence with the environment. Of course, like other political forms, environmentalism has areas of ideological overlapping in many paradigmatic areas, but the distinction between deep green radicalism and a 'shallow' compromise which tolerates high levels of pollution for profit can be clearly identified. The 'deep green' position, as articulated by Dobson (1990), argues for a 'limit to growth' and understands 'sustainable' to mean no sustainable damage to the earth rather than the 'sustainable pollution' ethic found in the concept of ecological modernisation. As such, deep green politics argues for an ecocentric society, which places an intrinsic value on the environment, above any consideration of profit or structural development.

It was Eckersley (1992) who first defined the distinction between the eco-centric and anthropocentric spectrums of green politics. By this distinction, Eckersley meant the politics of ethical environmentalism which included 'resource conservation, human welfare ecology, preservationism, animal liberation and eco-centrism' (Eckersley 1992 p.34) was separate from the accommodation of 'sustainable' development which placed that development at a higher value than the environment itself. This argument is at the crux of the environmental debate and is central to the definition and public ownership of a shared understanding of what environmentalism is.

Through a study of existing theory (Dobson, 1990, Eckersley, 1992, Pepper, 1993, Bahro, 1994, Bookchin, 1995, Dryzek, 1997) an understanding of deep green politics, and that paradigms variance with anthropocentric environmentalism, can be examined. We can also explore the ecological modernisation and sustainable development paradigms which gained currency in the 1990s through theorists such as Hajer (1995), Weale (1992) and Janicke (1997). By outlining the eco-modernist position we will place the deep green theoretical perspective within the 'concrete reality' of the type which sustainable development typifies. We can then identify Irish environmental disputes within the context of the shifting 'discursive opportunity structure' (Gamson 2004) surrounding sustainable development and ecologically modern initiatives in the Irish case.

Anthropocentric/eco-centric approaches

The dichotomy between deep green and eco-modernist paradigms has its basis in Eckersley's definition of an 'anthropocentric/ecocentric cleavage'. The distinction is made clear from the following quote:

> The first approach is characterised by its concern to articulate an eco-political theory that offers new opportunities for human emancipation and fulfilment in an ecologically sustainable society. The second approach pursues the same goals in the context of a broader notion of emancipation that also recognises that moral standing of the non human world (Eckersley, 1992 p. 26).

While both approaches are concerned with the environment, it is the emphasis placed on 'human emancipation' over 'the non human world' which demarcates the anthropocentricism of the sustainable development culture from an eco-centric perspective. Eckersley also cites the 'broadly similar distinctions found in the ecological theories of Naess ('shallow and deep ecology'), O'Riordan ('techno-centricism and eco-centrism'), Bookchin ('environmentalism and social ecology') and so on. The positioning of humankind in relation to other species and ecosystems is pivotal in regard to this theoretical contextualisation of two main distinct features of current environmental thought. While not aligned with a traditional understanding of the left/right divide within political ideology, the distinction between anthropocentric and eco-centric does have its basis in humankind's technical and industrial capabilities, which have become the basis for the type of environmental destruction evident in contemporary society. While traditionally the Left pinpointed control of the means of production as the crucial issue of political contestation, environmental politics is more concerned with how the means of production impact upon the environment and to what extent this is acceptable in society.

Nonetheless, mainstream political structures have continued to concentrate on the development of society which threatens the environment. Environmentalists have responded to this by addressing the technical nature of industrial development, and the need to critique that development through deep green politics, or alternatively, to try to compromise and regulate industry. A difference has been detected in both aspects of environmental thought in so far as perspectives vary as to whether industrial development should be slowed down, through eco-modernist principles such as 'BATNEEC' or 'the best available technology not entailing excessive costs' or 'The polluter pays principle', or whether industrial growth should be reversed and replaced with a more eco-centric social planning.

Techno-centrism versus Eco-centricism

Pepper (1993) and O'Riordan (1981) have defined such environmental diversions as that of a 'technocentric perspective as opposed to an eco-centric' view:

> Techno-centrism: recognises environmental problems but believes our current form of society will always solve them and achieve unlimited growth ('the cornucopian view') or more cautiously that by careful economic and environmental management they can be negotiated ('the accommodators').

> Eco-centrism: views humankind as part of a global ecosystem and subject to ecological laws. These…constrain human action, particularly through imposing limits to economic population growth. (Pepper 1993 pp. 33, 93).

In other words, the root of techno-centrism lies in social and political compromise between the earth's resources and human development with technology as the cutting edge of this manipulation of the earth's resources. Techno-centric approaches are determined with no overhaul of human social systems envisaged and despite recognition of the inherent ecological problems of this analysis. Eco-centrism, conversely places humankind not to the fore of the global eco-system, but rather sees humanity as part of an organic whole, with a moral imperative to restrain activity and growth and to interact and co-operate with the greater eco-systems that populate the earth. This view holds a respect for a pristine, natural world in its own right before any aspect of human economy and development is considered with human beings living in a spirit of cooperation and ecumenism with the environment. The 'deep green' view of environmentalism had its roots in the ecological, feminist and other new social movements of the 1960s and 1970s and has challenged the hierarchical hegemony of political dominance and technological development over social and ecological systems across the globe. Deep green ideology goes beyond old left wing attempts at 'controlling the means of production' or of deconstructing class systems and sets its point of origin before the era of revolution to the beginning of modernity and the age of Enlightenment. By questioning the concept of social order based on expansive development which had its roots in the Enlightenment project present day environmental protests have rejected the concept of a technologically driven modernity in itself, radically moving beyond the position of 'sustainable development' by questioning the validity of development from an ecocentric perspective. Bookchin spells out this premise with a view on these challenges of hierarchical systems of development:

> Ecology raises the issue that the very notion of man's dominance of nature stems from man's dominance of man. Feminism reaches even further and reveals that the domination of man by man actually originates in the domination of woman by man. Community movements implicitly assert that in order to replace social

domination by self management a new type of civic self...must be restored...to challenge the all pervasive state apparatus (Bookchin 1980 p.15).

Risk Society

One conceptual offshoot of deep green analysis has been put forward by Beck in his portrayal of a 'Risk Society'. Essentially, this outlook views the earth in a hazardous light as rampant industrialisation pushes the planet to the brink of a catastrophe caused by a 'bewitchment of reason' (Beck 1996) which holds that in the event of possible global calamity such as nuclear or chemical fallout prevailing attitudes are so transfixed by existing industrialised systems that no real provision has been made for such an event. Furthermore, it seems beyond the genius of current populations to envisage a system of human existence which, at least, doesn't threaten humankind and the planet we inhabit. Yet Beck sees no saviours in the environmental movement, which he claims is trapped in a naturalistic misunderstanding' (Beck 1996 p.7). He furthers this argument by claiming the ecological movement 'reacts to and acts upon a blend of nature and society that remains uncomprehended, in the name of a nature no longer extant'... which is held up as 'a model for the reorganisation of an ecological society' (ibid).

Criticisms of the environmental movement from industrialists are commonplace but Beck's analysis of an overriding confusion as to the positioning of the paradigms that intersect the bounds of society and environment point to the need for interrogation of the cultural and ideological backdrop to environmental politics. In doing so, this book addresses the varying strands of ecological discourses, by surveying the writers mentioned above, as well as undertaking to analyse recent theoretical conceptualisations in relation to the environment and post-modernity, as well as some of the more diverse examples of environmental consciousness.

Beck claims that 'ecological protest is a matter, not of natural but of cultural fact; a phenomenon of cultural sensibility and of the attentiveness of institutions' (Beck 1995 p. 49). This assertion has its basis in the argument which characterises environmental concern as a cultural rather than purely ecological expression. Essentially, the argument highlights the difficulty in explaining the inherent meanings underlying environmental discourses. Political protests, ecological or otherwise, invariably follow from cultural rather than ideological grievances. As western culture has industrialised so too has a new emphasis been placed on protecting an environment once seen as the very impediment of human aspirations for development.

All political ideologies shared at their core a belief in the betterment of humanity through the taming of the ferocity of nature. This is what makes aspects of deep green environmentalism distinctive from the rest of the ideological spectrum. While acknowledging the Left's position on the failure of industrialised capitalism to include large sections of the global population in its wake, deep Ecologism goes beyond protesting this as unjust and inequitable and goes on to advocate an overall rejection of human development based on industrialised, technologically driven expansion in favour of cooperation with the still ferocious natural world.

However, theoretical conceptualisation of environmental modernisation which relates to sustainable development of industrial and political processes does not always fit into policy agendas at the EU or national government level. Tensions remain between environmental directives and some policy objectives of economic and structural growth. To achieve some semblance of ecological consciousness many industries hire PR spokespersons that use ecologically friendly language to mask their true intentions. Such rhetoric allows multinationals to sell themselves (and their products) on an environmentally friendly basis and allows a greater threat to the environment to be sold to an unsuspecting public. As a result it is often left to enquiring bodies such as protest groups to oppose multinationals with many such groups and protestors portrayed as unreasonable extremists by the public relations mechanism of multinationals.

Such multinational posturing has blurred the definitions which underpin ecological politics. As a result environmental discourses have taken on the dialogue of metaphor and imagery, becoming a part of post-modern representations of the fragmented relations which concern humankind, nature and the building of social networks both globally and locally. As environmental definitions fragment and as the strategies and movements surrounding ecological politics diversify multifarious strands of 'green' political, cultural and social analysis vie with each other in an attempt to engage the public perception of what it is that 'environmental' actually means for them. These ecological discourses become central to the conceptualisations which define the environment. Furthermore, these definitions also challenge the discourses previously set by the parlance and paradigms of industrial society.

Through this discursive contestation of social paradigms, ecological political debate has changed society's vision of itself as well as altering the dynamic of social and political relations, through protest and dialogue, since the last decades of the previous century. In the forty years since the publication of works such as Rachel Carson's The Silent Spring (1961), the discourse of ecological consciousness and later protest has created new expectations of industrialised modernity, which perhaps for the first time since the Enlightenment led to the questioning of humankind's impulse towards expansive development. This questioning has enabled the growth of new approaches to many aspects of social and ecological relations and in turn has reshaped existing cultural and political discourses while also giving rise to new paradigms of distinct ecological expression. This new expression has come to be known as the 'green movement' or theoretically 'environmentalism'.

At this stage it would be beneficial to outline the various strands of environmentalism to better understand the meanings attached to these concepts. If, as Meyer (1999) contends, western thought contains elements of a 'dualistic' anti-naturalism, the theoretical conceptualisations stand aside from previous political aspirations in the Western sphere of influence, while fundamentally laying down a challenge to the social constructs which promote an ongoing form of accelerated development.

However, there are two variations of environmental theory which can be used to divide the various elements within ecological thought. One contends that the environment can be 'managed' in conjunction with industrial development. As such this viewpoint, which includes theories such as Ecological Modernisation and Sustainable Development, are in conflict with the 'deep green' school of thought. The 'managerial approach' contends that 'environmental problems… can be solved without fundamental changes in present values of patterns of production and consumption' (Hovden 1999). One of the central theories which underpin managerial approaches to the environment is 'Ecological Modernisation' (EM).

The development of EM theory has been linked to the publication of the Brundtland Report (WCED 1987) and other events such as the UNCED conference on environment and development (1997). Through these formalised declarations the diverse actions and agencies involved in environmental protection began a process of dialogue concerning the global effects of development on the environment and how agencies can have some input into the environmental issues in their region. In turn, environmental theorists such as Janicke, Weale and Hajer, began to examine the varying strands of social actors involved in environmental matters; these included multinational companies, national and local governments, social and environmental movements and other NGOs. Through this review of existing environmental paradigms a critical theoretical concept, Ecological Modernisation Theory (EMT) was advanced.

EM Theory has taken on a particular momentum in terms of environmental debate and had developed various localised aspects in different states. Huber has been credited with the earliest incarnation of EM Theory, which was significant for its emphasis on the role of technological innovations in environmental reform…a critical attitude towards the (bureaucratic) state, a favourable attitude towards the role of the market actors and dynamics in environmental reforms; a systems-theoretical and rather evolutionary perspective with a limited notion of human agency and social struggles; and an orientation towards analyses at the level of the nation state (Mol and Sonnefeld 2000).

However, EM Theory in the 1990s was redirected towards the cultural and institutional sphere of influence over the environment, through the works of Weale and Hajer, among others.

Weale defines 'the new politics of pollution' with a quote from Commoner, as the process by which affluent societies begin 'making peace with the planet' (Weale, 1992 p.1) and its levels of affluence which vary from country to country. There has also been a dichotomy between the rates at which different states have developed pollution controls and environmental policies. New forms of institutions, using sanctions and regulations, have become an integrated part of states' and regions' environmental policy. For instance, EU member states respond to the ongoing environmental directives emanating from Brussels and the regulations behind these directives go on to become that member state's internal environmental law. However, the complexity of the increasing challenges placed on the environment, when added to diverse cultural factors at a localised level, creates a multi-lateral, problematic response to centralised directives.

Ultimately, many environmental problems were 'unresolved or growing worse' (Weale 1992 p.23). Increased population trends, with resultant growth in infrastructural and consumption patterns have compounded responses to ecological crises. Among the issues involved in the growing ecological threat outlined by Weale are: 'Growth in population, pressure on food supplies, increased use of fertilisers, depletion of ozone, contamination from sewage and waste disposal, oil spillages, nuclear accidents, species extinction and global climate change are among the issues which currently threaten the earth' (Weale 1992 pp. 24,25).

While this has seen an increase in environmental concern globally and in eco-policies nationally, a 'sense of policy failure' (Weale 1992 p.26) remained in relation to ecological matters. This sense of despondency is due, in part, to the difficulty in coordinating a global response to environmental challenges, through existing agencies, when individual states have different levels of economies, industrialisation, environmental values and localised problems. It was also becoming apparent even to the industrial sector that levels of pollution were now beginning to threaten economic development, through costs and fears for market confidence. For political planners 'environmental protection is now a precondition of economic growth' (Weale 1992 p.32).

An understanding of new political approaches to the environment can be made clearer by examining some of the paradigms which have become part of this process. Among the theoretical concepts which can explain new approaches to pollution are Rational Choice Theory (RCT), systems analysis and what Weale calls 'the idiom of institutions'. Rational Choice Theory is used to examine the background to why pollution occurs and 'why does it take the form that it does?' (Weale 1992 p. 39).

'Market failure' is given as the origin of pollution conflicts in society, with the specific consequences of 'externalities' causing a 'spillover effect' (ibid). In other words, pollution caused by waste by-products affect many others outside the producer and buyer of the product, indeed the spillover effect often affects nations far away from the point of origin of that product. For instance, toxic waste produced in Europe or North America is often found in Asia and/or Africa, with a trail of corruption to enable such processes to damage local democracies. For Weale, Rational Choice Theory addresses these concerns through the creation of a public demand for environmental protection which 'takes the form of a public good' (Weale 1992 p. 41).

This 'public good' is acted on through 'public choice theory' which examines 'rational agents in the context of collective action' (Weale 1992 p. 42). Among the actors concerned with public choice theory in relation to pollution are politicians, individual citizens and interest groups. Politicians respond to demands from the electorate. Experienced politicians will know that the answer to environmental problems is only to be found in an area of policy acceptable to the electorate. In turn, individual citizens and interest groups grow concerned when the perceived generality of political responses to environmental challenges (formed in response to the perceived desires of the electorate) fail to deal directly with issues. The complexity of such responses, at once interdependent and yet at odds with each other, does much to create the state of chassis which has resulted in a sense of 'policy failure' surrounding environmental issues.

Systems and institutions are also identified as important aspects of collective action on pollution. Systems theorists examine the link between the functions of the state and economy in what is described as a 'system of relationships' which become problematic when the 'imperative of capitalist accumulation' (making profits) 'is in conflict with the imperative of political legitimacy' (meeting the democratic aspirations of its citizens) (Weale 1992 p. 97). This conflict is met by state regulations but in the case of multinationals and the globalisation of industry such regulations are discouraged in favour of capital investment, creating a crisis of legitimacy for the nation state. It is at this point that the role of the environmental movement impinges upon the state, as such movements respond to a perceived lack of activity by the state in aspects of ecological protection. This role is outlined as being that which is concerned with 'what could be saved from and defended against the state...trying to protect a sphere of life against the intervention of the state or state-sanctioned policy' (Offe 1984 pp.189-190).

The third 'idiom of analysis' in relation to ecological modernisation is that of institutions. Institutions are defined as: 'systems of rules governing electoral processes, the practices governing the use of resources' (Weale 1992 p. 52).

Furthermore, an institution is defined in relation to 'identifiable practices consisting of recognised roles linked by clusters of rules or conventions governing relations among occupants of these roles' (Young 1989 p. 52). A distinction is made in relation to their possession of 'physical locations, offices, personnel, equipment and possession of budgets' (Young 1989 p. 32). Institutions are often cast in the role of 'honest broker' in relation to common sense policy decisions. As such, institutions are used to pass on or retain information which, while crucial to policy processes, holds to an informal non-bureaucratic aspect which is often lost to other, relevant actors in the policy process.

As a result, institutional arrangements tend to exist between policy actors at local and international levels. Ultimately, the disparity in institutional influence shaped by cultural and historical factors, affects the regional outcomes of policy directives not least in relation to environmental matters. This complexity in the procedural apparatus of state and voluntary actors reveals the fragmented nature of the political arena which is charged with pollution controls and environmental protection. It is this very complexity which lends itself to the adoption of policies built from an ecological modernisation perspective, as a form of compromise with the labyrinth of bureaucratic agencies which are a feature of modern society.

By the late 1980s, in response to a growing recognition of an increased complexity in the strands of environmental discourses, attempts were made to create a new consensus in environmental politics. Among the most significant of these are the Brundtland Report in 1987 and the UN Earth Summit in 1992. In particular, the Brundtland Report outlined the concept of 'sustainable development', a concept which quickly began to take on many different meanings. This diversity in the overall understanding of what sustainable development actually means became further apparent at the UN Earth Summit in Rio, which began as a conference to herald a new ecological age, but ultimately highlighted the difficulty in even defining what the environment meant to people from differing cultural and political backgrounds. In Rio it had become apparent that 'Our Common

Planet' as defined by the UN Report on 'Our Common Future' from 1987, had failed to grasp the diversity of opinion as to how that future would be met.

It was the recognition of the failure of such conferences and official reports to grasp the concepts of overlapping or fragmented discourses as they existed in many areas of environmental politics (with the addition of regional variations and localised bureaucratic interpretations further complicating such issues) that ecological modernisation as a theory first began to take shape. With an initial emphasis on technology, theorists such as Huber and Janicke initiated an understanding of how environmental protection could co-exist with industrial expansion. With an emphasis on policy and directives, EM has been defined as: 'the discourse that recognises the structural character of the environmental problematic but nonetheless assumes that existing political, economic and social institutions can internalise the care of the environment' (Hajer 1995 p. 25).

EM as a policy concept challenged the notion of 'end of pipe or quick fix' solutions to industrial pollution. It promotes the 'polluter pays' principle, which places financial responsibility as well as blame at the feet of those responsible for environmental damage. Furthermore, the actual benefits of pollution controls for industry are highlighted, going beyond the issue of environmental protection itself. Science is also given a role through EM, in the area of providing an understanding of ecological problems and evidence of ecological degradation. This burden of proof has shifted, in certain cases, onto the industrial polluter and has become part of industrial planning. However, in many cases individuals or environmental movements are still left with the task of protecting the environment against industrial pollution. While EM "acknowledges new actors, in particular environmental organisations and to a lesser extent, residents" (Hajer 1995 p. 29) conflicts between authorities and industry on one level and environmental movements on the other remain a feature of the contemporary political landscape.

While undoubtedly eco-modernism has provided an outlet for the many competing elements in the Irish environmental arena and it has crystallised current understanding of what the environment means from an industry perspective, it is not without its criticisms. Although facilitating policy making at an administrative level and bringing diverse elements of pollution control together under holistic regulatory frameworks, eco-modernism has been criticised for being too inclined towards industry for an ecologically minded concept. This criticism may overlook the necessary role of EM in bridging the gap between business and ecology, in the face of the regulatory failure of the 1970s, as it has been the main point of contention between deep green ecologists and environmental agencies and has also affected the structures of Green parties across Europe.

EM may challenge industry into creating new markets from a reassessed vision of how business relates to the environment; it also 'turns the meaning of the ecological crisis upside-down: what appeared a threat to the system now becomes a vehicle for its very innovation' (Hajer 1995 p. 32). However this innovation has in itself created further tensions between capital and the environment as with each new innovation in business comes new and better concealed threats to the planet. In other words, it has become almost easier to pollute under eco-modernist guidelines due in part to the fact that such environmentally friendly practices are now considered to be 'dealing with the problem' while most industries now hire PR firms and consultants to 'sell' their angle on any particular issue.

A further criticism of EM is that the strengthening of the relationship between administrative policy makers and industry in relation to the environment, the independence of the legislative and regulatory process, has become compromised. This has become evident in terms of how governments attract multi-nationals for the purpose of job creation. In the event of environmental regulations hampering the operation they may often be altered or overlooked and in the easing of conflicts of interests, the public is often caught in a propaganda war over the merits of industrial progress vis a vis environmental protection.

This has become a recurring feature of environmental conflicts in Ireland, from the Raybestos dispute in Cork in the 1980s to the campaign against incineration in Galway or the Shell to Sea campaign. A feature of both these campaigns was the conflict between the PR section of the polluting industry, which was given practically limitless funding to give their viewpoint and the oppositional efforts of concerned citizens and groups who had little or no previous expertise and no funding beyond public contributions. Ecological modernisation as a discourse, while acknowledging the role of the citizen fails to address the social reality underpinning the politics of environmental protest, a reality which cast the modern protester in the role of David to an industrial Goliath.

By promoting a 'techno-institutional fix' (Hajer 1995 p. 32) for the challenges of the environment, EM has served to provide a 'Trojan-horse' for the potential polluter, In so far as that pollution is possible as long as an industry can provide funding for the potential fines incurred. In addition funding programmes for substantial public relations operations have to overcome incidents of localised hostility. This in an ironic twist has become central to our very understanding of what it is that the environment is, as our definitions are often driven by public relations and media images of 'the environment'. As a result many have felt the need to fully challenge the concept of industrial progress and have begun to question aspects of industrial development. To further understand meanings of the environment in this regard we will now go on to explore these viewpoints, which have come to be known as 'deep green' or 'ecocentric' concepts.

Deep green ecologism represents the embracing of nature, as opposed to the centuries old Enlightenment process of repressing nature. It has at its root an overall concern with a sense of global cooperation and species ecumenism which go far beyond the compromising elements of ecological modernisation. Where nature was once 'wild' and in need of taming, deep green ecology places the environment as the equal, or more fundamentally, a more important entity than humankind. Of course, this places most deep green activists in opposition to the onset of a society enthralled by rapid acceleration, over-consumption and environmental degradation in the name of profit. Moreover, while deep green ecologists may have been members of the larger environmental agencies, such as Friends of the Earth and Greenpeace, they have come to reject the bureaucratic nature of such groups, working instead in small clusters of committed activists, protesting about specific environmental problems, such as the protestors around The Twyford Downs protest in the UK, or the 'eco-warriors' of the Glen of the Downs in Co. Wicklow.

Theoretically, deep green ecologism has been part of the process of shaping an environmentalism which was 'understood within a liberation framework heavily influenced by the social criticism articulated by Marcuse and the emergent New Left' (1991 p. 59). As such environmental politics have been shaped by a critique of modern society as having a concern for nature itself. It is through this radical praxis, which fuses social protest with a rejection of industrial agendas such as globalisation and mass consumption, that deep green politics finds a basis for its support especially among the young, students and those previously involved in environmental agencies. In this way the environment became a key manifestation of the counter-culture and environmental lifestyle as a way of resisting destructive culture apparently bent on self destruction' (McNaughten and Urry 1998 p.47).

This view makes apparent the fears deep green ecologists have for an earth threatened by the actions of humankind, driven by greed and seemingly unable to separate these processes of expansive development from a culture of environmental degradation. It is interesting to look back at the recent history of the United States in relation to the rise of deep green political thought from its basis in the counter-culture movement of the 1970s. Writing in 1975, Bookchin claims: "'Environmentalism' does not bring into question the underlying notion of the present society that man must dominate nature; rather it seeks to facilitate that domination... The very notion of domination itself is not brought into question. Ecology, I would claim, advances a broader conception of nature and of 'humanity's relationship with the natural world. To my thinking it sees the balance and integrity of the biosphere as an end in itself." (Bookchin 1975 p. 123).

This contrasts greatly with current views on 'sustainable development' and places the earth's ecosystems on a higher plane with an almost spiritual dimension, to the compromising position offered by ecological modernisation. While undoubtedly radical in so far as advocating a rejection of modern industrial society (and even working to subvert this society), deep green politics is less volatile than left wing radical groupings as protest movements replace revolutionary cells. This distinction can be used to distinguish 'environmentalism' from Ecologism. It is from this perspective that a concept of ecology is developed, one which 'advances the view that humanity must show a conscious respect for the spontaneity of the natural world' (Bookchin 1975 p.123). In regard to social relations the same writer views ecology as affording 'a new relationship between humanity and the natural world in which society itself would be conceived as an ecosystem based on unity in diversity, spontaneity and non-hierarchical relationships' (Bookchin 1975 p. 133).

Conclusion

We have examined how competing meanings of environment contend with each other as society grapples with ecological issues on an increasing scale. Environmentalism has many separate meanings but for our purposes a distinction has been made between the type of radical green politics, which argue for a complete change in emphasis in humankind's relationship with its surrounding environment and the type of compromising pro-industrial approach of eco-modernist and sustainable development discourses. This distinction has come to represent the growing alienation that has developed between green political groups and the institutional agencies charged with implementing the bureaucratic and legislative infrastructure which derives from sustainable development, such as 'the polluter pays' principle. While both would claim to be pro-environment, per se, they remain essentially divided in relation to their theoretical interpretation of whether society can continue to develop as it has done since the Industrial Revolution and whether consumption and pollution levels can be sustained in their current forms.

It is from within the tensions of this societal dichotomy that the politics of environmental protest has grown as administrations, already faced with a crisis of legitimacy are now confronted by sections of the population not necessarily politicised until faced with a nearby environmental crisis. Recent campaigns, such as those undertaken by the Rossport 5 in Co. Mayo show that communities can become politically motivated by a looming environmental crisis, even if economic or legalistic difficulties or even imprisonment result from their resistance to an industrial polluter. This may not mean that community protest groups are all green political ideologists, but they take on the mantel of environmental activists, at least for the duration of their protest.

Theorists have argued that aspects of radical ecologism are disconnected from political reality, claiming that much of what passes for green politics is based on a form of 'anti-humanism' which lacks a rational basis (Bookchin 1995). It can also be argued that green politics has provided a focus for the type of community-based protest movements that can address the democratic deficit created by over-bureaucratic and hierarchical administrations, at both the global and national level. By providing an outlet for social protest deep green environmental movements are addressing the onset of democratic deficit in society. In so doing, green politics has provided a basis for political movement rather than the type of entrenched ideological positions which have emanated from traditional left or right wing politics.

In other words, the basis for green political protests may not necessarily be a strong belief in green politics. However, the types of protests which have become identified with the environmental movement have at their core not just ecological issues but also a representation of an understanding that the type of expansive capitalism which pits polluting industries against local communities in the name of jobs and profit. Moreover, a hegemonic response to the discord of public protest has been seen in what Dryzek (1997) has described as 'the Repertoire of Administrative Rationalism' which represents an institutional response to environmental issues. Dryzek describes aspects of this approach:

1. Professional Resource-Management Bureaucracies: Consisting of 'natural resource management' policy making, usually in the areas of national parks, marine, sea and geophysic concerns.

2. 'Pollution Control Agencies': The use of regulations and directives to control pollution.

3. 'Regulatory Policy Instruments': The use of regulations and directives to control pollution.

4. 'Environmental Impact Assessment': Administrative (and industrial) assessment of environmental damage.

5. 'Expert Advisory Commissions': The use of scientific and technological expertise in relation to environmental issues at the behest of senior tiers of government.

6. 'Rational Policy Analysis Technologies': The utilisation of the knowledge and methods of environmental science and engineering (Dryzek 1997 pp. 64-70).

Such a response to environmental issues places an emphasis on science and technology and 'takes the structural status quo of liberal capitalism as given' (Dryzek 1997 p. 74). Administrative Rationalism relies on a hierarchical approach and a regulatory response to environmental issues, within the existing bureaucratic and administrative structures of modern, capitalist societies. It assumes the 'subordination' of nature to development, people to state and experts and manager over communities. However, Administrative Rationalism, like the ecological modernisation discourse from which it emanated, is in a state of crisis as industrialised development impacts more and more on the environment. Weale has described this administrative failing as an 'implementation deficit' (1992 pp.17,18) which represents a deficit in the aims and actual achievements in relation to environmental matters at the administration level.

This has fuelled a sense of public doubt and mistrust of administrative bureaucracy on environmental issues. In turn, individuals and communities no longer deriving their understanding of 'the environment' from the administrative level are coming to terms with ecological issues from their own perspective which was shaped by environmentalists and NGO actors, green political discourses, media concepts of environmental and 'New Age' philosophies, which have come together with remnants of the old left, to form a New Social Movement based on community responses to environmental issues.

Moreover, as centrist and centre-right ideology have come to dominate the politics of Western Liberal democracies, many disparate elements of the old left have realigned themselves and their struggles with the agendas of deep green and eco-protest politics. This has been as much through necessity as ideological choice due to the lack of any real momentum in radical politics, outside of the globalisation protests, as seen in Seattle and Rome and eco-protests such as the eco-warriors in Wicklow. These eco-warriors have at their basis elements of an anti-globalisation youth movement, disaffected and disenchanted with liberal capitalism overall. They also provide a platform for the expression of environmental concern and even anger in a way which the substantive body of mainstream politics can not begin to represent, due to the embracing of models of liberal capitalist development by all shades of Western political expression.

Bahro (1994) has argued that this dichotomy represents a division between Ecologism and what he calls 'exterminism' in

Western society. While Ecologism is represented by the many disparate aspects of environmental thought their opposition to capitalist development (or the 'Imperial Consensus', as he terms it) ranges from strategies of environmental compromise to radical positions such as eco-terrorism. These various possibilities are outlined as follows:

'the restorative', represented by a 'necessary minimum of environmental protection'.
'the reformistic', with a 'concealed (ecological) fundamentalist intention'.
'radical conservative', which would achieve environmental goals through 'economic planning'.
'Left Radical (New Left)' uses 'hostile' approaches to environmental problems
'Terroristic' wants to 'terrorise liberal capitalism into insecurity'
'Radical-ecological-'human egoistic arguments'
'spiritual fundamentalistic', dissolve it from within   (Bahro, 1994).

Ultimately, these forms of opposition have come to take on as much in the way of understanding the protestation and rejection of industrial society's processes of capitalist development and being specifically about environmental concerns. As ecological management practices and sustainable development approaches become features of industrialism's compromise with a growing sense of ecological concern, the true nature of environmental protest has come to represent as much a challenge to and rejection of established agencies of bureaucratic administration as well as challenging the impingement of industrialism on the environment of 'unspoilt nature'. The cases studied in this book can be understood in the context of this wider contest between grassroots community campaigns and the technocratic alliance between industry and the state over the introduction of major projects or policies.

Chapter Three

Rural Sentiment as Environmentalism

Introduction

For many the changes that have occurred in rural Ireland over the last half century have mirrored a disengagement from the traditional patterns of life that had embedded a set of values and practices which allowed rural communities to co-exist with their surrounding environment. With the onset of a technologically driven agri-business sector, mass production and scientisation drove a wedge between rural dwellers and their hinterland. Farming would become synonymous with over production, fish kills derived from slurry spillages and images of EU subsidies for non-production in the wake of the 'butter mountains' and 'gravy lakes' which stemmed from unsustainable practices. In the era of globalised production local production for local markets came to be dismissed as small minded thinking. The damage caused to local interactions between communities and hinterlands was significant.

One response to this loss of local identity was the concept of 'rural development' which involved community based initiatives to reinvigorate local discourse in the face of outside challenges, both culturally and environmentally speaking. A combination of grievances relating to depopulation, unemployment and neglect of rural regions provided successive environmental campaigns with a groundswell of dissent to facilitate mobilisation processes against multinationals or the political establishment. When combined with the renewed confidence achieved by new middleclass figures bolstered by expertise on rural rejuvenation programmes learned during migrant experiences abroad, a significant form of rural based resistance emerged. This fundamental response came to be articulated around 'defence of space' territorial campaigns involving the imposition of industrial plants or infrastructural projects.

By addressing the political void which had opened around an increased sense of democratic deficit in a scandal ridden era, rural based environmental protests reclaimed a dominant sense of agrarian nationalism which could be traced back to Michael Davitt and the Land League. This potent mixture of traditional values and local sentiment created a persuasive moral frame for many environmental campaigns to build on. Furthermore, the increased sense of confidence that collective mobilisation in common cause can re-establish a sense of cultural resistance to the globalised hegemony of development and consumerism at a time when uneven economic growth and industrialisation threatened to create unsustainable imbalances between the rural and the urban and between developed sprawl and rural environment.

Community Politics in Ireland

The backdrop to the emergence of environmental disputes in Ireland has been the development of a form of community politics which has its basis in a rural identity which is embedded in Irish society. This identity has been born out of a traditionalist discourse which embraces local values over the modernisation projects of colonisers, state officials or EU bureaucrats (Tovey 1992b). Over time attempts to tame both the 'wild Irish' and their rugged landscape have cultivated an instinctive mistrust of officialdom and technological change in rural communities. One result of this has been a growth of an identity based community politics which challenges industrial policies and projects in the regions. This type of externalised community expression has taken shape in spite of the dependent nature of the industrialisation policies of the state, and illustrates a rural mindset that holds self sufficiency and local wisdom drawn from interaction with the hinterland in higher regard than the conventional wisdom of the representatives of politics or industry.

This form of 'rural fundamentalism' (Commins 1986. p.47) places an emphasis on localised structures that includes landowners, family-based farms and agrarian small-town life as the unifying component of social and political life in Ireland. While the lineage of this agrarian ideology pre-dates independence the protectionist policies of Eamon de Valera and his promotion of a vision of a nation built on rural values have bolstered this perspective (ibid). The state's policies of modernisation of agriculture through the application of science or through promoting industrialisation served to further strengthen this rural fundamentalism over recent decades. A wider sense of community grievance also developed in response to incidents of environmental and resource contestation.

Extreme emigration was suffered in rural communities between the 1930s and 1980s. Over these decades, a sense of 'rural decline' (Varley 1991 p. 83), due to depopulation and a perceived loss of traditional lifestyles led to a hardening of rural fundamentalism, allowing environmental challengers to construct grievance frames by drawing on the shared sense of injustice that had developed in rural communities. Seen in this light the sense of democratic deficit which existed in Ireland can be better understood, particularly in the context of an historical resistance to authority which had been at the heart of nationalist attempts to subvert the rule of authority, be it based in London, Dublin or even Brussels.

This form of political deficit is demonstrated by the low levels of membership of political parties, which was as low as 21 per cent (Hardiman and Whelan 1994, p.108). In the absence of a strong political culture, a parochial form of populism emerged, which created a growing sense of civic based 'political competence' (ibid) among citizens who wished to challenge the state. As mistrust of and participation in the formal political sphere went into decline protest politics emerged as a vehicle for dissent in Ireland. Many issues, such as civil rights for nationalists in Northern Ireland, equality for women or better economic conditions for farmers or trades unionists were characterised by public protests and marches across Ireland from the 1960s to the anti-globalisation marches of recent years.

Within that growing sector of a politicised civil society a reservoir of radicals, pacifists, nationalists and feminists was established, which provided both expertise and prior campaign experience that facilitated the mobilisation of environmental campaigns over the last forty years in Ireland. The 'interpersonal contacts' between these individuals and groups has created a network which can be mobilised around environmental issues, creating a strata of civil society which assists movements to emerge from their NIMBY inception and go on to build wider campaigns (Leonard 2005).

It is important to note, however, that this stratum of politicised civil society is very much in the minority in Ireland. Invariably that society was characterised by a conservative political and social culture where values based on tradition, moralism and a paternalistic authoritarianism held sway over time. While recent years have witnessed more liberalised social norms alongside rapid economic growth, it is important to remember that the 'Celtic Tiger' has by-passed many rural areas and has remained a largely urban phenomenon. The state's attempts to modernise through industrial or infrastructural projects have been presented as key components of spreading an industrialised wealth base across the country which would stem the tide of emigration. And yet, in spite of historical depopulation and economic stagnation, rural communities have resisted industrial or infrastructural projects which they have deemed to be too much of a risk to the local population or environment.

The basis for their community based environmental resistance has been non-party or 'non-political community groups' (Varley 1991 p. 85). The social networks which were established across a series of co-operatives and community groups created the 'platform for popular discourse' (Peace 1997 p. 67) which provided fertile ground for the germination of many community challenges in recent years. And while the state has attempted to reach out to communities through the 'partnership' model, the networks of civil society have also provided effective links for the dissemination of information that underscores the mobilisation process. Although the relationship between the state and community partnership groups has been weighted in favour of the authorities, the interaction between civil society and local and national government created a sense of efficiency and confidence amongst community leaders which has bolstered the leadership of environmental campaigns, in the guise of 'community primary resources' (Varley 1991 p. 100). While these individuals may have been involved with community development they were more likely to be familiar with the marginalisation experienced in their locality.

The position of many community development groups who were directed by the state to develop tourism, agriculture and fisheries was often diametrically opposed to the infrastructural or industrialisation projects which the state wished to impose from above. The emergence of campaigns of rural regeneration, such as the 'Save the West' movement or Irish language campaigns, have further served to create variants of rural fundamental discourse. In the late 1980s and early 1990s community politics gave rise to the 'single issue candidate' (Varley 1991 p. 105) based on the mobilisation of campaigns highlighting the need for or loss of local services, although the political potency of the single issue or Independent Candidate has been shown to be reduced significantly once the candidate crosses the threshold of the Dáil. On other occasions community groups have formed alliances with non-governmental agencies (NGOs) such as An Taisce (The National Trust) to preserve areas of scenic beauty (Curtin and Varley 1989 p. 216).

While rural community groups had the provision to appeal to An Bord Pleanála (The Infrastructural Board) to register their concern about projects in their areas, attempts to transplant their rural discourses into a legal setting was often lost in the constrained setting of the oral hearing or legal challenge (Peace 1997 p. 99). This inability to translate rural sentiment into legal efficacy stymied many environmental campaigns yet the legal route was retained by many campaigners as the primary external strategy.

For many campaigns the ability to create 'links' with 'influential allies' (Tarrow 1984 p. 88) from elite groupings became an essential component of the wider mobilisation process. By obtaining sponsorship from a 'primary sponsor' (Dear and Patti 1984 p. 189) community groups could attempt to gain access to the formal political structures of the state and thereby attempt to influence policy makers. By exploiting clientelist political arrangements in this way, community groups hoped to apply pressure on the state.

When local elites are linked with grassroots groups the combination of 'top-down' and 'bottom up' (Haggstrom 1984 pp. 222-229), goes towards creating effective community responses which can build a sense of local populist resistance to both state and corporate entities. This local opposition can draw on 'rural discourse' (Peace 1997), which can be found in even 'non-political' community and voluntary groups which form the basis of Irish life in rural areas (Varley 1991 pp. 84,85).

By exploiting the unstable alignments (Tarrow 1984, p. 88) that existed between the political parties of the Dail communities can also come to define themselves through their attempts to resist the policies of the state, as local viewpoints are shared and articulated, and grievances highlighted during the course of a campaign (Tucker 1988 p. 284).

However, a number of factors militated against outbreaks of widespread collective action in rural areas. These variables have their basis in a persuasive sense of conservatism that restricted a person's or groups' ability to respond to incidents or disputes. These factors included the intricate set of relationships that existed around property and land ownership as the most significant 'established institutional arrangement' (Varley 1988 p. 8) in the regions. Relationships are built around land ownership, so resource disputes impacted upon the very basis of community interaction. This stratified social structure also militated against wholesale class based collective action (ibid) and the resultant emphasis on individualism and independence reduced mobilisation potentials, as did practices of clientelism and political brokerage between individuals (ibid). Accordingly, only the cultivation of grievance frames built on rural fundamentalist discourse facilitated the establishment of a template for community mobilisation against projects or policy initiatives, based on the depiction of such projects as 'an intruder which exploits rural labour, destroys rural values and ruins the beauty and tranquillity of the countryside' (Gillnor 1986 p. 29). The dichotomy between the state's attempt to reduce dependency in rural peripheralities by promoting local self-reliance and the manner in which industrialisation or infrastructural projects were imposed 'from above' also provided campaigners with a basis to construct grievance frames by drawing on resultant societal strain.

Community Advocacy: The Role of New Middle Class Experts

Over time, rural community sentiment has come to depend on the leadership and expertise of an autonomous middle class. This social group, often residing in the suburban belts where environmental disputes occur, have both the independence and expertise necessary to sustain campaigns against multinationals or the state. The expertise of what has been termed the "new middle class" (Inglehart 1977) professionals has become a crucial component of Irish environmentalism. Whereas first phase campaigns in the pre-Celtic Tiger era were often dependent on external experts from the UK or North America, the emergence of a new middle class in Irish society in the post-boom years coincided with the increase in localised incidents of ecological and infrastructural disputes from the mid 1990s onward.

Expertise in communications technologies would become a vital part of this emergent group of advocacy entrepreneurs as returning emigrants brought back new skills gained during spells abroad during the unemployment blighted 1980s. Moreover, these returning professionals brought with them a sense of confidence combined with a determination to improve conditions at home for their families, economically, politically and environmentally. The role of indigenous expert became a significant aspect of the wider framework of environmental campaigning in Irish cases, as new and previously existing connections with international advocates were created and maintained, adding to the potency of the network circuits which provided the interest driven data necessary to contest the scientific arguments of the industrial sector and the state (Leonard 2005).

Furthermore, these new middle class advocates were autonomous from the neo-corporate partnership model which characterised Irish political life from the 1990s onward. In the absence of trade movement mobilisation, environmental advocates were well placed to mobilise existing dissent in an era shaped by a succession of religious and political scandals. Inevitably, neo-corporatism creates political opportunities for those excluded from the partnership table, particularly environmental activists who challenge the economic imperative of the neo-corporatist state (Scott 1990). While many members of the new middle class were in the employ of state, particularly in the university sector, their relative economic independence combined with their positioning on the apex where urban sprawl was causing ecological degredation gave rise to a suburban eco-consciousness which spawned many of the campaigns of recent years. In addition, many of the new middle class had become aware of their Gaelic heritage during their time in exile, and the connection between locals and their hinterland became a social trend alongside the emergence of the Gaelscoilanna, the local GAA club and the popularity of Gaelic names for children in recent times (McWilliams 2005).

The role of the new middle class advocate has become that of a disseminator of knowledge and expertise, and in many cases these advocates have become charismatic figures who project their concerns onto the national stage, as in the case of Emer Colleran or the Rossport 5. While these advocates have been described as "program professionals" (Zald 1987), invariably they are unpaid volunteers who compete with the highly paid consultants of the multinationals or the state. Over time, these advocates can suffer from "activist fatigue", as the strain of sustaining a campaign begins to weigh heavily on the shoulders of the main personnel or leadership group driving any protest movement. Many environmental campaigners I have spoken to have gone on to reveal the extent of the personal cost, or that suffered by their families, over the duration of a campaign.

Nonetheless, these campaigners have captured the imagination of the public at various times, as a sense of genuine sympathy has come to replace dismissive depictions of these "eco-warriors" in both the local and national press. Eco-advocates have also been able to benefit from the wider understanding of environmental issues which have resulted from better education in schools, as well as the initiatives and information drives of the state as it introduced a succession of EU environmental directives on waste management, plastic bag taxes and the introduction of smokeless fuels.

Without doubt, the mobilisation of successive environmental campaigns have had the effect of creating a degree of environmental consciousness across Irish society which has been evident in the support shown to campaigns as well as the rise in votes for the Green Party in recent elections. It remains a fact that the work of environmental advocates has contributed to the much vaunted social capital which has so enthralled both the media and political elites as a source of all that is good in Irish society. Regrettably, this hasn't as yet led to the ending of the isolation, harassment and at times, imprisonment of many of those who have fought to defend the Irish environment at various points in our recent history.

In order to better understand the nature of community mobilisation around environmental issues, an examination of some of the main aspects of social movement and resource mobilisation (RM) theory will be undertaken. These theories will be applied to the series of environmental campaigns discussed throughout this book. The development of resource mobilisation theory can be traced back to attempts to measure the outbreak of new left activism during the 1960's in the United State. Collective action by civil rights activists, anti-war protesters and women's liberation groups was defined as part of an attempt to 'promote or resist change in society' (Turner and Killian 1972 p.246). Arising from historical conditions or societal strain, new middle class students or professionals attempted to utilise collective action to promote either increased levels of resource distribution or further autonomy from the state in an era of 'post materialism' (Davies 1962).

The importance of charismatic leaders who influence and enthuse a wider activist base around key moments of social change has been documented by movement theorists. The significance of leadership groups or committees in interpreting grievances and creating collective action has been highlighted (Wilson 1973, Klandermans, 1989). While earlier theorists identified charismatic consensus forming, recruitment and fund-raising as the key focus of movement leaders, later works highlighted the significance of prior protest experience, political, legal and media expertise, and an ability to maximise the use of communication technologies as vital components of a potential leader's strategic portfolio.

In many cases, distinctive leadership types emerge, offering their expertise as part of a leadership collective or committee. In the era of mass communications, a leader's ability to open up network channels and effectively link with like minded groups, the media and the institutional sector can define a movement and enhance the outcome of a protest. Incidents of environmental collective action in Ireland, have tended to rely on local or internal leaders mobilising grievance frames, while external leaders or experts have provided updated information, strategies or contacts to regional campaigns, leading to a wider range of 'enriched options' (Morris and Staggenborg 2004, p. 178) for protestors.

Resource Mobilisation and Political Opportunity Structure

Leaders must also mobilise the resources available to them, in order to galvanise a movement over the duration of its campaigns. Over time, a movement's ability to access and utilise resource has been identified as a crucial factor in determining the effectiveness of any campaign, based on the generation of resource mobilisation theory (RMT). Through this approach, a model of movement development has been established (McCarthy and Zald 1973, 1977, 1979; Gamson 1975; Jenkins 1983), focusing on both the benefits and constraints of resource based movements. While the initial wave of RMT theorists comprised the first strand of that perspective, later analysis of collective action emphasised the political opportunity structure (POS) as an external resource which movements could exploit to gain leverage or access the political process (Kitschelt 1986, Tarrow 1984, 1988; Kriesi 1989, 2004). However, the nature of the POS in a state may influence the manner in which political opportunities emerge, thereby influencing the tactical approach of a campaign (Kriesi 2004). Eisinger (1973) initially defined the 'curvilinear' nature of POS, as structure 'open' and 'closed' at different states. For Tarrow (1994, 1998) this 'shifting dynamic' of POS created 'salient changes' such as 'increased access' or 'divided elites' (ibid) which movements could exploit to gain leverage or influence.

Master Frames, Grievances and Consensus Mobilisation

The evolution of a campaign of collective action may depend on the ability of movement 'entrepreneurs' (McCarthy and Zald, 1977; Della Porta and Diani, 1999 p. 7) to exploit an issue around a 'shared grievance' (Klandermans 1989) held by a community. Grievance can have its basis in a sense of injustice which has been harboured by a social group against the state or industry. Movement leaders or entrepreneurs can make issue out of the lack of facilities or the manner in which facilities are imposed through policy agendas. This form of 'grievance interpretation' (Klandermans 1989) can be revisited throughout the duration of a campaign. The 'mobilisation of consensus' (ibid) around issues is an important part of extending a campaign to the community. Movement leaders attempt to link their issue with the wider grievances held by the community, creating 'frame alignments' (Snow et al 1986) to build wider support for their cause. In time, a movement's interpretation of a grievance can become a 'master frame' (Snow and Benford 1992). Master frames come to define an issue, and can be used throughout a campaign, or by subsequent activists, to rekindle grievance issues. Such master frames come to define the key moments of the 'cycles of protest' (ibid), as movements attempt to change existing meanings, particularly through the forum provided by the media. Tarrow (1994, 1988) highlights the importance of 'media framing' for campaigners.

Environmental movements have been able to use media frames to highlight major incidents of pollution extending the wider sense of concern about 'risk society' (Beck 1992). This concern has persisted in the wake of large-scale technological accidents such as Three Mile Island or the Chernobyl reactor meltdown. By using media frames movements can communicate their aims to a wider audience, enhancing the presentation of their cause through relayed or documented events or debates. However, media frames are subject to editorial control and issue salience (Dearing and Rogers, 1996) as disputes ebb and flow through the consciousness of the public.

Incidents of collective activity take on many different forms. The 'repertories of protest' (Della Porta and Diani 1999) that define a campaign may include a range of approaches. Those most frequently used include protest marches, sit ins, strikes, petitions and public meetings. In Ireland environmental groups have traditionally used the legal or oral hearing approach (Peace 1987; Taylor 2001). A movements' readiness or 'flexibility' (Tilly 1977 p. 155) in relation to implementing tactical repertories has a significant relationship to the overall impact of their campaign. Innovation in repertoires is difficult to achieve, as the forums and meanings of protest frames have come to be defined. One recent area of innovation in protest has been the utilisation of communication technologies as a 'privileged tool for acting, informing, recruiting, organising and counter dominating' (Castells 2001 p. 137) The use of communications and internet technologies has become a basis for expertise information flows which creates support networks for disparate campaigns.

Many of the various components of environmental movement activism can be diffused across internet and media outlets, academic and scientific expertise, political strategies, legal frameworks and the location of national or global networks (Leonard 2003 p. 88). This innovation in technology has facilitated the creation of wider repertoires of contention for movements and increased the importance of leaders who can exploit both the new technologies and the expertise that emerges from their use.

The relationships between movement leaders, individual activists and like-minded groups allow movements to reconcile their aims, experiences and outcomes with other collective actors. Such links become the basis for the diffusion of expertise, grievance frames or pertinent forms of social capital (Diani 2003 p.109). Movements must create networks in order to partake in information flows and media debates. Networks are often based on the maintenance of 'interpersonal contacts' (Friedman and McAdam 1992 p. 158). These contacts can have a client-broker type of relationship between groups or individuals as experienced campaigners pass on information or expertise to fledgling activists (Diani 2003 p.108).

Many advocacy researchers or entrepreneurs play a key role at the centre of environmental networks. They provide a brokerage link between various regional campaigns, global campaigners and media groups, using internet technologies to provide a resource for activists, news corporations and even the institutional sector. The role of a movement broker may lead to the embedding of an advocacy expert at the heart of debates about social capital or environmental disputes (Ansell 2003 p.125). By igniting social ties movement advocates can illuminate relevant social grievances to the wider community. The role of the embedded entrepreneur of social capital has become a pivotal aspect of environmental disputes in Ireland.

Since the era of protest in the 1960s new social movements as represented by the environmental, feminist and civil rights movements have become an increasing feature in societies facing periods of political, structural and economic change. Here we will examine the phenomena of social movements in relation to their strategies and impacts. Aspects of social movement theory looked at will include the concept of 'social breakdown' which holds that social movements are a response to democratic deficit from the perspective of theorists such as Smelser (1962), Tilly et al (1975) and MacAdam (1988). This is followed by an exploration of 'rational choice theory' which holds that any movement that can point to the benefit of its proposed change over any cost incurred stands a better chance of mobilisation and success. Theorists examined in this regard include Klandermans. (1984 and Borgetta et al (1992).

Resource Mobilisation Theory which looks at the organisation of movements through the application of resources of finance or skills is examined next. Theorists analysed include McAdam, McCarthy and Zald (1988). The dichotomy between activism and parliamentary politics is then detailed briefly citing Bahro's critique of the mainstream. The strategies employed by social movements provide the next area of analysis. The use of traditional social movement strategies such as strikes and protests is shown to have been supplemented by scientific and technological expertise as movements go from street-level politics to professional campaigning. Social Movement theorists examined in the section include Della Porta and Diani (2000). The application of the resources of expertise to movement strategies according to Piven and Cloward (1991) and Gamson (1995) is then outlined. At this point an analysis of the Formation of Consensus is undertaken. Once mobilisation has begun movements must undertake to create an overall consensus maintaining focus on the original movement aims. This is developed through the perspectives of Klandermans (1988 and Kreisi (1986). When established a movement must engage with potential participants through organisational efficiency and reliable, sourced media statements amongst other factors. This aspect of movement organisation is examined through a review of writers such as Klandermans (1988), and Wilson (1973) while the concept of grievance interpretation is also outlined.

We also examine how the exploitation of a particular grievance in relation to societal shifts becomes a central focus for movements through the analysis of Ferree and Miller (1985), McAdam (1982, Snow et al (1986) and Taylor (1986). The transformation of a shared grievance into a platform for move4ment activism is the next area of focus. Theorists such as Kreisi (1984), McAdam (1985) and Melucci (1985) look at the micro social grouping which can be transformed into an overall movement. The conditions for this are then explored in relation to Snow et al (1986) who examine the concept of 'Frame Bridging, Amplification and Extension' leading to the sustaining of a campaign. This is further defined through an understanding of the concept of the 'vocabulary of motives' as defined by Snow and Bedford (1988) and is known as a system of communication that is utilised for the mobilisation sustaining of potential participants by establishing a dialogue of intent between existing micro groupings.

After the maintenance of campaigns we look at the achievement of movement objectives. This is usually measured over time as cultural changes stemming from original movement objectives become absorbed by mainstream society. The potential for reaching any particular movement objective is often a difficult prospect as movement participants must alter existing social attitudes on a particular subject. The need to challenge authoritarian perspectives together with a set of achievable outcomes are identified through the concepts of Gamson (1975) and Della Porta and Diani (1999) whose writings are examined in relation to movement strategies that have become one of the main focuses of social movement analysis.

Conclusion

The pool of discontent from which many Irish environmental groups draw support can be understood as part of a wider grievance frame which has emerged from historical circumstance. Culturally the articulation of rural sentiment has been intertwined with the many versions of nationalism that transpired in opposition to centuries of colonial rule. While rebellion and independence followed on from the evocations of such nationalist sentiment, rural meanalities were only reflected in the artistic renaissance of the Celtic revival by Dublin-based ascendancy figures such as JM Synge or WB Yeats. And while the daily life of the inhabitants of the capital city was brought to life through the works of Joyce and O'Casey it would be some time after independence before Kavanagh's 'stony grey fields' of Monaghan would project deeper insights of the relationships between country people and their hinterland on the consciousness of the nation.

Inevitably the enduring hardship and poverty which had come to characterise life in many rural communities, since the Great Famine, became an underlying source of communal grievance in the regions. Urban poverty in Ireland was just as obdurate but the huge rates of emigration from rural areas and the West of Ireland in particular, added to the sense of societal loss which left many rural communities concerned about the possibility of complete demographic and cultural extinction. Moreover, the deeply rooted sense of connectedness that defined rural communities through their hinterland created a strong sense of what Benedict Anderson (1983) has called 'the imagined community'. Within this fulcrum of grievance, folklore and opposition, a sense of place emerged and a set of fundamental beliefs have been cultivated alongside the ditches and hedgerows of the West.

In the years after independence, this sense of parochial grievance was strengthened by what was perceived as the heavy hand of officialdom. The state attempted to impose modernity on rural communities which used traditional methods of production. This model of development emphasises science and technology as a way of maximising the market potential of agricultural produce, with a view towards exports. In order to achieve a modern agri-business sector, the state set out to provide grants and technical assistance which would affect a transition form smaller family based farms with an emotive attachment to land, towards more 'efficient' larger farms which could service a globalised food-processing industry (Tovey and Share 2003 p.56). One result of these changes was a decline in the numbers involved in agriculture with countless thousands taking the emigrant boat to find work abroad. Viewed in this context, the state's attempts to generate employment through multinational led development were perceived with a degree of scepticism and hostility, even before pollution or health risks were discussed.

The grievances of rural communities which emerged from this perception of a loss of community have contributed to the growth of 'populist environmentalism' (Tovey 1992b p. 283) in Ireland. Populist environmentalism has been manifested as part of the 'rural discourse' (Peace 1997) which was a characteristic of anti-toxics and anti-multinational disputes during the pre-boom decades of the 1970's and 1980's. Populist sentiment had also been a feature of many of the anti-mining and resource disputes which occurred during the same period. It is quite interesting to see the re-emergence of rural populist discourse during the recent dispute about the Mayo gas pipeline involving the 'Rossport Five' as calls for local ownership of local resources were combined with concerns about the risk posed by on-shore pipelines as part of the framing strategies of that campaign.

The existence of strong parochial rural sentiment has been cited as a factor in the lack of acceptance of 'official environmental' organisations in country-based disputes (Tovey 1992b p. 286), as communities attempted to mobilise grievance based on local understandings and relationships. However, this localism has also left many populist environmental groups open to the accusation of being mere NIMBYists as opposition to industrial or infrastructural projects in a communities 'backyard' is identified as the primary rallying point for campaign mobilisation. Further challenges for populist campaigns such as the problems of translating rural discourses as part of normal legal hearings have also been identified (Peace 1997, p.99).

Essentially, the well of grievance which provides much of the underlying discontent for populist campaigns to exploit is the basis for an understanding of exactly how the various environmental campaigns that have occurred over recent decades can be characterised as components of an overall social movement (Tovey 2002 pp. 147-148). While populist environmental campaigns may 'wax and wane' (ibid), the significance of each campaigns' contribution to an articulation of community grievance has created a movement of sorts, where outcomes can be measured through an understanding of the extent to which populist fundamentalism has come to be seen as the very basis for traditional rural identities in the post-consumption, post-modern era. This is an outcome that can be measured as part of the social capital of all rural and rural-urban communities and which has far greater significance than the outcome measurement models which chart the impact of protest campaigns on policy implementation. The true measurement of the impact of rural populist discourse goes beyond moments of access to political opportunity structures and contributes to the shape and nature of the populist Irish political system itself.

There are many definitions of what the term 'rural' means. By and large, rural life is understood through an existence in a hinterland, defined by a relationship with the land, through agricultural production (Curtin, Haase and Tovey 1996 p. 11), or traditional cultural values and discourses (Taylor 1989, p. 19). In the Irish case rurality has also been associated with 'spatial peripherality' (Curtin, Haase and Tovey 1996 p. 13), as the communities west of the Shannon River came to define themselves through their distance from the 'developed core of society' (ibid). This sense of local embeddedness and hostility to the core can be traced back through Michael Davittt and the Land League. It remains a pivotal feature of the ongoing recreation of societal grievance which Giddens (1984) has described as 'practical consciousness', the basic opposition to officialdom due to an emergent sense of both 'ontological insecurity' and structural 'motivation' (Haugaard pp.104, 105) which stokes the embers of rural discourse, which Irish environmentalism exploits. Invariably, it has been the gradual translation of agrarian discourse into a form of environmentalism shaped by new middle class advocates which has influenced the emergence of a wider eco-consciousness in Irish society in recent years. This motivation can be traced through a succession of Irish environmental campaigns over the past forty years.

Over time, a pattern of rural resistance to the onset of globalised development becomes discernable in the Irish case. We can see that an overall combination of grievances around perceived threats to traditional processes and identities led to a growing sense of resistance which in many cases surfaced around environmentally-based contests and disputes. In many ways the culture of social and political acquiescence which permeated life in the years after Independence gave way to a community based political articulacy which sought to interrogate the grand narratives of industry or the state in the same manner as had been undertaken around issues of equality and religion across the nation. Moreover, at a time when the cycles of economic growth and recession sundered society through emigration and poverty in the pre-boom years or immigration and accelerated growth in the post 'Celtic Tiger' era, the values embedded in traditionalism rural mobilisation and concern for heritage became appealing and achievable for beleaguered communities when faced with the threat from 'outsiders', be they industrial or institutional.

Of course the student activist who took part in organising participation in the Carnsore Point Anti-Nuclear Protests in the late 1970s has emerged in adulthood as the concerned citizen protesting against the health risks of incineration for his/her children. In many ways the generation that has their feet planted on either side of the Millennium have grown up with and continued to be involved in environmental discourse as a facet of their lives, at a time when emigration and immigration, political scandal and economic success have been encountered. During the previous forty years environmentalism became part of the discourse of rights issues that have shaped modern Ireland. Many of the leaders of this generation were women, such as Mary Robinson, who took part in protests against the destruction of Georgian Dublin during her student days and who later became President of Ireland. Others, such as Petra Kelly, would go on to become leading figures in European environmentalism, with Kelly becoming a founder of the German Greens in her native Germany. Emer Colleran, who orchestrated the Mullaghmore protests with such effectiveness, went on to become the founder and Chairperson of the Environmental Change Institute which encompasses diversity to facilitate greater ecological awareness. A strand of eco-feminism can be traced throughout the successive campaigns that have come to make up the Irish Environmental Movement; this allowed that discourse to be more representative while locating it within the contexts of Celtic mysticism and a deep green connection between the cycles of nature, both of which inform the prevailing 'new age' attitudes now commonplace in alternative culture.

Another facet of the new environmentalism in modern Ireland has been the emergence of risk society and toxicity as a new issue of concern in our daily lives. With the onset of regular flights from the US and a series of low tax incentives in Ireland, American Multinationals began to set up across the country, primarily in rural areas. In the aftermath of the Love Canal and 3 Mile Island toxics scandals in the US, issues surrounding nuclear or toxic pollution came to be a part of modern culture. As multinationals availed of the lax regulatory regime in Ireland, communities grew increasingly concerned about the costs to human health and the environment in the vicinity of established or proposed industrial plants. At the same time, a culture of oppositional politics has become an integral part of civil society. Student, feminist and republican protests were routinely featured in the media and on the television news. These new social movements also provided a pool of activists who also found common cause with community and environmental campaigners. Issue salience was established around protest events throughout the 1960s and 1970s. By the end of the Millennium all relevant actors, ranging from campaigners and their adversaries through to the media and their audience became more adept at recognising the manipulation and framing of events to maintain an ongoing awareness around environmental issues. And while international movements such as Greenpeace became an integral part of both media and public understanding of environmental issues the institutional input from agencies such as the UN and the EU to the acceptance of concepts such as sustainable development across the globe has completed the acceptance of environmental issues as a significant component of life in the early part of the 21st century. As the paradigms of environmental discourse have come to be embedded in the public's consciousness so have the understandings of protest events and collective framing developed amongst campaigners and public alike. As a discursive tableau of environmental protest has emerged so too has a degree of acceptance of the components of protest frames and events occurred as the public's consciousness heightened and media focus increased around environmental issues.

The following chapters will apply a discursive and contextual protest event analysis to some of the most significant environmental campaigns which have occurred in Ireland in the years between the Carnsore Point Anti-Nukes protests in the late 1970s to the 'Shell to Sea' campaign of the Rossport 5 in 2005. By combining protest events with framing discourses as part of the analysis a combination of political opportunities, mobilised resources and framing contexts will be provided to illustrate the emergence of an environmental movement from a series of local campaigns. The tactical approaches of each campaign will be examined alongside the development of legal, political, moral and cultural frames to underpin instances of environmental collective action.

Chapter 4

Understanding Social Movements

Introduction

Social Movements have been described as 'collective attempts to promote or resist change in a society...' Emerging from a set of social conditions social movements undergo a process of recruitment, campaigning through various strategies such as protests and developing the movement through media relations and political participation. The organisation of social movements is undertaken through a variety of strategies. Social movements try to alter society through large-scale revolutionary change or by focusing on a specific aspect of social tension, often 'during times of rapid social change' (Smelser 1962). Thus social movements can be said to be a response to democratic deficit and 'systematic breakdowns' which become evident through periods of accelerated development that lead to social and environmental upheaval.

Large structural re-arrangements in societies such as urbanisation and industrialisation 'increase social breakdown and widen the democratic deficit' which increases 'the impulse towards anti-social behaviour'. However, the 'New Social Movements' such as environmentalism and feminism have been identified by theorists such as McAdam (1988) as 'simply politics by other means'. While participation in new social movements is sometimes met with repressive measures from the authority of the state theorists such as Klandermans (1984) have developed the 'rational choice' theory which argues 'that the anticipated benefits outweigh the expected costs of participation'. While these benefits may be related to an improvement in lifestyle or otherwise for social movement members some political or ideological advancement may be at the heart of those aims central to the social movement's organisational core. These political motivations may differ to the stated aim of the social movement but the use of such movements for anti-social or ideological purposes may meet a similar agenda to that of a previously existing political group. For example, anarchist groups may hi-jack an anti-globalisation protest to cause rioting and disruption as has occurred in Genoa in 2001 and in Dublin in 2002.

Thus many diverse social movements can develop around a particular issue. While the social movement organisations (SMO's) may share similar aims their strategies and ideologies are often diverse. However, SMOs hold their movements together and reinforce the overall campaign even through this diversity. 'They acquire and deploy resources, mobilise adherents and plot movement strategy'. SMOs become the central tenant of social movements according to Resource Mobilisation Theory through the raising of revenue, publicity, enrolling new members and planning campaigns. SMOs also become the 'command posts of movements' (McAdam, McCarthy and Zald 1988). It is interesting to note that McCarthy and Zald have also linked the affluence of society as a factor in both creating social change through development on the one hand while being an important factor in the resourceing of social movements on the other. As a result social movements tend to flourish in times of economic growth and prosperity.

> "There are simply more discretionary resources available for movements during these periods…the macro level (a society's surplus resources) mediated by SMOs affects the micro level (individual participation)".

Although many campaigns such as the anti-nuclear or anti-globalisation protests are comprised of a loose alliance of social movements these may sometimes come together to form a stronger movement often with a view of participating in the mainstream of politics. One instance of this was the rise of the Green Parties in Germany and Ireland where a once diverse set of environmental campaigners came together to form a political alliance which then took on the structures of a political party attempting to influence the political process from within the parliamentary system. This process is not without its critics who, like Bahro, argue that the compromise of parliamentary politics leads to a weakening of the movement's initial core aims while simultaneously leaving a void on the protest side of the movement alienating more radical members. Indeed, the process of becoming more acceptable to centrist voters led both Left and Green parties across Europe jettisoning their activist wings during the 1980s; a process only slowly being reversed (often from below) today.

Outside of parliamentary participation social movements are free to develop whatever strategies necessary to pursue stated objectives. Essentially, movements may then choose to develop these strategies along either legal or illegal lines and may incorporate violent or anti-social tactics to support them. They can range from the use of arms and explosives for revolutionary movements to the more widespread utilisation of marches, rallies, protests and strikes which have come to represent the tactics of the new social movements. In recent years the addition of expertise in relation to scientific legal and political process has been combined with the utilisation of internet technologies to reinforce social movement strategies. This represents a shift from the social movements of the part which tended to be based on industrial class mobilisation. With the onset of Social Movements 'conflict among the classes is of decreasing relevance'. By operating outside of the realm of economic confrontation with campaigns based on professional expertise new social movements are attempting to engage the political mainstream while resisting the increasing globalised industrial sector.

By incorporating both professional expertise and internet technologies new social movements allow themselves a wider range of strategic operation matching and often surpassing the government and private sector in relation to gaining public and crucially for campaigns, media support. In so doing new social movements set themselves up as major players in affluent, developing societies contributing to pluralistic society and to the public consultation process in relation to environmental matters. Advantages are gained from this diversity in approaches open to social movements. The confidence of members and the widespread public is gained through the utilisation of expertise while the individual contribution of members with expertise becomes more valued. As a result individual expertise can widen the range of strategies open to social movement through individual innovation.

Resource Mobilisation Theory

Theorists (McCarthy and Zald 1987) have focused on the importance of resources available to social movements. Resource Mobilisation Theory (RMT) examines resources as a factor in the mobilisation of movements. These resources, be they material or expertise based, become the dynamic that drives social movements in regard to the mobilising and sustaining of protests to the point of reaching an outcome.

> "The type and nature of the resources available explain the tactical choices made by the movement and the consequences of collective action on the social and political system".

The application of resources through a variety of strategies allows movements to mobilise a wider membership, organise protests and expand networks of activity with like minded movements. The utilisation of internet technology in recent years has allowed for the creation of a globalised network of social movement groups in areas such as environmental and anti-capitalist resistance. According to Piven and Cloward (1991) 'Resource Mobilisation theory defines the importance of institutional continuities between conventional social life and collective protest'. The sentiment underlying this analysis holds that social movements are not random occurrences of public protest but are instead part of an overall pattern of 'normative and non-normative forms of collective action'. This is a contrast with mal-integration theory which contends that socially disruptive or rebellious behaviour is less discernable as a facet of social functioning and more likely to represent an anti-social rejection of societal norms. As a consequence of this theoretical dichotomy RMT analysis has tended to pursue an examination of the organisational aspect of social movements concentrating on the links between the mainstream establishment of financing norms, media relations and conventional collective activity in regard to formalised procedures such as committee and meeting structures and behaviour.

Social movement strategies have shifted from a reliance on anti-social activity such as strikes to the incorporation of establishment knowledge based in the realm of science and technology together with a degree of political sophistication that enables campaigns to be undertaken through wider parameters. Resource mobilisation analysis in defining these procedural changes in social movement practices has come to emphasise the importance of organisation and access to both political and professional resources as critical factors in social movement development. Piven and Cloward (1991) cite Gamson's (1998) 'check list' in relation to resource mobilisation for movements taking into account the need to match the bureaucratic structures of establishment actors. These include:

1. The drawing up of a 'constitution'.
2. The establishment of 'an internal division between officers, committees and rank and file'.
3. The maintenance of a 'formal membership list'.

Formation of Consensus

Having established a movement structure based on the above criteria the generation of an overall consensus in regard to a movement's aim and direction is undertaken. This sets in motion the process that has been described by Klandermans (1988) as 'a spiral of mobilisation'…led by 'activists, political entrepreneurs or indigenous leaders'". One of the more dynamic features of the mobilisation process is the utilisation of media coverage. For Klandermans (ibid) a 'successful mobilisation draws mass-media attention especially if innovative action strategies are used'. From extensive media coverage a movement can build on its membership as awareness of the campaign increases. According to certain theorists (Kriese 1986 and Klandermans 1988) new social movements such as that led by environmentalists and feminists have a reserve of activists who maintain a loosely-knit network of 'already motivated campaigners'. These reserves 'are rooted in dense sub-cultural networks that serve as communication and mobilisation channels in case of need' (Kriesi 1986). Nevertheless, despite any previously existing network being already in place consensus formation and mobilisation must be created and maintained in relation to each new issue and campaign as it arises. In this regard the resource of expertise becomes a critical factor as the main unifier of participant opinions. New information routinely accessed helps to bring together various factions which can exist in many campaigns particularly as they expand and gain momentum that sometimes moves the overall group away from the control of the organisers. As expertly given information also wins media support the overall importance of maintaining these channels of expertise becomes crucial to a campaign's success. If maintained, the flow of expertly given information emanates throughout the movement creating consensus.

This form of consensus mobilisation allows individual participants to take the personal decisions necessary which in turn allow for a more committed participation in the movement's strategies. It is the sum of this form of personalised consensus that creates the overall strength of a movement. It also gives social movements a further underlying strength that oppositional agencies such as governments and large businesses lack in terms of a freely given commitment of support. Once this commitment is formed into an overall consensus an essential difference can be established between consensus formation and subsequent mobilisation. According to Klandermans (1988) 'Consensus mobilisation must be distinguished from consensus formation: it is a deliberate attempt by a social actor to create consensus among a subset of the population whereas consensus formation concerns the unplanned convergence of meaning in social networks and subcultures'.

Once established a campaign's perspective is then made coherent and disseminated throughout the community through the utilisation of the media, public meetings, rallies and through availing of the already existing support networks open to social movements. Once consensus on a movement's direction is reached it must be open to the competition of existing social discourse. It is through this form of open debate that a movement's aims can be seen to strengthen and gain momentum with the overall public as these aims challenge the orthodoxy of existing social structures. By presenting a new alternative, often to the excesses of injustice and greed, the agenda of a social movement can attract further consensus and participation amongst a disenchanted public.

Mobilisation of consensus

Once a movement or campaign has gained momentum participation is maximised in the following ways:

1. formation of mobilisation potentials
2. activation of recruitment networks
3. arousal of motivation to participate
4. removal of barriers to participation
                              (Gamson 1975).

These aims are achieved through the galvanising of political support through a widening of a movement's parameters to as wide a range as possible without losing focus on the issue at hand. Furthermore, Gamson has differentiated between what he terms 'consensus' and 'action' mobilisation. From this comes the understanding of what has been described as that which distinguishes 'the creation of commitment from the activation of commitment' (Gamson 1975). In other words a reserve pool of previously engaged activist support may already be in place around the scene of a new dispute. This support may be part of previously active and like-minded social movements. Or it may be part of an emerging population of academics and professionals who have gained a certain wealth and social status and form part of newly formed suburban belts. Both of these groups are faced with all the infrastructural and environmental difficulties urban sprawl can raise. Likewise urban renewal has, according to Castells (1983), led to social movements emerging from areas of strong trade union or radical political support.

Klandermans (1988) details the rationale for the mobilisation of consensus among potential participants. He cites Freeman (1983) in regard to how 'the desire to spread the marriage of the movement is even considered as one of the defining characteristics of social movements'. Beyond this a movement's ideology is given as the main framework for its medium. A set of factors introduced by Wilson (1973) can be used to demonstrate the role of movement ideology in regard to creating a series of conditions for protest including the following:

> 'Diagnosis (an indication of the causes of discontent)'

> 'Prognosis (an indication of what must be done)'

> 'Rationale (…arguments to convince the individual that action must be taken)' (Wilson 1973).

Having established a framework for mobilisation a movement must then engage with potential participants while attempting to enact their strategies. This process includes the mobilisation of both the already committed and the motivation of new forms of commitment. In order to maximise mobilisation potential activists are sought from groups that are hit the hardest by the negative consequences of modernisation processes.

In addition to locating a reserve of potential activists social movements are often mobilised around particular incidents that have a bearing on an overall issue for instance, a leak at a nuclear plant, an incidence of industrial pollution or a threat to a shared resource such as parks or woodlands. This leads to a collective grievance which can then be exploited by social movement organisers or 'incident entrepreneurs'. These entrepreneurs transform shared grievances into movement mobilisation through the utilisation of existing communication networks. Klandermans (1980) points to the existence of research in relation to what he calls 'grievance interpretation' theorists such as Ferree and Miller (1985), MacAdam (1982), and Snow et al (1986). From this research it is concluded that 'Grievances that are attributed to situational factors predispose people to participate in social movements'.

What becomes crucial in relation to a social movement's mobilisation of potential is the pinpointing of blame for whatever grievance is being exploited. At this point the utilisation of expertise becomes important as the institutions of authority are targeted as culpable agents in the grievance process. As institutional authority becomes the target for accusations of certain forms of injustice it becomes 'necessary that people come to recognise that this authority and these institutions are unjust and wrong. In addition, 'people who are usually fatalistic and feel that the existing order cannot be changed must start to demand change' (Piven and Cloward 1979 from Klandermans 1988).

In order to transform grievance into activism theorists such as Kriesi (1984), MacAdam (1986) and Melucci (1985) have examined the difference between shared grievance and activist potential in a 'micro' or 'intermediate' social grouping that exists before an incident around which a movement can be mobilised. Once aligned around an issue a group can be mobilised and strategies enacted. When linked, a movement can spread through the community as grievance and values become enmeshed thus increasing participant levels. It is not uncommon for a movement to hold a large scale protest, meeting or demonstration at this point to combine strength with the increase in participant interaction strengthening the channels of communication within the wider movement. Klandermans cites Snow et al (1986) in relation to the 'frames' of grievance interpretation:

    i)   Frame Bridging: 'Occurs when the individual and social frames are congruent'.

ii)   Frame Amplification: 'Occurs when an interpretative frame is clarified and strengthened by linking it to values or beliefs held by the public'.

iii)   Frame Extension: 'Occurs when values and interests of potential adherents become aligned with participation in movement activities'.

iv)   Frame Transformation: 'Occurs when individual frames need to be changed...to make them congruent with the movement frame' (Snow et al 1986).

Sustaining a Campaign

Consensus mobilisation in itself is not enough to sustain a movement. While the aspiration to unite a section of the population against a certain issue can be achieved through the methods discussed above further patterns of mobilisation are necessary to activate a movement. Strategies must be devised which are sufficient enough to create a consensus in relation to a movement's potential to be effective and create change. In order to best enact strategies the aims of a movement must be legitimised. These aims must be focused enough to maintain the interest of potential participants while being flexible enough to sustain the fluctuations and changing demands of an ongoing campaign. It is at this stage that core group members become crucial in maintaining an overall direction for a movement as peripheral actors may find shifts in movement direction confusing lessening the overall momentum of a campaign. In order to maintain a high level of activist mobilisation a movement needs to convince its members 'that individual participation contributes significantly to success or alternatively that non-participation threatens success' (Klandermans 1988).

Furthermore, movement activism can be reinforced by applying a rationale that justifies participation to those within the movement and those outside who may question the legitimacy of the strategies engaged in by the movement. This justification of activism has been described as a 'vocabulary of motives' (Snow and Bedford 1988). These justifications can be used 'as motivational prods to encourage sympathisers and adherents to take action on behalf of movement goals' (Borgetta 1992). The employment of 'vocabularies of motive' enables a movement to develop a system of informal commitment with participants. Activists identify themselves more closely with the movement as they participate in movement strategies and help achieve movement goals. Theorists have indicated 'that such conversion and commitment building processes are ... typically voluntary' (Snow et al 1986).

Achievement of Movement Objectives

As each movement has its own desired outcomes in relation to the fluctuations involved in each campaign it is fair to say that social movement outcomes are largely dependent on the parameters defined by any original set objective. In most cases the achievement of movement objectives is relative to effecting a change to the relevant area of policy. This change must be then measured in relation to the situation prior to the existence of the social movement. Nonetheless, the effects of a particular social movement campaign may not be immediately known as the central movement's activities gain mainstream acceptance over a period of years eventually making once radical social changes seem timely or overdue. Certainly, this has been the case in relation to the campaigns for equality in relation the feminist or US Civil Rights Movements. Ultimately, change is often effected on a cultural level as certain injustices become intolerable. The immediate impact of directly changing policy on an outstanding issue of grievance is an altogether rarer occurrence. In this regard the likelihood in achieving social movement outcomes has been identified as being dependant on the existence of certain characteristics within a movement. These include:

i)   'Selective incentives for participants'

ii) 'Unruly tactics (e.g. strikes, violence)'

iii) A 'Relatively weak, bureaucratic, centralised' target.

iv) 'The absence of factional splits within the group' (Gamson 1990).

Any social movement success is dependant on the challenging and changing of perspectives in the process of effecting structural changes either through their immediate campaign or through any subsequent cultural repositioning of society. As such, social movements must contend with deeply entrenched social perspectives regarding the legitimation of authority. Challenging the perceived legitimate authority is according to Gamson 'a formidable task'. The same theorist has identified the potential outcomes arising from social movement activity:

i) 'Full response, both gains and acceptance'

ii) 'Co-optation, gains without recognition'

iii) 'Pre-emption, gains without recognition'

iv) 'Collapse, neither gains nor acceptance'
(Gamson 1990).

What becomes clear from this analysis is that social movement success has varying degrees of success and failure from which it is measured often in regard to an overall time scale. In other words, social movement success is often measured over a long period of time subsequent to any initial phase of activity. In certain cases such as the Women's Movement, there has been a degree of success in relation to some issues (equality legislation in the workplace) which is tempered by some outstanding inequalities (the representation of women in politics) demonstrating the difficulty in measuring the outright success or failure of any movement. Consequently the success of strategies employed becomes the focus of any social movement analysis.

These strategies include questions such as:

1.   'Are movements which propose radical change more successful than those that propose moderate change or visa versa?'

2.   'Does violence work?'

3.   'Is a centralised and bureaucratic organisation a help or a hindrance for social movements?'(ibid).

Protest Event Analysis

Protest Event Analysis (PEA) is a quantitative, methodological approach which can be applied to the cycles of collective action in order to better understand the key elements of the processes of framing which surrounds consensus building and campaign enhancement.   While concerns have been expressed about protest event research methods which rely too heavily on media data, we will combine media reports with alternative data sources such as campaign websites and literature, together with academic research and inspired observation to create a wider 'issue history' (Szasz 1994) to underpin the argument model.

By combining 'media theory' and 'representational' approaches (Mueller 1999) an overview can be constructed which allows a protest amalgam which avoids the biases of media or campaign sources becoming the explicitly dominant elements which shape conceptual findings.   By applying a protest event analysis to these findings, further understanding of how the cycles of environmental protest in Ireland have come to be influenced by events, both internal and external, in a diffuse set of campaigns. This analysis makes it possible to develop a coherent account of how these campaigns have come to represent a nascent environmental movement in the country.

The protest event analysis which is used in this book identifies the cognitive frames established by each of the environmental campaigns which developed in Ireland since the 1970s.   By applying this diachronic analysis to the key events which shaped these environmental action frames, a discursive overview can be established which demonstrates a convergence of campaign collectivity which reveals evidence of an articulate environmental movement built on national and global linkages. Recent critiques of protest events have purported to use news reports as the basis for their analysis.

However, the event analysis utilised in this book allows for a wider understanding of the manner in which framing processes create issue salience. This may shape subsequent media coverage of protest events. What results is very often a form of ideological diffusion from media which is often bound up in reporting accurate data, while becoming increasingly reliant on activists for material in an era when the public has grown tired of political 'spin'.

There are many additional variables associated with protest event analysis such as the impact of mobilisation processes or access to political opportunities (Kriesi 1995) or the alliances and alignments which emerge from the fluctuation shifts of political opportunity structures (Tarrow 1998). This methodological approach is developed by applying a political discourse analysis (Gamson 1992) (Koopman and Statham (1999) to the collective action frames outlined in each campaign. As each campaign identified new understandings of environmental contests within the framework of dominant social and political relations a new discourse of cultural opposition emerged.

Over time this cultural discourse has come to be a feature of Irish modernity as territorial localism has encapsulated a type of community opposition to the grand narratives of the state. By establishing a discourse of environmental opposition successive campaigns have established an articulate reservoir of community actors who have at their disposal an accumulated network of experts, campaigners, strategists and communicators who can advocate the concerns of those citizens who have come to question the wisdom of unfettered growth and development.

Moreover, the emergence of a cultural discourse that has at its core an embedded concern for the environment provides each campaign with a template for their own mobilising and framing processes. As the internet has become an integral part of environmental protest, the patterns and cycles of collectivity have become enmeshed, with mobilisation of dissent and the framing of the cycles of protest centring on major events which promote not just current concerns, but also established environmental values.

Protest Event and Framing Process Analysis Movement theorists have developed understandings of protest cycles (Tarrow 1998) and tactical innovation (MacAdam 1983). These developments have highlighted the interconnected linkages that allow a fragmented series of protest campaigns interact with elements from prior activist movements as well as with agencies of the state, industry and media (Oliver and Myers 1999). Successive events can create a momentum towards collective responses to the imposition suffered by civil society as a result of state policy, technologically-led development or multinational greed.

The cycles of protest which underpin the spread of collective action frames as a cultural response to impositions 'from above' provide us with a framework with which to develop a framework of analysis. The methodology applied to the Irish environmental case studies in this volume will combine protest event and framing process analysis, drawing on the integrated protest event analysis and political discourse approaches established by Koopman and Statham in 1999. The categories of this discursive analysis can be seen in the diagram on the following page.

Table 1

| | *Categories of* | *Protest Event and* | *Framing Analysis* | |
Type of Frame	Type of Campaign	Type of Protest / Tactics	Framing Outcome	Political Outcome
Political	Concerns for democratic deficit and party support/opposition; local political allies, national political allies exploiting political opportunities, electoral leverage	Locally alliances, national alliances, global alliances, embedded advocate framing issues, political opportunities	Mobilisation of grievance consensus at local and national level; heightened awareness of environmental issue and democratic deficit	Increased political access and leverage
Social	NIMBYism grassroots alternative energies new middleclass professionals, working class	Populism supported or opposed by local interests, health risks, marches, demonstrations	Evolving from NIMBYism into wider movement	Increased politicisation of civil society
Cultural	Rural discourse / eco-feminist discourse, moral discourse / religions, use of interest-led expertise, nationalist discourse	External advocate Mobilised resources Cultural and heritage frames Media campaigns, celebrity advocacy	More expansive media coverage. Discursive interpretations of culture and heritage.	Enhanced socio-political and cultural discourse

Legal	Oral hearing, High Court, European Court	Legal challenges to policy or projects	Establishing precedents or overturning laws or policy	Redefined policy agendas. Changes to Legal framework.
Institutional/ Agencies	EU-UN-Sustainable development, local authority support or opposition, the State, An Taisce, An Bord Pleanàla	Legal campaigns, expertise advocacy, institutional allies, political allies	Enhanced understanding of overall issue from grassroots grievance to institutional frameworks	Redefined policy agendas Changes to legal framework Reinforced linkages between institutional sector and community
Economic	Pre-growth – pollution, resource protection, post-growth – infrastructural	Anti-multinational, anti-state, Opposition to sitings	Establishing grievance over costs and location of projects	Projects delayed or shelved
Scientific	Global networks	Interest-led advocacy	Counter arguments to established scientific viewpoints presented	State and industrial science challenged

Many approaches to protest event analysis have come to rely heavily on press reports of protest events (Fillieule and Jimenez 2003 pp. 258-60). We will place this protest analysis in the wider contest of an 'issue history' (Szasz 1994), a wide-ranging longitudinal study, which measures the mobilisation, political access and overall impact of a series of environmental disputes, ranging back over forty years. In order to facilitate such a comprehensive overview, a broad series of materials will be consulted and analysed. These materials will include the body of literature surrounding Irish sociological and political inquiry, as well as case studies, articles, methodological debates and wider media coverage. Such an integrative approach will provide an in-depth understanding of the contexts from which incidents of environmental disputes emerge in the Irish case, in an era when Ireland has undertaken a transition which Tovey and Share (2003) have defined as going from tradition to modernity. Some of the primary environmental contestations which have characterised the underlying social and political tensions surrounding that transition will be outlined.

Chapter Five

Anti- Nuclear: Carnsore Point

Introduction: The Issue of Nuclear Power

Campaigns against nuclear power plants emerged from the
concerns expressed by some U.S. medical and science experts
about the dangers of radiation exposure in the decades after the
Second World War. While the horrors of Hiroshima and
Nagasaki and fears of Cold War nuclear arms proliferation
created a combination of grievance factors for many people, the
global oil crisis of the 1970s had led to a renewed interest in
nuclear energy as an alternative to fossil fuels. Many western
nations such as the United States and Britain had developed their
nuclear energy capacities, and as Ireland had little in the way of
natural resources, some favoured the nuclear option as a
potential policy for consideration. While many opposed nuclear
power due to fears about the harmful effects of radiation, others
saw it as a futuristic and efficient energy source.

By the late 1960s and early 1970s the anti-war movement which
had emerged around Vietnam War protests developed an interest
in building up a resistance to nuclear power plants. Protests
emerged in West Germany and France as activists, students and
citizens came together to prevent nuclear plants from being
constructed. Common cause was established between the anti-
war protestors and environmentalists, while many feminists
joined the anti-nukes campaign with the Greenham Common
Women becoming synonymous with the movement in the UK by
the 1980s. Anti-nuclear campaigns had already commenced in
the US where the site for one nuclear plant was occupied to
prevent further construction. The nuclear accident at Three Mile
Island proved to be a fundamental moment for both the industry
and the anti-nuclear movement providing as it did a visible
manifestation which seemed to validate the grievances of

concerned activists. With its pacifist inception the anti-nuclear movement came to be characterised through its strategies of non-violent protest, occupation of nuclear power sites or military installations and the involvement of concerned students and women's groups. The emergence of the Campaign for Nuclear Disarmament (CND) came to replace the nuclear energy protests particularly in the aftermath of the Chernobyl disaster in 1986. This accident put grievances about nuclear power to the fore across the globe and certainly set nuclear energy back in the public's eye. Many states began to call for the phasing out of nuclear power in its wake (Kriesi et al 1995 p. 151).

In recent years the Irish state, which tried to develop their own nuclear energy policy in the 1970s, began to challenge the UK government over the nuclear power plant at Sellafield, North Cumbria. In June 2005 the Irish government's legal team claimed that the discharge of nuclear waste into the Irish Sea was a breach of UN conventions. Despite the Irish state's poor record on environmental regulations the British government was taken to the European Court of Justice by their Irish counterparts but the case was rejected in January 2006. It was a far cry from the Carnsore protests in the late 1970s when the WISE 'nuclear power – no thanks' logo began to appear on the back windows of Volkswagen vans across the country. The debate about nuclear power has recently re-emerged in the wake of some environmentalists such as J.F. Lovelock proclaiming that nuclear power was still a viable and green alternative to the fossil fuels which have caused global warming.

Background

Recent announcements by the All-Ireland Nuclear-Free Local Authorities Forum, which embraces councils from both sides of the border, calling for clarification on plans for a nuclear power station in Northern Ireland (*Irish Examiner* 30 December 2005) rang a familiar, if somewhat alarming note with those who had opposed nuclear power in Ireland during the 1970s and 1980s. The campaign against the state's decision to build a nuclear power station in Carnsore Point, County Wexford in 1979 was the first large-scale instance of a collective response by environmentalists in Ireland. Many of the initial networks of the Irish eco movement were established as a result of the Carnsore campaign. Links were established with environmentalists at home and abroad. The anti-nuclear issue would become an iconic one, characterised by an energetic alliance of many of the 'new left' social movements such as feminist, anti-war and student groups, as well as environmentalists who would go on to form the basis of the new social movements of the modern era.

A significant amount of popular opposition to nuclear power was mobilised through the Carnsore protests, creating the resource of a collective pool of environmental consciousness which future campaigns would draw upon. Perhaps more importantly, the state's plans for nuclear power were defeated by the Carnsore protestors, a victory which established a precedent which Irish environmentalists would aspire to, as policy was seen to be reversed through political protest. Plans for the use of nuclear power for the generation of electricity were first put forward in 1968. It was hoped that the nuclear option would help to meet projected increased demand for power in the 1970s. As the electric grid between the Electricity Supply Board, (ESB) and the Northern Ireland Electric Services (NIES) had been connected, the Irish state attempted to bring their policy of power generation in line with that of the UK, where the nuclear plant at Windscale, later Sellafield, had been in operation since 1951.

The fact that the Windscale plant had been involved in Britain's military nuclear project was one of the first issues picked up on by Irish anti-nuclear Protestors. Indeed, British and European anti-nuclear groups, who were primarily pacifists concerned about nuclear arms proliferation during the Cold War, provided important links with Irish anti-nuclear protestors.

The state's project for nuclear power took a few different turns throughout the 1970s. Initial plans were put back in 1972, in favour of the development of the Kinsale gas field in County Cork (Dalby 1985 p.3). The onset of the global oil crisis in 1973 forced the state to again consider nuclear power as a possible option. As oil prices rose considerably as a result of oil shortages, a Nuclear Energy Board (NEB) was established to examine the feasibility of a nuclear power plant (ibid). The planned location of this plant was Carnsore Point, a peninsula in County Wexford. In September 1974 the ESB applied to Wexford County Council for planning permission to build four energy stations, without specifying which technology was involved (ibid).

Although all of the parties of government had examined options for nuclear power, the populist Fianna Fail government led into power by Jack Lynch in 1977 became most associated with the Carnsore project. Under the supervision of the Minister for Industry, Commerce and Energy the momentum for a nuclear plant at Carnsore increased, while energy demands in the economically buoyant late 1970s grew.

The brash "men in mohair suits" who led Fianna Fail at this time equated national growth and nation building with large-scale industrial projects. Historically, Fianna Fail had promoted campaigns of self-sufficiency, characterised by the protectionism of the 1930s. Major projects such as the Ardnacrusha Hydro Electric Dam on the Shannon River or the industrial zone at Shannon airport were overseen by Fianna Fail governments in an attempt to promote industrial infrastructure and economic growth. Carnsore nuclear plant was seen as a project which would bring Irish industry into the future.

This form of 'economic nationalism' (Baker 1990 p. 50) was central to the political platform of Fianna Fail, combining that party's inherent populism with a policy framework which would allow Ireland to grow beyond the economic constraints traditionally associated with dependency on the United Kingdom. The partitioning of Ireland into northern and southern states in 1922 had also shaped this post-colonial mindset as membership of the European Economic Community (EEC) in 1973 was seen as facilitating Ireland 'taking its place among the nations of the earth'.

The development of an industrial sector in Ireland remained a key objective for successive governments. The Industrial Development Authority (IDA) was established in 1959 to encourage direct foreign investment by US multinationals in Ireland. Carnsore nuclear plant was seen as a vital component for presenting Ireland as a good destination for industrial investment. In many ways, the contestation of environmental disputes in Ireland can be placed in the context of the state's attempt to impose modernisation from above, through industrial and infrastructural projects and community resistance to such projects 'from below' in an attempt to retain traditional ways of life and autonomy from the sate, particularly in rural communities.

Seen in this context, the campaign against nuclear power at Carnsore Point can be seen in the fullest cultural context as part of an attempt to resist aspects of modernisation by a sceptical community. A number of objections to the application for planning permission for the Carnsore plant were received by Wexford County Council in 1972. There was also an initial wave of enthusiasm about the plant, led by local businesses. As early as July 1971, local groups including An Taisce, The Irish Heritage Trust, and the local Chamber of Commerce had formed an impact study group to examine the potential affects of a nuclear plant in the area.

The first attempts to create a local campaign against the plant began in Rosslare in late 1973 (Dalby 1985 p. 6). The Rosslare Development Association hosted a meeting of local groups and the Nuclear Safety Committee (NSC) was established. This group began to research the nuclear issue focusing on safety and environmental concerns. In June 1974 a debate on the issue was held featuring Sean Coakley of the ESB and Dr. McCauley of the Physics Department, Trinity College. The morality of nuclear power's potentially toxic legacy for future generations was questioned from the floor of this meeting (ibid), indicating the degree of existing local concerns.

Throughout that year, the National Safety Committee became the Nuclear Safety Association (NSA), as the campaign grew (Baker, 1990 p. 53). Meetings, events, newsletters and a letter writing campaign were established to promote the aims of the NSA (Dalby 1985 p. 7). The antinuclear movement began.

The ESB had put forward their planning permission application by the end of August 1974 and held seminars and meetings on the issue to which the NSA and local politicians were invited. While all political parties supported the nuclear plant, local opposition on moral grounds was growing, reflecting the concepts of a finite and fragile 'planet earth' and concern for future generations represented during the first 'Earth Day' held globally since 1971. The NSA framed their objections to the plant on moral grounds, putting forward the following objections:

- A nuclear plant conflicted with high amenity area
- Cancer and leukaemia risks
- Disruption to local bird sanctuary (Lady's Island Lake)
- Radioactive waste as a national security risk
- Aggravation of fresh water consumption
- Long-term hazard of radiation in local eco-system
- Disruption to tourism
- No provision for domestic storage of radioactive waste if export proved impossible   (Dalby 1985 p. 7).

A further mobilisation tactic of the NSA was the collection of 2,200 petitions against the plant in February 1975 which were presented to the local authority (ibid). During 1974 potential supporters for a nascent anti-nuclear movement could be found in branches of Friends of the Earth which had opened in Dublin and Cork (Baker 1990 p. 3). However, reduced demands for electricity due to economic recession in 1975 saw the plans for the plant put back again. By 1977 the recession had ended and Fianna Fail was back in power. The Carnsore plant was back on the political agenda. This was reflected in the appointment of Professor C.T.C. Dillon from the Nuclear Energy Commission to become the chairman of the ESB in the spring of 1977. By that autumn the public inquiry at Windscale had revived local concerns about nuclear power.

The inquiry debated the nature of the future of Windscale as British Nuclear Fuel Ltd. (BNFL) attempted to make that plant the largest nuclear reprocessing plant, through its thermal oxide reprocessing plant (THORP) facility, in the wake of growing popular resistance to nuclear power in the United States. The subsequent protests became a unifying (2002 p. 416) force for the UK's anti-nuclear movement which would also benefit the Carnsore campaign.

Movement Expertise, Leadership and Expansion

The original committee of NSA was led by local people such as Harvey Boxwell and Helen Scrine. Having mobilised local opposition to nuclear power based on health and moral issue framing, the local campaign was expanded into a larger group known as the Council for Nuclear Safety and Energy Resource Conservation (CONSERVE) in January 1975 (Dalby 1985 p. 8). This was an attempt to increase the levels of expertise available to the campaign while networking more effectively with the regional branches of Friends of the Earth. FOE had undertaken a leafleting campaign highlighting important issues about nuclear power and radioactive waste and at the same time promoting alternative energies such as solar and wind power. The CONSERVE Committee produced their own document in July 1975 titled Legislation, Energy Conservation and the Balance of Payments which outlined the dangers and inefficiencies of nuclear power (ibid). The alternatives put forward in this document included better energy legislation, decentralised electricity stations and the co-generation of heat and power (ibid).

FOE extended their campaign against nuclear power by promoting alternative strategies. Another group to emerge at this time were the Solar Energy Society (SESI). At the same time a coalition of anti-nuclear groups was growing across Ireland in Cork, Limerick and Galway (Baker 1990 p. 54), with support from the student populations in those cities. As the anti-nuclear movement expanded, cleavages began to develop between the various strands of the movement. One of the central areas of discord was based on the tactical approach to a campaign against nuclear power. Friends of the Earth favoured a strategy of legal challenges and organised themselves with formal structures, leaders and members with links to the global FOE organisation (ibid).

Another section of the anti-nuclear movement had a more radical and grassroots basis. Following on from the radical origins of Italian anti-nuclear groups which had links with revolutionary movements, groups such as Revolutionary Struggle, Trotskyist and anarchist collectives became involved in the campaign. These groups advocated violence as part of their resistance to nuclear power (ibid). The radical groups did not have formal structures and wished to oppose all forms of capitalism, rather than promoting alternative power (ibid). However, both sets of groups worked together on a casual basis producing literature, newspapers and organising protest events.

The area of expertise was becoming more important for the anti-nuclear campaign, as academics such as Dr. Robert Blackith of Trinity College became more involved in the articulation of a critique of the nuclear issue. Dr. Blackith's book *The Power that Corrupts* was issued in 1976. This text included criticism of the ESB's approach to the nuclear issue in regard to providing the public with answers to these concerns (Dalby 1985 p. 9). During 1977 the newly formed Friends of the Earth branch in Dublin continued the debate in a series of letters to the media. The national press featured articles on the subject of nuclear power, providing an outlet to those for and against the issue.

Another ally of the anti-nuclear campaign was John Carroll, president of Irish Transport and General Workers' Union (ITGWU). Carroll spoke at many anti-nuclear rallies, helped launch and would also edit a book with Petra Kelly of the German Greens who was doyen of the European environmentalists, called *A Nuclear Ireland?* (Baker 1990 p. 55).

The link between trades unions and the nuclear industry had been noted in the anti-nuclear World Anti-nuclear Service on Energy (WISE) newsletter in 1978. In their first edition, WISE, which developed the famous 'sun-smile' symbol with the 'nuclear power – no thanks' logo stated that workers were beginning to question their role in the 'energy – jobs link':

> They are beginning to realise that they are effectively terrorised by governments and energy monopolies with threats of mass unemployment unless atomic plants get built...In some cases, links are starting to be established between the trades unions and the environmental and anti-nuke lobby...to find out the real relationship of energy to jobs (WISE Bulletin, May, 1978).

In the same issue, a list of trades unions sympathetic to the anti-nuke movement stated that the ITGWU was 'opposing the plans of the Irish government for giving Ireland its first atomic reactor' (ibid) and included John Carroll's contact details. Its round-up of global anti-nuclear protests included the following article:

> *Ireland: Opposition Starts*
> Ireland is about to go nuclear. The government has decided in favour of a first atomic reactor, to be built at Carnsore Point in County Wexford. The decision is the result of heavy pressures from the industry, and discreetly from the EEC...An opposition front is already forming. The biggest Irish trades union is opposed....Opposition to the scheme will be a major concern of the Irish Friends of the Earth, which has come to life again (ibid).

As a result of increased networking by the various components of the Irish anti-nuclear movement, a wider consciousness developed around related issues such as Windscale's dumping of nuclear waste in the Irish Sea. The global campaign against nuclear armaments was also gaining strength and these issues increased interest in the anti-nuclear movement. Many people were concerned that the Carnsore plant could become involved in these processes in some way, particularly with groups such as Sovereignty Ireland (ibid). Student groups such as the Student Christian Movement (SCM) continued to press the moral argument against nuclear power, with the support of 'new theology' Catholics and other Christian groups (Baker 1998 p. 6). Another issue which came to light was the campaign against uranium mining in Donegal which involved direct action and the destruction of equipment (Baker 1988 p. 9).

"Get to the Point": Cultural Mobilisation

By September 1978 a decision was made to seize the land at Carnsore, with further plans for an anti-nuclear festival. A new group, based on the various elements of the anti-nuclear movement was formed for this purpose, called the Carnsore Collective (Baker 1978 p. 10). At the same time Friends of the Earth began a national campaign encouraging people to lodge planning objections to the proposed site with Wexford County Council. These two tactics would form the main mobilisation strategy for the anti-nuclear campaigns with both the planning protest and the festival receiving prominent national and even international attention, with reports of the event featuring in the WISE Bulletin:

> *Irish anti-nuke show*
> An anti-nuke show will be held on August 18-20 [1978] at Carnsore, planned site of Ireland's first power plant. A local farmer has made his land available. There will be a weekend of practical work-shops and education on nuclear power, "plus enjoyment". An Irish decision on whether to go nuclear is still pending. It has now come out that the Irish electricity board plans a battery of four reactors at Carnsore, total capacity 3000 MW (as compared with present total Irish electricity generating capacity of 2540 MWs! (WISE Bulletin July 1978).

As anything up to between 7,000 and 25,000 people descended upon Carnsore on the weekend of the 18th of August, the scale of the free festival was given front page coverage in the national press, with both the BBC and RTE featuring the protest. Special buses and trains brought the crowds to the site and a team of volunteers was on hand to provide stewarding, parking and crèche service (Dalby 1985 p. 11). The festival was called "Get to the Point", and featured a mixture of popular and folk musicians led by Christy Moore. Local activist Jim "Doc" Whelan provided Moore with a song called "The Ballad of Nuke Power" which was used throughout the Carnsore protests as an unofficial anthem of the movement. The opening lines of the song set the tone:

> *My name is Nuke Power, a terror am I*
> *I can cause such destruction on land, sea or sky.*
> *Your Minister tells you I'll do you no harm*
> *If he locks me up in that house down in Carne.*
> (Whelan, J. / Moore, C. 1978)

Onstage, between luminaries such as Clannad, the Atrix and the Roache Band, speakers included Petra Kelly, John Carroll and Dr. Blackith. In the crowd, radical left wing and anarchist groups were well represented.

Gales and heavy rain on the Saturday of the festival made heavy going of the festival site but there were no reports of criminal activity. On Sunday, a choir from the local church sang as festival goers swam at the local beach (Cassidy 1998). There were many tents which became forums for alternative politics, energy and lifestyles. Stalls sold books, newspapers and distributed leaflets and badges while most groups recruited new members at membership and information posts. By the end of the festival, it was suggested that over 7,000 letters objecting to the nuclear plant had been lodged with Wexford council (Dalby 1985 p. 12).

Following the festival the national press and opposition spokespersons such as Fine Gael's John Kelly, began to call for an inquiry into the Carnsore Plant, something that was rejected by the Minister of State, Desmond O'Malley. By November the Minister had the support of the Confederation of Irish Industry which claimed nuclear power was 'essential for industrial development' (ibid). Throughout the autumn of 1978, the anti-nuclear movement built on the momentum of the Carnsore festival, as events were held around the country. A major anti-nuclear meeting was held at the Mansion House in Dublin, while the ESB began to bulldoze the memorial cairn at Carnsore. Additional large scale meetings in Dublin and Cork were followed by the 'Roadshow' tour of artists such as Christy Moore and Freddy White, together with an anti-nuclear play. One resource which was established was a newsletter for the combined anti-nuclear movement in Ireland. This was used to promote the 'Monster Meeting' held on the 25th of November in Dublin.

This meeting included all-day seminars followed by a performance by the 'Roadshow' artists. The meeting was unstructured and led to a frenetic exchange of ideas (Dalby 1985 p. 13). In January, RTE broadcast a programme exclusively on the nuclear issue. This special edition of the popular 'Late Late Show' was hosted by Gay Byrne and featured speakers such as John Carroll and Petra Kelly. The programme was aired in the aftermath of a series of radio programmes on the issue. The show was a raucous affair, with the panel's statements being subject to interjections and booing from the audience. In between the lively debate, Christy Moore sang anti-nuclear ballads (Dalby 1985 p. 14). The issue began to crystallise in the minds of the viewing public.

A Nuclear Ireland?
In May 1978 an Energy Symposium was held under the auspices of the now defunct Irish Transport and General Workers Union (ITGWU) at the Royal Marine Hotel in Dun Laoghaire. Among the contributors to the Symposium were Dr. Blackith, Petra Kelly and Dr. Michael Flood, who was the Energy Consultant for Friends of the Earth (FOE) in London. The Unions were represented by John Carroll, the ITGWU's vice president, who chaired the symposium alongside union president Senator Fintan Kennedy and Dr. James Kavanagh, Auxiliary Bishop of Dublin. The State was represented by Minister Ray Burke. Submissions were divided into five sections. The first considered 'the Case

for and against Nuclear Energy' with pro and anti arguments being presented by Ray Burke and Dr. Blackith. John Carroll addressed the subject of 'Jobs and Nuclear Energy' while Petra Kelly discussed 'Nuclear Energy and the European Community'. 'Medical Considerations' were the subject of presentations by three medical doctors and paediatricians from the UK and the US while the 'Ethical, Moral and Social Ramifications' of Nuclear Energy were debated by Sr. Bertell from New York State University and Dr. Michael Flood of FOE. The proceedings of this Conference were published under the title of *A Nuclear Ireland?* This text highlighted a number of the frames which the No Nukes campaign had already employed. The first of these was the moral frame.

Moral Frame:

The preface to *A Nuclear Ireland?* opens with a poem from Karol Wojtyla, otherwise known as Pope John Paul II, whose iconic status was confirmed by the hundreds of thousands who flocked to see him on his visit to Ireland in 1978. The poem, entitled "The Armaments-Factory Worker" makes a connection between the sin of war and the participation of workers who build armaments. At the time the Cold War between the US and the Soviet Union was at its zenith with thousands of nuclear missiles primed for catastrophic destruction if launched by either side. The use of Pope John Paul's poem on the need for conscious responsibility on everyone's behalf at a time when fears about possible nuclear war were heightened allowed the anti-nuclear campaign to grab the moral high ground.

This moral frame was underlined by the participation of the Auxiliary Bishop of Dublin, Dr. James Kavanagh, as well as through the submission of Sr. Rosalie Bertell, who had a Doctorate in Biostatistics, from New York. Sr. Bertell presented some of the ethical problems posed by nuclear proliferation in her contribution to the symposium. She claimed to have been politicised after being intimidated by a utility company after publishing her findings on links between nuclear power and leukaemia. Her findings demonstrated that the ageing process was advanced by one year for each rad exposure experienced, which was the equivalent of the yearly exposure for a worker in the US nuclear industry. This damage also causes increased susceptibility to leukaemia tumours and heart disease (*A Nuclear Ireland?* 1979 p 162). For Sr. Bertell these side-affects, which were more pronounced for at-risk groups such as infants or the elderly, posed a series of moral and ethical problems. These included the following issues:

(i) a shift from the father working to provide for his family to the father's exposure to radiation threatening his family including the unborn child;

(ii) community exclusion from the nuclear industry's decision-making process on workers' health, community protection and family compensation;

(iii) increased secrecy from industry and the state over nuclear power;

(iv) the threat of nuclear pollution (ibid).

Sr. Bertell made the moral point that a link between technology, jobs and health should coincide with increased civic participation and awareness. At the same time she called for increased controls over technology which should be employed for human good (ibid). Sr. Bertell echoed the UN's call for sustainable development when she stated that a balanced approach was needed on energy:

The energy source we pursue cannot sacrifice the needs of future generations to satisfy the desires of present generations. The energy source we pursue cannot sacrifice truth-telling and concern for public health for economic good (*A Nuclear Ireland?* 1978 p 166).

The Health Risks Frame:

The Health-risks frame was presented by Dr. Helen Caldicott of Boston's Children's' Hospital. Originally from Australia, Dr.

Caldicott had lobbied the French government about a decade before the sinking of the Greenpeace ship, the Rainbow Warrior, in New Zealand by French agents. In her submission Dr. Caldicott challenged a statement by Ray Burke that nuclear power would be 'good for the people'. Nuclear power 'had produced epidemics of leukaemia, cancer and genetic disease' (*A Nuclear Ireland*?1978 p 106) according to Dr Caldicott. She linked nuclear power with the armaments industry. The health risks of radiation were seen in instances of cancer and leukaemia in the US, she claimed. The doctor also made reference to the threat of genetic engineering, a subject that would re-emerge in Ireland decades later. For Dr. Caldicott the damage caused by radiation to the human genetic system would have dreadful repercussions over generations. Another health risk raised by the doctor was the carcinogenic radioactive waste from nuclear power which remains toxic for half a million years (ibid). Dr. Caldicott also predicted the dangers of terror groups stealing or obtaining materials for nuclear weapons.

The Economic Frame:

The economic frame was put forward by the union chief, John Carroll. While he acknowledged the wider acceptance of the hazards of nuclear proliferation among the public Carroll wished to highlight the economic fallacy involved in the nuclear option. The 'doubtful economics' as he termed it, involved the development of an energy plan that would leave Ireland's grid in the hands of the international cartels which controlled multinationals. In addition to the health risks highlighted by other speakers, Carroll argued that nuclear power plants were expensive due to the high security costs associated with similar projects elsewhere. The transportation of raw materials and nuclear waste was both expensive and hazardous in the extreme and would be subject to 'severe security measures' (*A Nuclear Ireland? 1978* p 44). Furthermore, a nuclear plant at Carnsore would have been achieved at a high cost of over £300 million with US cases indicating rising costs for nuclear power plant construction and maintenance. Some American plants were unable to operate due to the scarcity of uranium supplies, which had rising costs of nearly 10 % per annum. Another cost outlined by Carroll was the 'vast sums of money which the nuclear industry has spent on propagandising its wares' (ibid).

Carroll was concerned that the high costs for building, maintaining and promoting a nuclear power plant would be taken from social services or other aspects of the state's development plans. Moreover, he anticipated only minor employment levels at the Carnsore plant with no extra employment that would have been achieved from a conventional power plant. At the same time resources for alternative energies such as wind and tidal power would be diverted to fund the nuclear plant which itself, would struggle to reach full capacity due to 'shut downs and infrequency of operation that performance entails', with 'no guarantee that such a plant will operate during its lifetime at anything like an average 60% capacity which will add to the costs of the energy produced' (ibid).

The European Frame

Petra Kelly outlined her vision for a better Europe which embraced 'a civic, non-violent community of various member states' (*A Nuclear Ireland?* 1978 p 89). For Kelly, a German of Irish extraction, Ireland still remained 'ecologically intact' (ibid). Kelly outlined a cultural discourse which contextualised Ireland as a place of rural culture with an enduring 'loyalty to locality' (ibid), which reflected a European ideal of traditional values. The shift to nuclear power would see Ireland become reliant on a centralised and erratic form of energy. The security threats surrounding nuclear power would affect Irish politics and society, leading to an over-emphasis on centralised technocratic power. The risks inherent in nuclear processing were so great that a controlled society would emerge in its wake, with implications for democratic freedom, according to Kelly. The results for Irish society were stark:

> The delicate web of social life called democracy will be torn and ripped apart due to the very nature of nuclear power and the monitoring and protection and

surveillance necessary for the worker, the general population and the environment (*A Nuclear Ireland?* 1978 p 91).

This combination of economic, cultural and ecological frames allowed Kelly to invoke a familiar rallying call for the Irish audience, that of dependency on a foreign source. This dependency would range from various supplies to nuclear expertise, while security demands would challenge the social fabric of the countryside. Kelly called for Ireland to resist the type of technocratic power which had been introduced in other EEC member states. Kelly also appealed to the Irish sense of independence to argue that the country could stand out as a type of ecological beacon for a Europe which had become engulfed in an economic and political morass. She also raised concerns about the need for democratic participation in the nuclear debate, saying the state's endorsement of Carnsore 'already demonstrates that the right to complete and objective information of every citizen is being squelched' (ibid).

Kelly then argued that across the EEC political and scientific expedience was replacing accountability, while the true health costs of nuclear power were being withheld throughout the Community's member states. Ireland's involvement with nuclear power would also pave the way for an erosion of her traditional neutrality, with European military cooperation focusing on nuclear capabilities. Such a scenario would draw Ireland closer to membership of the North Atlantic Treaty Alliance (NATO), according to Kelly, in order to fulfil the EEC's ambitions to increase its global political power. This was being resented by anti-nuclear and pacifist groups across Europe and Kelly asked Irish citizens to join their campaign of resistance to nuclear energy. For Kelly, Ireland could still choose 'two minutes before midnight, whether or not it will accept the two headed monster – nuclear power and NATO' (ibid). Kelly would subsequently go on to found the German Green party and win a seat in the European parliament before her tragic and premature death.

In the aftermath of the anti-nuclear campaign calls for a public inquiry increased. The Labour Party, under pressure due to its pro-nuclear stance, called for a referendum (Baker 1988 p. 12). Fine Gael limited itself to calling for an inquiry while adding that the concerns of the public should be addressed. While the radical left and the ITGWU opposed nuclear power, the Worker's Party continued to support the Carnsore Plant placing itself in the mainstream (ibid). Fianna Fail conceded on the public inquiry, hoping to reduce the public pressure which was building on the issue. Not for the first or last time would Fianna Fail be caught between an economic nationalist infrastructural project and growing populist opposition. In February, Minister O'Malley announced that a public inquiry would take place. However, this did not have the desired effect, as opposition to the state's nuclear policy increased after the announcement (ibid). An Interdepartmental Committee was established but again the government provided further political opportunities for the anti-nuclear movement by referring to the Committee's Report. In addition, the planned public inquiry never took place. The public felt misled on the issue, and the anti-nuclear campaigners appeared to be justified in their stance.

The campaign against nuclear power in Ireland and globally had been bolstered by concerns raised by the Three Mile Island reactor core meltdown in March 1979. By that time in the US the anti-nuclear movement, led by Ralph Nader, had captured the public's imagination in the wake of the 'No Nukes' concerts and film featuring contemporary artists such as Jackson Browne, Bruce Springsteen and Crosby Stills and Nash. The threat of hazardous nuclear waste was also becoming part of popular culture featuring as a threat in films and on television programmes (Szasz 1994 p. 55). While people lacked the expertise to fully understand all of the issues, popular culture had branded the nuclear industry and any client governments as the 'bad guys' in this dispute. This populist framing of the nuclear issue helped to mobilize the national and global anti-nuclear movement to a considerable extent.

The summer of 1979 gave rise to plans to hold a second festival at Carnsore. This rally was more politically focused but lacked the national impact or serious media coverage of the first event (Dalby 1985 p. 14). The second Carnsore festival called "Return to the Point" also provided a forum for radical European groups, and some of the increased political debates led to splits and disagreements on tactics (Baker 1990 p. 56). Three more festivals were held at Carnsore and the Irish anti-nuclear movement began to network and interact with the international movement particularly the French movement (ibid).

Conclusion

Mobilisation

Movements mobilise 'internal' resources such as expertise, leadership, finances, in order to improve the 'process of increasing the readiness to act collectively' (Gamson 1975). What was interesting in the first phase of the Carnsore protest was the willingness of locals with expertise, such as doctors who were concerned about the health risks of nuclear plants, to involve themselves in a campaign opposed to state policy. From that point on personnel, such as leaders, experts or support volunteers made themselves readily available to support the anti-nuclear cause. The emergence of a 'new middle class' (Inglehart 1977) in Ireland during the 1970s represented a section of the population that was educated and understood the potential threat posed by nuclear power.

Culturally, these new middle class activists were conditioned by local and international events ranging from the 1960s new left student, feminist and anti-war movements to the emergence of an environmental consciousness in the aftermath of the first Earth Day in 1970. The emergence of a post 1968 radical left in Europe also brought their influence to bear on the Irish anti-nuclear campaign (Baker 1990 p. 56). The ecopopulist 'no nukes' movement in the United States also provided a context in which Irish activists could locate their campaign. The ability of the Irish movement to frame the anti-nuclear issue as a moral question also appealed to the wider public who were less interested in radical or cultural politics. In contrast the state seemed unable to present a strong case in favour of nuclear power.

Political Opportunities

As the political process embarks on shifts to existing policy frameworks new opportunities open up for social movements (Eisinger 1973). As the state attempted to shift its energy policy in the aftermath of the oil crisis in the mid 1970s, the less than comprehensive knowledge about the links between nuclear energy and nuclear arms created a political opportunity for Irish activists to exploit. This opening in the political opportunity structure of the state allowed anti-nuclear activists to frame the issue as a moral one, thereby extending the grievance frame surrounding the issue in a way which would add pacifists, radical leftists and even the largest trades union to their list of allies. This facilitated the mobilisation process allowing a local protest in County Wexford to grow into a national movement.

Due to the nature of the populist Irish political system politicians are vulnerable to the demands of the public, if these demands are mobilised in a significant and politically coherent manner, as the state attempts to accommodate vested interests (Scruggs 1999 p 9). Therefore, the nature of the Irish political system could be said to have facilitated the wider mobilisation of the anti-nuclear movement. As the Fianna Fail government of 1977 had been elected on the back of a populist surge in their vote, they were vulnerable to a potential electoral backlash from the public, a concern which outweighed their desire to introduce nuclear power in Ireland.

Outcome

The government eventually abandoned its plans for nuclear power, due to a series of factors including 'the Three Mile Island accident and the Kinsale gas find, combined with Des O'Malley's expulsion from the party' (Edward Walsh *Irish Times* April 26 2006). However, the Carnsore anti-nuclear protests were also a factor in the reversal of the government's nuclear energy policy, a significant victory for any social movement. Nonetheless, the anti-nuclear protests also represented the birth of a wider populist environmental movement in Ireland. This movement was distinct from the 'official environmentalism' (Tovey 1992 b) of groups such as An Taisce. It was a coalition of many green and new left groups across the island of Ireland. Some of these groups would go on to form the Green Alliance, which later became Comhaontas Glas and the Irish Green Party. Petra Kelly returned to Germany to co-found Die Grunden, the German Greens, making a significant imprint on European environmental politics until her death. The ITGWU would ultimately go into neo-corporatist partnership in the 1990s while Christy Moore became an Irish folk hero.

Moreover, like so many radical Irish movements this nascent environmental movement experienced many splits over tactics and strategies, leaving many members to surface at times of local 'NIMBYism' (not in my backyard) in the intervening years. Many groups such as Friends of the Earth, continued to be active, particularly on University Campuses. By the 1980s the global Campaigns for Nuclear Disarmament (CND) would become a major political voice against nuclear arms proliferation. Despite the Chernobyl disaster in 1986 and the end of the Cold War, nuclear power has again come to the fore, ironically, as an environmentally friendly alternative to fossil fuels in the post Gulf War era. A recent Forfas report (April 2006) has also indicated that the nuclear option may have to be considered by future governments as Ireland's dependency on external, fossil based fuels will become unsustainable, while Dr. Edward Walsh of the University of Limerick has argues that Ireland might need 'a cluster of nuclear plants' to deal with any impending fuel crisis resulting from the decline of fossil fuels (*Irish Times* April 26 2006). The advocacy campaign of Adi Roche and Ali Hewson, who run the Chernobyl Children's Fund and bring children affected by the Chernobyl disaster for recuperation with Irish families serves as a reminder of the perils of nuclear power. It may be some time before people are willing to consider the nuclear option as a future energy policy for Ireland, despite the UK government's plans to redevelop

Sellafield as a potential site for the next phase of their nuclear energy production.

Chapter Six

The Anti-Toxics Movement

Introduction

During the 1970s and 1980s the issue of toxic pollution from multinationals gained international significance while anti-toxics campaigns became widespread. With increased understandings of the risks posed by toxic pollution, due to heightened media coverage a 'new issue' (Szasz 1999) developed in community politics, initially in the US and subsequently across the globe, including Ireland. As with most new social movement activity there was a good deal of interaction between various campaigns as anti-war and anti-nuclear protests came to provide momentum and influence for anti-toxics groups across the United States. Issues such as the use of 'agent orange' herbicide defoliant in populated areas during the Vietnam War and the risks posed by radiation informed the stance of anti-toxics campaigners who framed their protests around health-risks and corporate indifference to host communities.

One of the multinationals involved in the production of 'agent orange' was Merrell-Dow, who planned to escape the onset of the increased environmental regulation in the US by relocating a pharmaceutical plant to Youghal in County Cork. Dow had planned to manufacture the antihistamine terfenadine at the plant (Whitty 1988 p 9). Dow's involvement in the production of 'agent orange' and subsequent publicity about the health affects which affected US soldiers who came into contact with the chemical provided anti-toxics campaigners in Ireland with a set of pre-existing arguments which assisted the formation of discursive health risks and the 'uncaring and deceitful' multinational frames. US campaigns against corporate groups such as Merrell Dow also provided an established portfolio of advocate driven scientific data that could contest any scientific positions held by the multinational or state officials. In addition the success of the 'no-nukes' protests at Carnsore were underpinned by the Chernobyl nuclear power-plant meltdown in 1986 which sent a radioactive cloud across Europe increasing communities' concerns about the motives and culpabilities of industries or the state, in cases of widespread industrial pollution.

Ireland's favourable low corporate tax regime attracted many US pharmaceutical industries including Merrell-Dow in the 1970s and 1980s, such as Pfizer, Merck, Syntex, SmithKline and Schering-Plough. Factors which these multinationals found attractive included the IDA's presentation of Ireland as a location with wage restraint, purpose built factories, compliant local authorities and lax environmental regulation (Jones 1988 p 19). With a potential of halving operating costs being one of the favourable results for multinationals that relocated from the US to Ireland this increase in multinationals coming to Ireland was hardly surprising. However, the onset of the toxic multinational would also result in a series of protests about the environmental and health risks of corporate pollution across the nation.

Background

Multinational-led development

The abandonment of protectionist policies in the 1950s was followed by the state adopting multinational-led development as a means of securing growth. This process began with the relaxation of corporation taxes while the introduction of the Shannon Free Airport Development Company and the industrial zone were significant components of this new economic restructuring. By the 1970s import tariffs were abolished as the state prepared to join the EEC (Travers 2000). The Irish Development Authority (IDA) was given greater flexibility in the task of attracting multinationals to Ireland. Other policies introduced by the state to improve the climate for multinational investment included a zero rate of corporation tax on export profits and a combined analysis from the state, industry and trades unions to increase Ireland's competitiveness and manufacturing potential (ibid).

In addition, specific sites were targeted as potential destinations for multinational plants that were offered generous incentives to relocate to Ireland. One such area was Cork Harbour, which was identified in 1972 as a site for significant industrial development due to its deep-water port and on land facilities. Overall, Ireland's attempts to attract US investment in the early 1970s were very successful. Between 1970 and 1973, the US chemical industry alone invested up to $173 million in Ireland (Allen 2004 p. 3). Major US chemical industries such as Beecham, Pfizer and Schering Plough opened manufacturing plants in Ireland during this time. While IDA led programmes were a significant factor in this investment drive, so too were the changes in legal frameworks and public perceptions of the toxics industry in the United States.

Just as the anti-nuclear movement had become a vehicle for the expression of dissent on a range of issues, the anti-toxics movement in the US had become a significant political rallying point for communities that were concerned about health issues as well as local corruption and a wider democratic deficit on a national level. As technology and science were perceived as the vehicles for the capitalist state's imposition of modernity on local communities, communities led by new left activists in the United States began to resist toxic dumps and plants, leading to a rise in 'ecopopulism' (Szasz 1994). As the federal government in Washington responded to ecopopulist resistance by passing increasingly stringent anti-pollution laws, US multinationals began to look elsewhere for potential sites for their manufacturing plants.

These moves coincided with Ireland's liberalisation of their regulatory corporate legislation. As individual multinationals found out, local authorities were in competition with each other and offered deals which included further regulatory laxity at local level in return for investment in their areas. In addition, powers to inspect or close down polluting plants were scaled down or removed altogether (Taylor 2001 pp. 16, 17). In this context the difficulties faced by community groups opposed to toxic plants becomes evident.

Throughout the early 1970s, a number of communities resisted multinational sites in their localities, due to concerns about toxicity and pollution. As many of these plants were being sited in rural areas the alliances between local farmers and their political representatives was enough to lead to plans for any potential multinational plant being abandoned. The farming community was still the source of considerable local power and both Fianna Fail and Fine Gael were reliant on the support of the agrarian sector.

However, as the decade went on, the state's prioritisation of multinational-led development over agriculture and tourism meant that local political alliances did not have as much political clout as they once had in Ireland's traditionally clientelist political system. As the economy went through periods of fluctuation rural communities facing high unemployment and emigration had become more reliant on the state and multinationals to provide jobs. In this context, the emergence of local anti-toxics groups is significant as new middle class professionals, unrestricted by dependency on the state or agricultural sector, began to oppose multinationals due to the threat of health issues.

Mobilisation

The localised nature of community resistance to multinationals meant that the groups were NIMBYist in nature, often emerging from concerned meetings led by residents' groups. One of the primary tactics used by communities against multinationals was in lodging planning process objections in large numbers, primarily citing health concerns and pollution potentials. In order to achieve any sort of success, community groups had to organise committees, hold public meetings to highlight their grievances to both the wider community and the authorities and engage with sympathetic experts such as lawyers and scientists, to support their arguments. The emergence of new left politics in the late 1960s meant that there was a small but significant pool of environmentalists and radicals to draw upon as a source for activists willing to donate time or money to the cause.

As community campaigns against Beechams in Clare and Pfizer in Cork indicated even in the early 1970s, communities that were determined to resist multinational plants in their areas could be successful. However, as the state began to prioritise multinational-led development from the mid 1970s onward, the pressure to present Ireland as a suitable region for investment without major industrial or community unrest began to build. And while the conflict in Northern Ireland began to intensify, the state's desire to placate local radicals began to diminish. External pressure from corporate headquarters in the United States increased the constraints faced by the Irish state in dealing with concerned communities. As authorities attempted to impose unpopular policies from above, political opportunities for grassroots campaigners increased, as the initial concerns about health risks and toxicity could be combined with a portrayal of the state as undemocratic as part of a framing process (Leonard 2005 pp. 63-65).

The campaigns against toxic multinationals have been characterised by a community group's ability to forge alliances with scientific experts who can present an argument which demonstrates why any political site would be harmful to the local population and environment. This contestation of science has been the basis for 'populist' environmentalism's (Tovey 1992 b) resistance to the professional expertise employed by the state or multinational. The use of science as an empowering resource (Phyne 1996 p. 3) to be mobilised by communities has emerged in an era of 'risk society' (Beck 1992) and 'legitimation crisis' (Habermas 1972), where people are no longer convinced of the rationality of the argument put forward by the state or scientists in defence of new technologies or industrial processes. In a time where oil spills from super-tankers, chemical accidents and even nuclear reactor core meltdowns became a part of people's lives, attempts to mobilise communities against the potential threats posed by a multinational were enhanced by an increased sense of risk and sceptiscism.

By the time of the first Carnsore protests, Friends of the Earth in Cork also began to organise protests about toxic plants around the Cork Harbour area. Cork Harbour was central to the state's multinational-led development policy and was seen as a base for many of the chemical plants now having to leave the United States due to the tighter regulatory regime operating there. FOE combined with local residents' associations to mobilise large scale opposition groups such as the Bandon Valley Protection Association and the Cork Noxious Industry Action Group which also had members of the Cork Anti-nuclear group on their committee (Baker 1990 pp. 58, 59).

This creation of networks and larger groupings represented the next phase of mobilisation for the anti-toxics movement as localised campaigns of opposition began to unite together pooling the resources of expertise and campaign strategies, while bringing together a wider activist base. Toxic waste was becoming a political and cultural "icon" (Szasz 1994 p. 38) for environmental groups, both in Ireland and globally. In 1978, the discovery that thousands of tonnes of toxic waste had been illegally dumped over decades at the Love Canal site in New York catapulted the issue of toxic waste into the media while simultaneously confirming the worst suspicions held by environmentalists and concerned communities about the shadowy nature of some components of the chemicals industry. As information about the long term health issues of toxic chemicals became common knowledge through the ongoing media coverage of Love Canal, communities became concerned about the potential for birth defects, miscarriages, leukaemia and cancers resulting from exposure to industrial pollution, reinforced by the decision to evacuate pregnant women and young children from the Love Canal region (ibid). The destruction of the community at Love Canal, who were left with traumatic health problems in an unliveable, toxic, neighbourhood illustrated to many the potential price to be paid for inviting a multinational into a region.

While Ireland was particularly vulnerable to long periods of economic recession and unemployment many communities, particularly those comprised of middle class professionals or affluent farmers, were not interested in importing the threat of toxic pollution into their areas. As local concerns about health risks clashed directly with the state's policy of multinational-led development the late 1970s and early 1980s were characterised by a series of antitoxics campaigns against the siting of factories or toxic dumps. A number of well documented campaigns came to signify the Irish anti-toxic movement, including the Hanrahan family's challenge against Merck Sharpe and Dohme in County Tipperary (Allen and Jones 1990, Allen 1994, Baker 1990), the Ovens residents' groups' successful campaign against Raybestos Manhattan between 1976 and 1980 (Allen and Jones 1990) and the Womanagh Valley Protection Association campaign against Merrell Dow in 1988 (Peace 1993), or the people of Derry's challenge against DuPont in Northern Ireland (Allen 1992), a campaign that united environmentalists against both the Northern administration and the Southern state.

All of these campaigns against multinational-led development shared certain mobilisation strategies and their campaigns took on sinister characteristics despite a range of differing outcomes. All of the anti-toxics groups built their challenges around a contestation of science as they framed their arguments around the health risks posed by chemical pollution. This allowed the challengers to build up a dialogue with the wider public, who may not have had the same views or benefited from a similar middle class autonomy. By creating a sense of 'shared grievance' the anti-toxics groups widened their appeal amongst the general public. In order to promote their concerns about health risks with the public the anti-toxics groups needed to create events which the media would cover at local and national levels. In order to maximise any media coverage, protest events played on cultural images of 'risk society' (Beck 1992) as activists dressed in industrial protective clothing and boiler suits and wore face masks to highlight risks of airborne toxins. Women and children were often prominent at protests carrying hand made placards against pollution while creating a sense of inter-generational grievance against the threat of toxics, which could take years and decades to repair after spills or leakages.

Anti-toxics campaigners also exploited a traditional sense of hostility to officialdom and 'outsiders' that existed in Irish communities as part of their attempts to create a sense of shared grievance. Exploitation of populist localism was a feature of the Irish political scene and was part of a culture of opposition which could be traced back to the days of British rule through to the post-independence, inward looking protectionism which had shaped cultural and political activity over time. This 'populist' environmentalism (Tovey 1992 b p. 283) was part of an emerging backlash against the modernisation projects of the state, the EEC, or multinational corporations, and had a particular resonance with rural communities and suburban professionals who combined in their opposition to toxic plants in their areas.

Raybestos Manhattan (1976 – 1979)

When Raybestos Manhatten began to experience regulatory difficulties with their asbestos manufacturing plants in the United States, a decision was taken to relocate its production base to 'non regulated peripheral' (Allen 1990 p.95) locations. One such location was Ovens, near Ringaskiddy, County Cork. Planning permission was granted for the Raybestos plant at an early stage, denying concerned locals a chance to lodge objections to the project. The first attempt to frame a challenge to the plant focused on the lack of clarity over the nature of the production at Raybestos' proposed plant, the toxicity of asbestos and the lack of planning notices in the local Cork press (Allen 2004 p.96). This approach gave the Ovens residents an opportunity to open up two action frames: one focusing on health risks and toxicity, while the other portrayed the state and Raybestos as engaging in dishonest collusion about the nature of such risks.

By focusing on 'hard grievances' (Walsh, Warland and Smith 1997 p 45) such as the threats posed by the toxicity of the asbestos manufactured at the plant, the Ovens residents were able to benefit from a wider mobilisation of concerned residents in the surrounding Ringaskiddy area. This form of 'hard grievance' highlighted the wider risks posed by a toxic industry in the overall geographic area and allowed the NIMBY style Ovens residents' groups to extend their campaign at an early stage. Further mobilisation opportunity for the residents emerged when Raybestos began to attempt to locate an asbestos dump in the area. This provided an opportunity to object to the planning application for the dump, which the residents took in July 1976 (Allen 2004 p. 196). The residents achieved some access to political structures through their consultations with the planning committee of Cork County Council (ibid). The residents' tactic of objecting to the dump led to a new site being sought in a nearby area providing the residents with further alliances and wider mobilisation.

Associations' involvement in the dispute grew from the wider mobilisation through the spread of 'shared grievances' against Raybestos across the area. Local womens' groups also came to the fore during this campaign. These groups favoured direct action over the legal process and began to engage in a high profile picketing campaign at the Raybestos plant, IDA offices, and even the US embassy in Dublin (Allen 2004 pp. 95-99).

By early 1977, as Raybestos were granted planning permission for their dump site, the residents' campaign had grown to encompass residents' groups and civic organisations across Cork city and County, as well as encompassing allies such as John Carroll from the IGWU (ibid) who had led the Carnsore anti nuclear protests. At this stage, the residents had developed an 'Eight point programme' as part of their tactical approach to the campaign. This incorporated strategies such as appeals, a rates strike, pickets against local IDA and trades union offices, as well as against waste haulage contractors and the withdrawal of children from a nearby school (ibid).

Raybestos responded by taking out an injunction against the picket at the dump site which was being held 24 hours a day to prevent any dumping taking place. Pickets were also being maintained at the Raybestos plant. Threats of jail terms did not deter the protesters and by May of 1979 Raybestos' attempt to use the dump was blocked by picketers. The brutality of the police response has been documented in local press reports as having involved excessive force against the picketers, who were mainly women and children (Allen and Jones 1990 pp. 109, 110). This form of hostile response from the authorities provided the residents with an extension to their frame of multinational and state collusion against local communities. Press reports describing the police assault on the picketers shocked the wider community. The negative press coverage also weakened Raybestos' resolve and the residents responded to this incident by smashing the gate and fences at the dump while returning dumped bags of asbestos to the Raybestos plant overnight. A bomb scare was also directed at the Raybestos plant from an anonymous source (Allen and Jones 1990 pp. 109, 110). The residents took on a more belligerent tone in their communications with Raybestos and the IDA after these incidents. Raybestos claimed they were making millions in losses (ibid).

The residents employed some innovative tactics in response to Raybestos' continued dumping of asbestos, including photographing materials found at the dump (Allen 2004 pp. 103, 104). They were able to convince Cork County Council that Raybestos was engaged in violation of its planning permission (ibid). Ultimately, it was the poor condition of workers employed at Raybestos that would lead to the plant's closure and after a series of spills in the factory Raybestos announced the closure of their Cork plant in October 1980. The workers had been able to draw on the resources and expertise of the Cork Noxious Industry Action group, which had emerged at the time of the first Carnsore anti-nuclear protests. The networking potential of the nascent Irish environmental movement was established through these links and communities on the South coast had seen off a nuclear plant and an asbestos factory through their campaigns of resistance to aspects of the state's industrialisation policy. While the issue of toxic pollution had provided a localised sense of grievance which campaigners could mobilise, the indifference shown to the local communities allowed protests against toxic multinationals to 'go beyond NIMBY' (Szasz 1994) through the creation of a more extensive network of activists and experts who supported campaigns with 'interest- driven' (Grove –White 1993) data with which to frame their arguments.

Merrell Dow (1988 – 1989)

The Rural Response

In the aftermath of the announcement that the US multinational, Merrell Dow, was going to open a chemical factory in their region, the farming communities in east Cork began the process of mobilising a campaign against the proposed plant. Their first tactic was appealing to An Bord Pleanála (Peace 1993 p. 189). This dairy farming community was different to the new middle class residents of Cork Harbour. It was a mixture of small and large farm holdings combined with shopkeepers and publicans in an area of relative affluence (ibid, p. 191). However, one area of commonality this community shared with its urban professional neighbours was a desire to maintain their autonomy from state or multinational interference in their region.

As in many such disputes the secretive approach taken by the technocratic state and regulatory fearing multinational provided a significant opportunity for the local community to mobilise a campaign of grievance against any proposed plant. Resourceful local families were able to open up links with environmental sources in Ireland and the United States. Through these links Merrell Dow and Dow Chemical's extensive history of pollution at their US plants in Michigan were uncovered. This pollution involved discharging effluent into local weirs (Peace 1993 p. 194). This had created a history of discord between Dow and the US EPA. Concerned locals were able to construct a frame of shared grievance with this information, allowing their campaign to envelop the concerns of the wider community.

At the centre of this campaign was the Womanagh Valley Protection Association (WVPA). This group was determined to mobilise a wider support base for their campaign and engaged the support of a new ally with scientific credentials, Dr. Rory Finegan. His expertise was a vital component of the communities' attempt to expand their grievance and link frames to incorporate some of the negative impacts the Merrill plant could have on the locality. The impacts included a reduction in property and land values, air and water pollution, increased health risks to humans and livestock, which would create major changes in the local way of life (Peace 1995 p. 194).

The mobilisation of internal links by the WVPA's committee was also successful due to a series of meetings in local communities at which the latest information on the campaigns was disseminated. The hazards posed locally by Merrell Dow were placed in the context of other environmental disputes, both in Ireland and internationally, to combine local concerns with a growing ecological consciousness taking place globally after major incidents such as the meltdown at Chernobyl nuclear plant in 1986 (Peace 1993 p. 195). The recognition by community groups about their need to mobilise against the state's 'integrationist approach' whereby community development and legitimacy was equated with job creation (Curtin and Varley 1995 p. 380). Seen in this context the mobilisation of a community response in east Cork against a multinational could be seen to be as much a part of a contestation about the state's capacity to implement policy initiatives in the face of a community's desire for greater autonomy, as it was about any emergent environmental consciousness.

Herein lay the nature of the political opportunity structure surrounding Irish community campaigns against the state's policy agendas. While the state wished to 'modernise' rural areas by facilitating multinationals who wished to set up plants in Ireland communities become concerned that the state was failing to prioritise the safety of those living in that region. Sociological research has indicated that rural Irish communities invariably identify themselves in reaction to change rather than in response to it and the community remains the core component of individual identity in rural areas (Curtin 1998 p. 80).

Community groups which organise themselves in 'defence of space' campaigns see themselves as custodians of not just their hinterland, but of their very way of life (Curtin and Varley 1995 p. 392). It is this area of commonality through shared identity which community campaigns such as the WVPA can exploit for the purpose of mobilising around understandings of shared grievance. Attempts to understand what lies at the heart of Irish community opposition to state policy on environmental issues must first identity the strong sense of local identity which is rooted in the hinterland. This form of environmental 'consciousness' is different to learned behaviour such as concern for the state of the oceans or of the future of the planet. As such, two forms of environmental consciousness can be said to exist simultaneously. One is based on a shared identity which is shaped by relationships with the local environment which is largely instinctive and the other is based on a concern borne primarily out of media depictions of global environmental degradation.

In this context, the WVPA's ability to mobilise a significant section of the population of east Cork against Merrell Dow's plant could be understood as part of a deeper rural antipathy to outside interference. This form of grounded opposition held sway despite Merrell's attempts to convince locals that safety at the plant could be achieved by investing more money there (Peace 1993 p. 195). The WVPA could draw on themes of morality, local identity and opposition to multinational ruthlessness to frame their grievance campaign. Their tactic of bringing public meetings to the towns and villages in the area was successful serving both as a vehicle for disseminating information about the potential hazards of the site while simultaneously fostering a sense of community resistance to the plant in defence of their locality.

Another opportunity for the campaigners arose from the decision to let Merrell Dow with its history of polluting communities near its plants in the United States to monitor its own pollution levels. The problems stemmed from the practice of local authorities granting multinationals a lax regulatory regime in order to attract investment in their areas and acting as 'both gamekeeper and poacher' (Taylor 2001 p. 27). The benign and facilitating approach of both the state and local authorities became a focus for the WVPA who highlighted the scant regard that the authorities or multinationals had paid to local concerns (Peace 1993 p. 195). However, the WVPA didn't attempt to build any significant alliances with political figures and those who attended their meetings were rounded upon sharply (ibid). In the absence of any attempt to bring their campaign to the political level the WVPA missed an opportunity to bring the mobilisation process to another level. However, such was the strength of their mobilisation of a sense of local grievance, borne out of a community under threat, that any need for alliances with key political figures was unnecessary. The depiction of a toxic multinational attempting to alter a traditional way of life with the support of uncaring bureaucrats was a potent image for the campaigners and attempts to create links with formal political figures may have compromised that image.

"Hard grievances" and scientific discourse

It is interesting to note the ability to shift the basis for the campaign from 'hard grievance' to 'soft grievance' (Walsh, Warland and Smith 1997 p. 45) as the situation required. At times the WVPA highlighted the hard grievance of the hazardous waste plant being imposed by Merrell Dow on the local community. On other occasions their campaign focused on the 'soft grievance' of the rights of local communities to control their own future. 'Soft grievances' based on autonomy, equity and social justice concerns are often the basis for campaigns of cultural mobilisation and resistance. And while anti-toxics movements are usually characterised by the 'hard grievances' of campaigns against technology the combination of hard and soft grievances can become a potent one. Strengthening the mobilisation of a campaign by combining grievances based on technological risks while also acting as a cultural rallying point (ibid).

This form of emotive mobilisation also allowed the WVPA to build up a critique of the state which was selling out the local way of life in order to promote 'modernisation'. Farmers in small communities had been subjected to an ongoing offensive by the sate, which wanted farmers to introduce more scientific and technological practices into agricultural production. At the same time the state had prioritised the development of an 'agribusiness' sector in place of small holdings, in an attempt to shift Irish agriculture 'from Co-ops to capitalism' (Tovey and Share 2003 p. 61). Deviation from supporting local knowledge to importing scientific approaches from abroad created a sense of grievance in rural communities which campaigns like the WVPA could draw on. As grant-aiding for scientific technology was introduced small holders that were deemed to be inefficient by the state were encouraged to give up farming despite its centrality in their way of life (ibid).

The WVPA's gathering of over a thousand signatures from concerned locals led to An Bord Pleanála's decision to grant the group an oral hearing. This transformed the WVPA's challenge from a campaign which had focused on the mobilisation of grievance through a rural 'discourse' (Peace 1997 pp. 196-199) to an urban based legal challenge where legal and scientific fact held sway over community values. The WVPA spokespersons were cut off from their community at the Dublin based hearing and their arguments, which had lit up many a meeting in east Cork, became lost in the bureaucratic arena. The WVPA also found that their key allies such as tourism and fisheries board representatives only provided input into how a plant could be improved rather than prevented. They also had difficulties establishing exactly what Merrell Dow were going to do with the plant which undermined some of their scientific projections about the plant's hazardous potential (ibid).

Conclusion

The many campaigns against toxic multinationals in Ireland occurred in the 'first phase' (Leonard 2005) of environmental campaigning which occurred during the 1970s and 1980s, particularly in the rural counties of Munster which the state had targeted for multinational led development since the introduction of heavy industry to areas such as Cork Harbour or the Shannon Industrial Zone from the 1960s onward. The protracted dispute at Raybestos Manhatten, as well as the well documented Hanrahan dispute against Merck Sharp and Dohme in County Tipperary (Allen and Jones 1990), were among many disputes were local communities rejected industries that threatened local health and environment. These campaigns occurred despite longstanding patterns of unemployment and emigration which had blighted many of these regions. While in essence these campaigns were primarily populist in nature, the cycles of community based activism which began at Carnsore Point with the anti-nuclear protests led to an overlapping pattern of territorial protests with an emerging element of environmental consciousness which demonstrated a move towards a type of political response rooted in the landscapes and hinterlands these communities were attempting to protect. This development can be observed in the campaign which occurred at Womanagh Valley.

The WVPA's attempt to extend their campaign beyond its populist inception ran aground amid the scientific discourse created by both Merrell's experts and the WVPA's own key allies such as Rory Finnegan. The forum provided by an oral hearing did not allow the WVPA or their key allies to frame the issue in the manner they had hoped for: applying a populist discourse to oppose the threat of pollution in their region. While this process may have compromised the impartiality of An Bord Pleanála's hearing due to their deviation from an evaluation that was independent (Peace 1997 p. 159) the loss of potency experienced by the WVPA and their sympathetic experts served to underline the weakness of a planning process that was too reliant on populist sentiment without the legal or political connections to support the challenger's scientific arguments.

Ultimately, the WVPA's attempts to resist Merrell Dow's plant through mobilisation of populist rural dissent gave way to a bureaucratic exercise in keeping the plant's pollution levels to an 'acceptable' level (Peace 1993 p. 201). The anti-toxics campaigns which occurred throughout the 1970s and 1980s were part of the 'first phase' of environmental campaigning in Ireland (Leonard 2005).These campaigns had a localised or territorial aspect to them, but were part of a emerging consensus across rural and suburban communities in the west of Ireland that had come to consider toxic industries with a somewhat jaded eye, due to a series of factors which pointed towards the exploitative nature of the relationship between external multinationals and their host communities. Although these communities were often economically disadvantaged, they valued the resources of clean air and water or unspoilt agricultural land over any 'quick-fix' solution which came with the siting of a toxic multinational in their area.

Chapter Seven

Tynagh, Donegal and Croagh Patrick:

Campaigns against Mining

Introduction

Throughout the economically stagnant decades of the 1970s and 1980s a number of local disputes about national resources emerged across the country. The diverse and varied geological make-up of mountainous areas in the north-west or in County Wicklow were identified as holding potentially lucrative reserves of gold, zinc and uranium while the off-shore oil and gas fields of the Atlantic Shelf remained untapped. The extent to which successive Irish governments disposed of the nation's natural resources became the subject of considerable controversy leading to many campaigns which combined a resource protection frame with one of concern about democratic deficit as the activities of government ministers was called into question in regard to their dealings with mine and exploration companies. The legal framework for resource protection was also criticised by campaigners who feared that Ireland's natural resources were being sold off in a series of over-generous deals which provided no financial gain for the Irish taxpayer in addition to extensive ecological damage and limited concern for the local communities involved.

The methods employed in the process of mining became an issue of contention for communities. The use of highly toxic chemicals such as cyanide in the mining process threatened the landscape as well as the livelihoods of locals who were dependent on agriculture, tourism and fisheries in the regions.

The threat to these industries was threefold:

from the chemical agents such as cyanide or mercury used to separate gold traces from rock, in the toxic sediment that accumulates in the land and lakes surrounding a mine wiping out local fish stocks and poisoning livestock and in the heavy metals found in tailings (Laffan and Wall 1988 p 12).

The process of mining employed in these rural areas created an extensive threat to local ecosystems and agriculture. The use of open cast pits, the transportation of unrefined extractions for disposal and the storage of toxic residue on site exacerbated the threat to local communities. The process of leaching or washing out gold extracts from the base rock with cyanide created a series of toxic rock piles which allowed cyanide residue and dust to come into contact with the surrounding landscape and water tables, in addition to carrying the threat of airborne particles being spread across a wide area (ibid).

One mining dispute which encapsulated many of these issues was the Northgate operation at Tynagh in County Galway. The response of Northgate to the concerns of locals was somewhat dismissive, leading to widespread devastation across the area. This response to the pollution in Tynagh allowed their opponents to frame the industry and their state allies as greedy and disinterested in the welfare of the Tynagh community and surrounding environment. However, this dispute never emerged as a fully-fledged environmental campaign despite the high concentration of cyanide extracts used at the mine. At the time the potential for enhanced networking with other campaigns was limited due to the isolated nature of the local community and the hopes of economic benefits generated by the industry's promises to local landowners. The company's entrenched decision not to restore the area came to head decades later when the issue of ongoing pollution in the Tynagh area was raised in the Dail and in media reports.

With the emergence of the Shell to Sea campaign in County Mayo in 2005 the issue of resource protection also came to the fore with some of the Shell to Sea campaigners having been involved in the Mining Awareness protests in Galway and Mayo throughout the 1970s and 1980s. While individual farmers were afraid to take on the mining industry a group called 'Mining Awarenes' brought hundreds of people to meetings in the West with the protection of the West's 'holy mountain' at Croagh Patrick gaining considerable support from across the community. At the same time the Resource Protection Group, a left-wing movement which protested the sell-off of Irish resources to multinationals, actively led a campaign against the exploitation of mineral and off-shore reserves. The unveiled nature of Ireland's off-shore resources meant that campaigns would fall into abeyance until the dramatic campaign of the 'Rossport 5' gripped the nation. However, the 1970s and 1980s witnessed a series of mining disputes which brought environmental and community issues to the fore in previously tranquil rural areas.

Background

The state's predilection for multinational led development can be traced back to the 1950's when overseas mining companies were provided with incentives to exploit the mineral resources available at certain points across the country. The state's inability to extract these mineral resources led to a situation where local concerns and even domestic law were 'manipulated' (Curtin and Shields 1988 p. 109) by multinational mining companies who had no interests other than the exploitation of the local mineral base for profit. This form of dependency development resulted in a number of disputes between communities, the mining companies and the state. This chapter examines the mobilisation of two disputes against mining: uranium mining in Donegal and the lead and zinc mines in Tynagh, County Galway.

Concerns about the exploitation of the country's natural resources began to surface in the late 1970's. As a result of full and half tax exemptions for mines over the first two decades of their operations, in addition to a regime of compulsory purchases of lands and mineral assets by the state, a number of foreign mining companies came to invest in mining operations around the country (Curtin and Sheilds 1988 p. 112). One of these companies was the Canadian operation Northgate Explorations, which was run by Irish Canadians and listed as a public company in the Toronto Stock exchange (ibid).

Explorations at the Tynagh mine site had begun in the early 1960s. The granting of a mining licence was unusual as the first mineral finds were made by Northgate before any licence had been issued and without any consultation with local farmers (ibid, p. 114). While some in the local community felt that a mine would bring a degree of prosperity to the area many in the extended community became concerned that their way of life and local environment had come under threat. The local community's attempts to organise against the mine were hampered by their inability to mobilise either sympathetic experts or political allies. Farmers also felt that they had not been given a fair price for any local land that had been purchased as they were unaware of its new valuation in the wake of the mineral finds or that the state exercised control over all of the country's mineral wealth in spite of local ownership (ibid pp. 114, 115). The farmers' inability to forge alliances with any legal or scientific expert provided an indication of just how significant such key alliances were for subsequent campaigns.

In the absence of any local expertise networks the farmers were unaware of their ownership rights. The Irish legal system had not been involved in such disputes up to that point and was unable to provide local farmers with any legal framework with which to base a challenge (ibid). Seen in this context the lack of resources available to the Tynagh farming community made the mobilisation of a campaign very difficult. The key components of internal mobilisation such as finance, legal expertise, scientific data or political alliances were all missing. As a result the protests of the farmers lacked clarity or momentum. Certainly the risk of being defeated by the authorities and Northgate's representatives seemed to outweigh the chances of a victorious outcome to any challenge undertaken by the community. Faced with this dilemma many farmers simply sold off their land to Northgate as they were faced with the prospect of Northgate occupying and destroying their farmland anyway with the tacit approval of the state.

The legal anomalies which provided Northgate with legal protection from the state for unlicensed mining were compounded by the farmers' uncertainty as to the extent of damages they would be entitled to (ibid p. 116). Faced with a lack of resources and poor prospects for compensation individual farmers took whatever price Northgate offered for their lands which was detrimental to the communities' overall unity and resolve.

Community resistance was further weakened when recruiting began for the ore extracting process. In an area of high unemployment compounded by the loss of land and livelihoods, due to Northgate's enforced purchases, many local farmers signed up to work as manual labourers at the mine. The workforce at the mine was also divided into various components leaving little room for mobilising dissent. The Tynagh workers had different roles, capacities and ranks and didn't come from any one area in the locality thus heightening the sense of division therein (ibid p. 117).

The main area of dispute was economic rather than environmental. By the late 1970s the mine began to face closure as a consequence of exhausting its mineral base so unions began to press for improved redundancy packages for the workforce. Northgate's response was to look for increased productivity under the threat of closing the mines. Workers hoped to use extracted ore as leverage in their dispute and refused to load it onto ships in Galway (ibid p. 118). This action was unofficial and led to the workers being left without strike pay or unemployment benefit. As their desperation increased a mass picket and lockout shut down the mine. In August 1978 an injunction was given against the strike and the workers were forced to back down. The legal process had backed industry over the workers' concerns and they received little support from local politicians or business interests. Local community grievances about perceived injustices had no bearing and while the court recognised the depth of local feeling the overall imperative was that 'the law must be maintained' (ibid p. 120). Not for the last time would the Irish legal system fail to recognise the concerns of a rural community under threat from the manipulations of a foreign industry whose sole aim was the repatriation of profits.

Although the nature of the Tynagh dispute in 1978 wasn't perceived to be environmental the mine left a legacy of pollution in the area in addition to the disruption of a rural way of life. Laxity in the conditions for restoration of the land and a lack of pollution controls during the period when the mine was in operation led to thousands of acres of land in the area becoming unsuitable for agriculture (ibid). Over the years that the mine was in operation livestock had to be removed from local land and local produce was replaced by packaged food from local grocers paid for by the mine. Irish Base Metals had used a large amount of cyanide in their ore processing works and when the pollution from this process was highlighted by local councillors in 1982 the company refused to restore the affected areas (ibid p. 121). It was only then that the Irish Farmers' Association (IFA) lent their weight to the Tynagh community, ordering a members' ban on prospectors from Irish Base Metals. The perceived short-term benefits of the Tynagh mine were offset by the considerable pollution of that region.

The extent of the pollution was compounded by the acquiescence of the state which was prepared to support the mine company at almost any cost despite local concerns about the damage that was being done to the farming community around Tynagh. The short-term gains of local employment and corporate profitability were perceived as part of the modernisation of the state. The legacy of toxic pollution at the site of the mine indicates the fallacy of that perspective. Mining companies were able to repatriate their profits without taxation while family members of prominent politicians were appointed as directors of other mining companies, a situation that was indicative of the type of cronyism that was endemic at that time (Allen and Jones 1990 p. 50). Clearly the enforcement of pollution controls was not a priority for the state during these years.

While a succession of mining controversies eventually led to the formation of the Dublin based Resources Protection Campaign, the Tynagh community was unable to open up links with any form of political support group leaving them isolated during their dispute. Indeed the workers' prioritisation of improved redundancy packages over land restoration could be said to stem from a lack of the scientific knowledge which links with experts could have provided. The absence of state regulations on the use of toxins such as cyanide, together with the communities' lack of external expertise links, gave the mine company a free run in regard to toxic pollution in the area. The farmers' lack of legal expertise (and the legal sector's own limitations at that point) also allowed Northgate to occupy land and begin operations with impunity. The only criticism of the mine came from left-wing radicals and trades unionists who wanted to see better conditions for workers and more state control of the mine (Allen and Jones 1990 p. 50).

During the 1980s concerns about pollution in the area increased and in 1983 it emerged that 2,000 acres of land in the area were contaminated with lead, zinc and arsenic with local accounts of the devastation describing toxic dust blowing across the area killing plant life around the ravaged landscape and dead water pools near the mine site. Large numbers of livestock deaths were reported (Allen and Jones 1990 pp. 54, 55). The eight tonnes of sodium cyanide used at Tynagh mines also had a devastating affect on the local bird population and workers had to be deployed to collect the dead swans and ducks from the cyanide pools (Friel 2005 p. 3).

The Donegal Campaign (DUC)

The 1970s also witnessed mobilisation of a campaign against uranium mining near County Donegal. In the mid 1970s the European Economic Community (EEC) provided significant financial aid to mining companies in Ireland to extend explorations for uranium deposits to increase supplies for Europe's burgeoning nuclear industry. Local alternative groups made links with Belfast's Just Books Collective run by the

Belfast Anti-Nuclear Group and began to mobilise a campaign around meetings, information sessions and rallies across Donegal (Baker 1988 p. 8). Anti-nuclear groups which had emerged in the aftermath of the Carnsore protests provided support and expertise for local campaigners.

The Belfast group also produced a pamphlet titled "Uranium Mining in Donegal: The Dangers and Deceits" which was a free sheet that was distributed to over 6,000 people across the county. The pamphlet detailed the links between the EEC's desire to expand uranium mining and the nuclear arms industry as well as highlighting the environmental risks posed by uranium mines (Dalby 1985 p. 30). Locals in Tintown formed the Donegal Uranium Committee (DUC) and set about mobilising resources such as funds and scientific data with which to launch a campaign. DUC's campaign was the first such protest in Ireland to link the issues of health risks with that of environmental degradation (Baker 1990 p. 68) and as such provided a strategic breakthrough for Irish environmental campaigning.

This template of mobilisation which combined anthropocentric and ecocentric concerns (Eckersley 1992) about human health and ecological degradation was bolstered by the strong networks established through 'interpersonal contacts' (Friedman & McAdam 1992 p. 158) built from Carnsore to Belfast and from Belfast to Donegal. The local Tintown community became very involved in the dispute and members of the town's development committee as well as local teachers and doctors became prominent figures in the campaign by 1980 (Allen and Jones 1990 p. 61).

Despite the extent of their initial mobilisation phase the DUC were unable to create sufficient links with Donegal County Council and were unable to get funding for a monitoring study of the mine by An Foras Forbatha (the Planning and Construction Institute). Initial attempts at drilling in the area were halted by local families concerned about contamination of water supplies. The DUC continued to gather information on the topic and by March 1980 they held a large public meeting which was attended by DUC spokesperson Brian Flannery as well as local physicians who highlighted the health risks posed by the mine (Dalby 1985 p. 31). The campaigners were also able to highlight a number of structures that were erected without planning permission at the mine site (ibid).

The DUC began to create a sense of grievance in the wider community through their health risks frame. Early press releases stated that their aim was to protect the environment and health of the people of Donegal (Allen and Jones 1990 p. 61). They also promoted their local cause as one component of a wider national campaign against nuclear power in Ireland. In August 1980 the DUC took part in the third anti-nuclear rally at Carnsore Point. The focus of the Carnsore rallies had come to encompass the issue of uranium mining by that stage and the DUC had a large exhibition on the issue providing an information resource while establishing wider networks at the festival. Members of the Cork anti-nuclear group had also attended and addressed DUC's rallies in Donegal (Allen and Jones 1990 p. 64).

While representatives of the state had refused to meet the DUC they were able to successfully mobilise external expertise links with the Oxford based Political Ecology Research group who said they would take on the monitoring study. Another expert who supported the DUC was Dr. Blackith from Trinity College who had been active in the Carnsore protests. The DUC's most successful mobilisation strategies included links with experts such as Dr. Blackith who provided scientific evidence at the hearings set up by An Bord Pleanála. As a result of this evidence, many of the mine company's operations in the area were halted. In fact, it was the DUC's ability to highlight possible breaches of planning laws that brought about this halt to mining in the area as the state had already provided the companies with licences (Dalby 1985 p. 31). The DUC also turned the tables on the state's own scientists and health experts who had claimed that nuclear power would not harm the locals. The DUC were able to mobilise local mistrust of officialdom by pointing out that their experts were Dublin based and had no knowledge of, or concern about the communities in Donegal (Allen and Jones 1990 p. 66).

The DUC acted as a coordinating committee for the various local groups that had been mobilised against the mines. These rural based groups set up signposts on their land stating their opposition to prospecting, a tactic which legally blocked the mining companies from prospecting in those areas. By establishing such a strong grassroots support network mining companies could not continue their operations (Allen and Jones 1990 p. 68). The DUC were also able to eventually forge key alliances with local political figures in Donegal County Council and some politicians returned donations given out by the mine companies during the by-elections in the Autumn of 1980 (Dalby 1984 p. 32).

The DUC were able to mobilise local sentiment, forge alliances with experts and other anti-nuclear groups and provide local politicians with reasons to oppose uranium mining while opposing the mining companies' attempts to rally business interests to support their operations. However, some differences of opinion about the manner in which anti-nuclear groups opposed state policy and the nuclear industry meant that links at a national level, while mutually supportive, did not ad up to an overall national anti-nuclear movement. One offshoot of these campaigns was the revival of the Irish Campaign against Nuclear Disarmament (CND) in the 1980s (ibid). Other campaigns against mining included the opposition to lignite mining in County Tyrone as well as protests against gold mining in Connamara, County Galway and at Croagh Patrick in County Mayo. The West of Ireland campaign against gold mining drew on traditional West of Ireland politics to create awareness campaigns about national resource protection from multinationals as well as creating demands for greater input from local communities into state policies affecting the region (Baker 1990 p. 69).

By 1988 one group in the West had formed around concerns about the ecological damage caused by such mining and the ease with which mining companies were able to get licences from the state. This group, Mining Awareness (MA), mobilised a campaign around three objectives: the dissemination of data on the degradation caused by mining, lobbying for changes in the legislation surrounding provision of mine licences and highlighting the need for an environmental impact assessment (Allen and Jones 1990 p. 79). The group's campaign emerged around an array of tactics which included the distribution of an information leaflet, holding a series of meetings and creating expertise links with academics that highlighted the pollution risks of mining (ibid).

The group were hampered by the secrecy surrounding the technocratic decision making which formulated mining policy and legislation. However, the MA overcame this by making presentations of videos and photographs of mining degradation while further cultural mobilisation took place through exhibitions and concerts by supportive artists and musicians who played at benefits in Dublin and throughout the West of Ireland for the group (ibid). However, MA's most successful mobilisation strategy was provided through the establishment of links with the Mayo Environmental Group and Gold Environmental Impact Assessment (Gold EIA). The latter group wanted to see a proper impact assessment based on European Community (EC) directives before mining licences were granted (Baker 1990 p. 69). This utilisation of EU legislation as part of a legal framing process was an indication of the options becoming available to environmental campaigns at this point.

Gold EIA and the MA framed both environmental and economic arguments highlighting the risks posed by the use of cyanide in the process of extraction for ecosystems as well as to the local water supply in the region. The campaigners also identified the damage which could be caused to local farming, fishing and tourist interests (ibid) as they attempted to broaden their shared grievance frame across the region's social categories. The anti-mining campaigners were also able to create a frame which incorporated local culture and religious practice based on the significance of Croagh Patrick for the local Catholic population as a popular site for religious pilgrimage. The campaigners were able to forge links with key allies such as the Archbishop of Tuam who condemned any mining on the 'holy mountain' (ibid). Gold EIA, who created significant networks and links with a variety of groups which were the basis of Non-Governmental Organisation (NGO) civil society in the West of Ireland which included An Taisce (The Heritage Trust), Bord Failte (The Tourism Board), the Irish Farmers Association (the IFA) as well as a number of environmental and wildlife conservation groups and small business associations (Allen and Jones 1990 pp. 80, 81). By extending their networks and support base in this way Gold EIA and the MA provided as their cultural frame a type of in depth coherence which could counter the arguments of the state and mining companies about the benefits of mining. By focusing on the implications of mining rather than being seen to be anti-mining per se the discursive process involving the extension of cultural, economic and risk frames could be merged into an overall stance against a fostered image of greedy mine companies and distant officialdom.

However, some activists who wanted to see a more direct approach to the campaign established the Mayo Environmental Group (MEG) in 1989 who more vocal about their outright hostility to mining in the region (ibid). At their height the MEG mobilised over 3,000 people for a public meeting in Castlebar and established expertise links with well known figures such as the British environmentalist, David Bellamy. They were also able to collect a petition with thousands of signatures at the annual Croagh Patrick pilgrimage in 1989 (ibid).

Such high profile events made mining in the region difficult for the companies while a groundswell of grassroots support built on populist cultural framing led to an undercurrent of opposition to environmental risk projects in Mayo which can be traced through to the opposition to the gas pipeline in Rossport in 2005. This lineage represents a form of sustainable community development 'from below' based on the mobilisation of a 'unifying ether' (Varley 1999 pp. 48, 49) which transcends social divides in rural Ireland. In the case of Gold EIA, their ability to create support networks across social divisions created an 'elite consensus' (Dye in Waste 1986 p. 33) which combined a concern for local communities and the environment with a sustainable platform for local agrarian business interests. This shift in the local power base from fragmented and localist activism towards a more coherent campaign was strengthened by local control of their most significant resource: ownership of the land in the area (ibid p.48).

Conclusion

The history of mineral resource management in Ireland has been littered with sporadic campaigns against local mining operations and multinationals with state support. In most cases disputes about mineral resources follow a similar theme: initial euphoria at the prospect of an economic boom for hard-pressed communities followed by concern about ecological degradation during mining operations. There has also been a residue of grievance due to the lack of any clean-up regulations at disused sites. Another concern for communities regarding the operation of mines was the transportation and dumping of waste made toxic from the use of cyanide in the mining process. Property rights and rights of access for prospective mining operations to private lands were also a matter of local community concern (Curtin & Sheilds (1998), Allen and Jones 1990 p. 46).

One of the most controversial aspects of resource management in Ireland concerning mineral or oil reserves was the lack of proper compensation for local communities or the taxpayer. In addition disregard was shown for communities from the Tynagh mines dispute in the 1970s through to the contested zinc and uranium mines in Tipperary or Donegal and the 'Shell to Sea' campaign of today. In all cases state backed multinationals were given access to the resources of the nation for little return. At the same time the multinationals have displayed scant regard for either local communities or their environments. It is from this arrogant disregard for the local grievances that the initial networking of the Irish environmental movement emerged as anti-nuclear campaigners from Carnsore made common cause with opponents of uranium mining in Donegal in the 1970s. From that inception a disparate group of anti-war, anti-nuclear, environmental and feminist groups from across the island combined to oppose the sell-off of Irish resources while protesting environmental degredation. Some of those involved with opposing mining at Croagh Patrick in the 1980s became involved in the current 'Shell to Sea' controversy demonstrating the extent to which the resources issue has retained its salience. However, the nascent Irish environmental movement did not impinge on the rural community of Tynagh in East County Galway whose lives were dramatically affected by the controversial Northgate mining operations in the 1970s. While the Tynagh community had to defend themselves the subsequent ecological degredation remains a concern for environmentalists today. The scarred landscape around Tynagh became an issue for environmental groups with the high levels of cyanide in the local hinterland a particularly controversial issue. While attempts to have the site at Tynagh reclaimed were less than successful a recent announcement by a company called Tynagh Energy to open a power generating station in the area was made in early 2006 (*Galway Advertiser March 10 2006*). The power plant may be able to reclaim some of the disused land at the site of the mine. In addition some enduring local employment may result from the plant, something that Tynagh was promised but ultimately never delivered in any real way despite the extensive degredation caused to the local hinterland.

The residue of pollution which resulted from Tynagh mines was the subject of an investigation by the Environmental Protection Agency (EPA) in recent years. The investigation's key findings concluded that there was considerable concentration of metals around the mine site and streams in the Tynagh area. The study was undertaken by the EPA together with Galway County Council and the Tynagh Protection Group. The report recommended a long-term project to rehabilitate the site as well as precautions to protect the local environment and human health in relation to any development of the area around the mine. Recommendations for ongoing monitoring of the site for any disturbances which could release pollutants or of unauthorised access to the site and the prevention of entry to the site by livestock with fencing which would be regularly maintained were also made (EPA 2003 pp.1-3). More recently the European Union has sued the Irish state over its inability to protect or rehabilitate mining sites including the Tynagh site. Similar concerns were expressed about contaminated water levels around Silvermines in County Tipperary with finishing plants in the area being criticised for disposal methods.

While many of these problems can be addressed the predisposition of the state is still one of lax enforcement of regulation in favour of industrial competitiveness. In addition the refusal of mining industries to address site rehabilitation increases the salience of the issue adding to the notion of corporate greed and indifference to host communities and their environment, a notion that fuels the simmering opposition to projects in rural areas. The incidents of degradation and protest at Tynagh, Donegal or Croagh Patrick may have taken on differing levels of environmental awareness or articulation. However, each dispute added to the tapestry of environmentally-led rural opposition to industrial projects creating a reserve of sentiment which contemporary campaigns such as 'Shell to Sea' can draw upon as part of their mobilisation and framing processes. The Irish state's consistent disregard for the establishment of a domestically orientated resources policy which would benefit the Irish tax-payer and protect the Irish environment has been heavily criticised over the years and has persistently resurfaced during campaigns from the Croagh Patrick dispute through to the sell off or our off-shore resources and the recent 'Shell to Sea' campaign. The fact that these domestic resources have be sold off to the multinational sector means that not only will local communities not benefit from the exploitation of such resources, but that the Irish environment is forever under threat from future projects by a sector that has shown scant regard for community or environmental concerns in the past.

Chapter Eight

Mullaghmore

Heritage and Conservation

Introduction

The conservation of areas of ecological significance or heritage value lies at the heart of many people's understanding of what essentially defines environmentalism. With the onset of accelerated levels of growth in Ireland since the 1990s urban sprawl has encroached upon the rural countryside in an alarming fashion. Furthermore, attempts to conserve scenic areas as heritage parks has led to the imposition of the apparatus of a tourism infrastructure on the very areas of natural importance that were meant to be protected. Inevitably this paradox has led to increased levels of contestation as local communities, state agencies and environmentalists debate the meanalities and selection of areas of heritage and conservation.

While the frames of reference for conservation debates invariably divide actors into pro and anti development camps, these competing paradigms contain their own internal areas of divergence. Within the ranks of environmentalism, cleavages and alliances can become manifest between 'deep green' ecologists who may veer towards radical beliefs and strategies and the rather more grounded conservation lobby, in many cases represented in Ireland by An Taisce (the Heritage Trust). The key points of divergence for deep green radicals and established conservationists develop around many issues: the framing of environmental meanings, tactical approaches and demeanour during campaigns and perception of both sectors by the wider public. And while deep green radicals may wish to challenge the prevailing dominance of capitalism and consumerism across society established conservationists work within the institutional frameworks of the system, be they political, legal or cultural. However, both sides of the conservation lobby utilise a moral discourse to frame their arguments. For deep green radicals the issues of environmental protection are based on an ecocentric perception that privileges nature over humankind. Established conservationists on the other hand are less interested in challenging the existing structures of society but many of them have ecological expertise and concerns about conservation. For many conservationists the issues need to be considered on a case by case and sometimes species by species level.

As economic buoyancy has come to support agrarian dependency in rural areas the issue of conservation has taken on a wider moral significance for many in a changing Ireland. Economic growth had for many embraced a form of development which has been likened to 'a Godless mammon' and the construction of moral frames around areas of natural significance had taken on an increased primacy. In the Irish case this can sometimes be qualified by debates about property rights, commonage and access (Marsden et al 1993 p. 9). Furthermore, the emergence of 'eco-tourism' in recent decades has led to a new commoditisation of the landscape (ibid pp. 27, 30). With such a range of competing interests and definitions it is little wonder that the rural landscape has become the site of so many disputes. As the spatial geographies of territory and location continue to dominate plans for development and conservation in rural areas it would appear that disputes such as that which occurred at Mullaghmore in the Burren throughout the 1990s will continue for some time.

Background

The Burren or 'stony place' is home to one of Europe's largest and most scenic areas of limestone landscape caused by glacial drifts. Hemmed in by the Atlantic coast in Northern County Clare, the Burren holds a diverse range of flora and fauna, some of which are often found in Alpine or Mediterranean climates. The area is also the site of human settlement stretching back to the monolithic age and many ancient ring forts and stone ruins can be found in the area. In the early 1990s the debate over designating the Burren as a National Park with an Interpretative Centre to facilitate large numbers of tourists became a full scale dispute about the manner in which areas of special scenic and natural beauty need to be conserved. The dispute divided environmentalists, politicians and the local community and affected understanding about heritage and environment in the ensuing years.

Framing the Mullaghmore Dispute

The primary framing issues surrounding the disputed Interpretative Centre at Mullaghmore can be divided into the following components:

- Property Rights
- Rural Development
- Heritage and Tourism Policy
- Social/Economic Restructuring
- Consumption/Commoditisation
- Cultural Debates (McGrath 1996)

These issues can be examined in the context of understandings about the consumption of rurality and landscape (Marsden et al 1993) through the advent of a tourism and heritage industry. The state began to implement plans to develop a largely unfulfilled tourism sector utilising EU policy initiatives and the European Structural Fund. One aspect of this policy would focus on developing amenities and infrastructure to facilitate increased tourist numbers (Dept of Tourism and Transport 1989 in McGrath 1995 p. 17). Areas targeted for development included those with eco-tourist potential, such as:

'cultural, heritage and entertainment with natural heritage and business, including incentive tourism' (ibid).

This model of rural development incorporates market rationalities into the processes of rural change (Marsden et al 1993 p. 27). Under this equation the rural sentiment, or attachment to local land or property, is replaced by market-driven values under the guise of economic maximisation and efficiency. Nonetheless, this model of change can be highly contentious as the emotive dispute about the Mullaghmore site would prove. The interaction between individuals and rural property has been identified as having a crucial, symbolic resonance which extends beyond mere enterprise or legal interpretations (McGrath 1995 p. 25). However, as with many of the manifestations of rural discourse this perspective can become extremely problematic in the vapid legal arena (Peace 1997). The rootedness of one set of actors, as represented by the local community in County Clare created one understanding of the value or commodity of the lands of the Burren while the market analyses of EU or state bureaucrats would provide a different evaluation of the site entirely.

It is necessary to explore further this dichotomy between cultural and economic evaluations of the landscape. Both are part of a wider representation of heritage and landscape; both are interchangeable and yet remain 'bottom up' interpretations of the institutional or community sectors. In an era characterised by high unemployment tourism was prioritised by the state as providing 10% of GNP with revenues of over IR£1,000 million (McGrath 1995 p. 27). As the tourism industry developed it came to be associated with certain environmental impacts as the infrastructure of tourism – hotels, camping sites, holiday homes and marinas – began to dot the landscape. Further impacts were created from the increased road building, traffic and waste or sewage plants associated with such developments (Kousis 2002 pp. 451, 452). Interpretative centres were seen as a necessary part of that infrastructural development in order that better understandings of Irish history and culture would be provided for visitors – 'creating interpretive "gateways" into our heritage' (O'Toole 1994 from McGrath 1995 p. 29).

One such 'gateway' chosen by the Office of Public Works (OPW) was Mullaghmore. It was the OPW's view that the interpretative centre should be located within the heart of the Burren rather than in a nearby village such as Corofin, to facilitate greater visual access for tourists in order to provide a 'first-hand experience of the park' (EIS Statement 1994 cited in McGrath 1995 p. 57). The result of this decision would lead to a sometimes rancorous dispute which impacted on both sets of local groupings that were for or against the project, and lead to a series of legal challenges at national and European levels.

The Campaign

The debate around Mullaghmore can be characterised as the mobilisation of competing sets of representation. This contestation began in April 1991 when Minister for state Vincent Brady announced the state's intention to proceed with plans to build on the Mullaghmore site. The OPW was traditionally exempted from planning permission, as well as being in a position where it did not have to consider results of consultations with Local Authorities. In the months following the announcement of plans for the interpretative centre, The Burren Action Group (BAG) which had been formed to oppose the development forged links with An Taisce, The World Wide fund for Nature (WWF) and Plant Life International to present a joint submission to the EU Directorate General for Environment at the European Commission or request an independent Environmental Impact Statement before funding for the centre could be released (Colleran 2000 p. 1). The joint submission framed the following issues and impacts:

i)   to freshwater systems from on-site sewage treatment;
ii)   trampling pressure around the proposed site;
iii)   creation of a development precedent;
iv)   traffic Impact (burrenag/histhtm p. 1 2005).

This submission frames the main impacts which the BAG felt would result from the large numbers of tourists that would visit the centre. It is interesting to note that in addition to concerns about damage to the water and lands around the centre the challengers were also projecting their vision into the future where any precedent set on developing sites in an area as fragile as the Buren would make future attempts to protect heritage sites very difficult. This framing approach was successful for the BAG and in August 1991 a significant ally was found in the figure of Dr. Ludwig Kramer, a senior official with the Environmental Directorate at the EU, who agreed on an environmental impact assessment and that structural funding would depend on evidence that no significant degradation would occur as a result of the centre's location (Colleran 2000 p. 1).

The Action Group was also able to forge links with local opposition politicians such as Michael D. Higgins who was environment spokesperson for the Labour Party. Higgins was in a position to interact with Dr. Kramer at the EU through formal channels, something which gave the BAG access to the wider political structures surrounding the issue. As the EU had the ultimate say over environmental policy as well as structural funds the ability of the BAG to achieve access at key points of the political opportunity structure in this case provided that group with a degree of leverage over the OPW and the state. These networks led to the first strategic outcome for the BAG in October 1991 when Minister Brady, under pressure from Brussels, announced that there would be an EIS prepared on the centre.

The various components of political opportunity were located at particular points of influence or access on either side of this debate about representation. The Burren Action Group developed links with sympathetic political figures as well as building a social network which encompassed a range of locals including academics, clergy, teachers, artists and environmentalists. This coalition of activists produced their own alternative to the interpretative centre, one which would incorporate the needs of tourism with contributions from local businesses, farmers, craft workers and the arts, creating links between local agricultural and environmental practices while including the local population as part of the tourists' experience of the area (BAG 1992 cited in McGrath 1995 p. 32).

This representation of a centre that allows for greater interaction between the visitor and the local community provides an example of a grassroots response to the OPW's plan, one which would have involved the community rather than being an imposition from the political core. At the heart of the BAG's representation of an alternative centre was the idea that local practice and custom was an essential part of life in the Burren which was inextricably linked to any wider understanding of heritage or environment. Notions of a landscape devoid of local inhabitants can be traced back to a neo-colonialist perspective whereby the 'tourists gaze' (Cronin 2000) is uninterrupted by indigenous society, preserving the relationship between colonisers and their conquest, allowing the traveller to maintain a privileged vantage over the landscape. The BAG's alternative vision of the relationship between tourist and locality is summed up in their proposal where they argue for greater recognition and harmonisation between the three main actors in 'the tourism triangle – the visitor, the host community and the host environment' (BAG 1992 cited in McGrath 1995 p. 32).

The alternative proposal set out by the Action Group also challenged the notion that the Burren National Park should be run by the state, as was the practice in the US. Rather, a model was put forward that drew on existing UK practice of shared management with local communities based on the incorporation of traditional methods of agriculture which have preserved the fragile ecosystem over time. Funding for this type of partnership model was located through the Common Agricultural Policy (CAP) and the EU Habitats Directives (ibid). However, the local Community was divided on the issue.

Many in the local community felt that the Interpretative Centre would have provided economic benefits for the region including an increase in employment. The employment issue was significant as the early years of the 1990s were blighted by a downturn in the economy. This pre-Celtic Tiger recession saw huge numbers of young people leaving the West of Ireland. The issue was a highly emotive one, with television news reports featuring tearful families saying goodbye to their young and then turning roundly on politicians for not creating the conditions which would have prevented this demographic haemorrhage, known as the 'brain drain' due to the loss of so many highly educated young people. In this context, many locals in County Clare wanted any project which could enhance job-creation to go ahead. The lack of any obvious health risks to the local community also gave the Mullaghmore dispute a different stance to previous disputes as mobilisation frames focused on the aesthetic resources of the Burren as an area of global significance.

The existence of competing sets of views in the local community led to a counter-mobilisation against the BAG as prominent representatives of the local civil society such as the Irish Farmer's Association (IFA) and the Gaelic Athletic Association (GAA) and political figures from the centre-right (McGrath 1995 p. 32). This group came to be known as the 'Burren National Park Support Association'. The project's support group would present their own discursive framing arguments which favoured developing the economic potential of the Burren in order to facilitate the creation of local jobs in an area traditionally hard hit by unemployment.

From a mobilisation perspective the importance of the campaign 'entrepreneurs' (Della Porta and Diani 1999) on either side of this debate about the representation and conservation of heritage was a crucial aspect of the framing process and campaign extension for both the Action Group and the Support Association. Significantly, both campaigns drew on understandings of rural discourse to underscore mobilisation and issues framing with contesting perspectives and meanings arising from the particular values either group were projecting on to the issue. Moreover, this contestation of rural sentiment went to the heart of established understandings of what rural community had been and would become from that point on. One of the central issues at hand was whether a sustainable rural community should use models of development, be they economic or environmental, to proceed with when planning for infrastructural projects such as the interpretive centre.

While the BAG put forward a cultural and ecological frame locating heritage and conservation with the local community the

Support Group emphasised the need to draw down cultural interpretations and methods of development from the core based on a bureaucratic rational. This division in understandings of conservation can be seen as having two distinct objectives: one having its basis in the concerns stemming from the environmental sciences, where expertise and research was used to promote the protection of wildlife and landscape wile the other combines concepts of protection with a desire to maximise the use of scenic areas as a resource for tourism and recreational pursuits creating two competing 'preservationist' and 'utilitarian' streams in the heritage movement (Green 1995 p. 101). Both groups drew on the same set of environmental directives and laws to frame their arguments but with a differing set of values applied. In attempting to manage heritage sites as amenities both lobbies had to contend with a major increase in visitors to a limited set of destinations, often to the point where the area of scenic beauty came under threat of degradation (ibid p. 173).

The framing of amenity management methods was crucial to both sides in the Mullaghmore dispute. Once large-scale visitor patterns have been established conservationist groups must measure the impact of their presence. One way of doing this is to examine the 'physical capacity' (ibid) on maximum influx that the local ecosystem can endure. Infrastructural considerations such as the provision of car and bus parking or sewage treatment which were central to the Burren dispute can be measured through capacity frames. An extension of this measurement is 'perceptional capacity' (ibid) which takes into account the diminished enjoyment of a site due to overcrowding or degradation due to infrastructural sprawl. In addition, an 'ecological capacity' (ibid) frame can be constructed around measurements of how much usage can be sustained by a site in relation to the maintenance of its ecological features.

The Burren Action Group utilised each of these capacity frames to structure their argument. For the BAG the Burren contained such a fragile ecosystem that its physical and ecological capacity was very limited and would not sustain the imposition of an interpretative centre and its additional infrastructure. The extent

141

of its fragility also attracted a particular type of visitor or group such as botanists or environmentalists whose perceptional capacity was intrinsically linked to a desire to see the Burren preserved in its entirety. With these frames established the BAG undertook a capacity measurement process, drawing on the considerable expertise of one of its campaign leaders, Professor Emer Colleran, who was the national chairman of An Taisce and a microbiologist. At a conference on aquaculture organised by An Taisce in 1989 just before the Burren dispute began Professor Colleran set out her concerns about ecological degradation stemming from development. Her response was to argue for an inclusive model that brought regulators, industry and conservationists together with the public (Colleran 1989). This inclusiveness is further developed in the following quote from her address to the conference:

> The development of any industry is dependent on public acceptance of the industry and public confidence in its control by the regulatory authorities. Involvement of interested and willing non-governmental organisations is essential in order to win such acceptance and confidence should be encouraged rather than discouraged. The public has a right to concern itself with job creation, economic development and environmental protection and must demonstrate this concern in an informed and balanced way. Presentation of only one side of the argument, misquoting of scientific literature and exaggerated accounts of environmental damage....is not in anyone's interest (ibid).

This balanced perspective provides us with an example of a prominent environmentalist's vision of how matters of ecologically sensitive development could be framed as in the case of the BAG's inclusive model of an alternative approach to the Mullaghmore issue. This framing process also provided an opportunity for the Action Group to acknowledge initiatives such as the Environmentally Sensitive Areas (ESA) schemes which targeted national parties run by local agrarian communities with funding provided by the Habitats Directive for Areas of

Scientific Interest (ASI), or National Heritage Areas (NHAs) (McGrath 1995 pp. 32-33). This framing strategy led to the BAG gaining support from a key ally, the Director General of the EU Environmental Directorate, Mr. Brinkhorst, who announced in June 1992 that arguments against the centre were 'compelling' and that he was recommending a withdrawal of European funds for the Centre (Colleran 2003 p. 2).

The BAG framed their objections to the centre around a critique of the OPW's plan citing spatial and sectoral problems and a lack of managerial planning particularly around the spatial siting of the centre within the Burren to facilitate interpretation of nature by tourists (McGrath 1996 p. 33). While acknowledging the significance of tourist engagement with the natural setting of the Burren the BAG utilised an existing Heritage Interpretation model proposed by Bord Failte (The Tourist Board) as an acceptable set of guidelines. The main points in Bord Failte's interpretation model included avoiding arbitrary developments, preventing wilderness erosion or commercial outlets and restriction of new developments which could cause degredation of the site (Colleran in Feehan 1992, cited in McGrath 1996 p. 33).

By November of 1992 seven key members of the Burren Action Group had taken a legal challenge against the OPW in order to obtain a High Court Judicial Review and sought an injunction against the development of the Mullaghmore site. From a mobilisation perspective, the emergence of the Acton Group's campaign from its local inception through to the creation of networks with key allies such as Professor Colleran and on to a legal challenge, established a route followed by many Irish environmental campaigns (Peace 1997, Taylor 2001). The need for key or 'influential' (Tarrow 1994) alliances with scientific, legal or political experts was a necessary part of the mobilisation process. The Action Group framed their legal challenge around the main issues: that the OPW lacked the statutory power to build the Centre and that the OPW's exemption from planning laws was unconstitutional. According to Justice Costello the presiding judge at the hearing the BAG's arguments 'raised an appalling vista for the OPW' (Colleran 2003 p. 2). The seven Action Group members taking the legal challenge represented a cross section of relevant actors who ranged from local farmers, such as James Howard and Patrick McCormack, local priest Fr. John O'Donohue, media figures P.J. Curtis and Lelia Doolin as well as Professor Emer Colleran (McGrath 1996 p. 34). This cross-section of people came from the immediate vicinity of the Burren or interacted with it in a professional capacity, which provided a sufficient interest for them to take their case. The General Election of November 1992 provided the Action Group with another political ally, Dr Moosaji Bhamjee, who supported the BAG and won a seat for the Labour Party in County Clare. Labour would then go on to form a government with Fianna Fáil, much to the chagrin of many who had supported them electorally. This coalition let to Noel Dempsey replacing Vincent Brady as the Junior Minister with responsibility for the OPW. However, Minister Dempsey was 'marked' by a key political ally of the Burren Action Group, Labour's Michael D. Higgins, who became Minister for Arts, Culture and the Gaeltacht, with responsibility for Heritage.

Despite a request from the Action Group's solicitor not to develop the Mullaghmore site before the Judicial Review, the early weeks and months saw considerable activity there *(Clare Champion January 1992)*. A car park was cleared and sewage works commenced as well as foundations and structures for the Centre itself (Colleran 2003 p. 2). However, two of the NGOs with which the Action Group had created links, WWF and An Taisce, challenged the European Commission's decision to provide £27 million in Structural Funds for the Centre, through the European Court of Justice (ibid). This approach provides an interesting example of an Irish environmental movement using European legislation and processes to support their challenge, a somewhat under utilised strategy for Irish environmental campaigns. Undoubtedly, these NGO's had enough resources which made such action easier. Nonetheless, the Court ruled against the NGOs and the OPW gained access to all EC information on Mullaghmore (ibid).

One strategic success for the Action Group came in February 1993, when the Irish High Court, in the person of Justice Costello, halted the development of the Mullaghmore site, due to the following reasons:

- the OPW's lack of relevant statutory powers to build which gave rise to an injunction against further building;

- the unconstitutionality and illegality of the planning permission obtained by the OPW (McGrath 1996 p. 34).

The Action Group had won a major victory against the OPW and was awarded costs. The state's response was to enact legislation legalising all previous OPW developments under the Local Government (Planning and Development) Bill 1993. The Act also covered all other state agencies (Colleran 2003 p. 3). The BAG also won a victory when the OPW's appeal was overturned and the injunction upheld. However the legal process also went against the Action Group and in June 1994 the High Court ruled that the state and the OPW had the right to re-commence work at the site under the State Authority Management Act.

Over the course of that winter the Labour/Fianna Fail government gave way to the 'Rainbow Coalition' of Labour, Fine Gael and Democratic Left, with Michael D. Higgins becoming Minister for Arts, Culture and the Gaeltacht with responsibility for Heritage. The Heritage aspect of this Ministry included areas of heritage which involved the OPW and Minister Higgins used his power to veto a response to the OPW by Clare County Council for more information on the Visitors' Centre, effectively suspending the project (McGrath 1991 p. 96).

By March of 1995 the state abandoned plans to complete the centre and Minister Higgins withdrew the OPW's planning application to Clare County Council while simultaneously stating that he wanted the Mullaghmore site to be restored. In addition, the Minister commissioned a Management Plan for the Burren National Park within the context of an overall Strategy Plan for the North Clare region with Conservation Guidelines

(Colleran 2003 p. 4). The restoration of the site was to incorporate existing car parks as part of the Management Plan and that the majority of EU funding would be retained as part of a new centre built with greater consensus and input from the community. Some money was delivered from the fund to pay for the demolition of the partially built centre at the Mullaghmore site (McGrath 1991 p. 97). Of course this decision drew heavy criticism from those in favour of the site, such as the Support Group and local Fianna Fáil politicians. This contestation of how Mullaghmore could have been represented through an interpretative centre was still strongly felt with many supporters of the centre arguing that planning permission would have been forthcoming from Clare County Council and the centre would have been of great benefit to the Community. Minister Higgins and the Labour Party were accused of being biased against the project (ibid) demonstrating the extent to which the BAG had forged successful links with those in power, such as Michael D Higgins, who had openly supported their cause.

A decade after the Mullaghmore contestation appeared to reach a resolution the issue re-emerged as the state announced that it would employ the firm of Croskerry Solicitors to reclaim the state's legal fees to the amount of €35,000 from the seven plaintiffs to the Burren Action Group's High Court challenge in 2000. The decision caused considerable dismay amongst the Action Group advocates who had moved on with their lives. Many observers felt that the decision to seek financial redress by the state was part of a wider campaign by the authorities to create unpalatable conditions for high profile activists in order to deter future activism by concerned communities. The pursuit of the balance of the state's legal fees in the Mullaghmore case can be seen in the context of other anti-activist initiatives by the state such as the 2004 National Monuments Act and the Infrastructural Bill which was due to be announced in 2006.

The government's new Infrastructural Bill was designed to fast-track the type of major infrastructural projects which second phase environmental groups have opposed since the 1990s

(Leonard 2005). These projects have been at the heart of community opposition to state policy and include interpretative centres such as Mullaghmore and Wicklow, sewage treatment plants such as that which led to the Save Galway Bay' campaign in the early 1990s as well as plans for incinerators and superdumps contained in the state's regional waste plans. While certain local protests about small-scale or low-impact technologies such as wind turbines or phone masts caused problems in the pre-construction phase many of these issues petered out after the erection or completion of the project. However, large scale projects such as heritage centres, roads or incinerators were met with considerable opposition during the decades either side of the Millennium. The protracted nature of these disputes and the extent to which projects were delayed resulted in attempts by the state to create legal and financial impediments to environmental activism. While these issues were contested in a legal framework there was a political subtext to the cases contested by activists and the state in recent years.

In addition to infrastructural projects the distinctive sites of heritage which dot the Irish countryside have faced considerable degradation. Successive governments have attempted to address this threat by implementing a regulatory framework for Special Areas of Conservation (SAC) through the EU Habitats Directive. Emerging from the social constructionist and discourse analysis approaches that became a feature of EU state bureaucracies since the 1970s the regulatory discourse of environmental protection was introduced as an attempt to circumvent territorially-based environmental disputes (Hajer 1995). One of the core elements of this institutional response to degradation and community concern is the concept of a proactive and reflexive response to ecological regulation. By the 1990s EU member states had embraced ecological modernisation (EM) in an attempt to address widespread perceptions of regulatory failure and democratic deficit. EM approaches to environmental regulation combines sustainable development with cost efficient regulatory models, ideas which informed the bureaucratic implementation of wildlife and heritage zones across the European Community (Leonard 1999 p. 11).

By implementing forward looking environmental regulations for conservation and heritage areas member states planned for a rejuvenation of the process of environmental regulation implementation. However, this standardised approach did not take on board areas of unique distinction such as the Burren, a region without equal across the world due to its unique flora and fauna and fragile ecosystem. The hoped for reflexivity which was anticipated through the adoption of a regulatory discourse approach to conservation was further hampered by the Irish state's ongoing performance as an environmentally 'laggard' state (Weale 1992) which failed to provide any significant input into the formulation of European Union environmental policy.

Furthermore, the horizontal dialogue necessary to make a regulatory discourse approach successful has been conspicuously absent from the state's approach to environmental policy implementation. In many instances, such as Mullaghmore, a heightened awareness of local concerns on both sides would allow the state to anticipate inflammatory problems rather than embroiling the sate or Office of Public Works in a protracted dispute. One of the central features of ecomodern practice is increased consultation in order to facilitate more efficient implementation practices. The Mullaghmore case demonstrated the problems which emerge in the absence of dialogue on the ground as competing interests respond to a perceived gap in existing understandings of local issues. By failing to address either set of diachronically held grievances the state was merely widening the extent to which perception of a democratic deficit regarding an overly technocratic approach to conservation was held.

Of course, the failure of regulatory conservation as a discourse is not a recent phenomenon. In the United States conservationists competed directly with Federal authorities over control of the Minnesota national park. After a century of contested lobbying, Congress passed legislation to create the park. However, the existence of opposing sets of interests each maintaining that they were taking on the mantel of environmental advocates led to a dispute between both competing sets of interest and the authorities. What resulted was a series of legal challenges to federal attempts at land acquisition in the area in order to evaluate wildlife habitats. A central feature of the dispute was whether the area should be used as a recreational and tourist amenity or preserved as a wildlife sanctuary (Lewicki et al 2003 p. 94). As in the Mullaghmore dispute the lack of consultation compounded local interest group responses to an environmental issue that required an element of local knowledge due to the distinctive nature of the region. However, the Minnesota case resulted in the appointment of an independent mediator, the type of consensus building approach the Irish state has successfully utilised throughout the Northern Ireland Peace Process and the creation of the social partnership neo-corporate model. The inability to apply mediation to environmental conflicts disputes such as the one at Mullaghmore is thus all the more perplexing.

There were striking similarities in the framing processes surrounding the Minnesota and Mullaghmore disputes. In both cases some sections of the population feared that tourist infrastructure would have negative environmental impacts in addition to challenging traditional ways of life in the hinterlands surrounding the intended heritage parks. Opposition to tourism and heritage infrastructure in both areas was taken despite anticipated economic benefits from increased visitor numbers. Each case presented expertly organised defence of space arguments with the added component of unique local ecological characteristics which would be threatened by any development. Furthermore, the officials who represented the authorities in both cases were framed as uncaring technocrats with little understanding of or feel for these ecological treasures. However, both campaigns also faced trenchant opposition from local economic interests who saw benefits from the expansion of tourism in cases of wilderness. For local tourist interests these areas represented an untapped resource which could ignite economic growth while simultaneously introducing a conservation plan through the development of heritage parks.
Both the Minnesota and Mullaghmore disputes were characterised by a great deal of emotive debate with a residue of resentment dividing locals into for and against camps. Those in

favour of development in both cases were quick to dismiss opponents as 'extremists' and 'yuppies' in the Minnesota case (Lewicki et al 2003 p. 101) or as 'blow ins' and 'outsiders' in the Mullaghmore dispute. The involvement of US federal officials or EU bureaucrats in the disputes served to cause further resentment particularly when local politicians stirred up populist opposition to environmentalists in order to appeal to local economic interests. The two cases also featured the issue of heritage becoming a political issue at government level with opposing parties championing causes for electoral gain. One strategic difference which separates the two cases was the tactical purchasing of land within Minnesota national parklands in order to complicate the federal compulsory acquisition process. Ultimately, legal challenges proved to be the most successful strategy for both campaigns.

Anthropologist Adrian Peace has written about the 'contested space' of Mullaghmore which is embedded in an unwritten cultural code that can at times defy characterisation. He cites a definition of the contested space as a location where 'social positions are defined by differential control of resources and access to power' (Low and Lawerence-Zúñiga 2003 p. 18 cited in Peace 2005). This analysis of a territorial distribution of power allows us to understand the mobilisation of the campaign to protect the Burren in addition to the counter-mobilisation by sectional interests to develop the site. For Peace, rapid growth and social change in Ireland have led to the rural landscape across the nation becoming 'perennial site for struggle' (Peace 2005 p. 496). The onset of disputes such as the one at Mullaghmore has, for Peace, led to a display of previously unconscious sentiments that were shaped from national interaction with local hinterlands and landscapes. This unspoken cognisance of space has a very personal basis formed within the core of personal or family experiences in an area. When that area is as geographically unique as the Burren this sense of psychological mapping and definition becomes all the more resonant. Peace has divided the competing sets of protagonists into two groupings. The first of these is 'The Supporters Camp' whose view of the area around Mullaghmore is one of an 'old crag' which could be exploited for its tourist value. The other group are characterised as 'the Opposition Movement' who perceive Mullaghmore as 'a sacred site' (Peace 2005 pp.498-502). This group was a collection of disparate groups that came together under the umbrella of the Burren Action Group (BAG).

Peace highlights the fact that the BAG was 'well endowed with middle class cultural capital' (ibid). However, he fails to acknowledge that supporters and activists from both camps came from across the class and social divides. It could be said that members of both groups recognised that the Burren was a sacred site and that it could also be a resource for tourist activity. It was the siting of the Interpretative Centre that became the focus of attention. For 'supporters' the site should be in the heart of the Burren to increase its tourist attraction in a county characterised by its location as a tourist destination. One local travel agent, Gearóid Mannion explained his own views on the issue. For Mannion, Mullaghmore was indeed a select area with a sacred aspect to it. For many locals it was a place of pilgrimage where a sense of spiritual rejuvenation could occur in the manner of their forebears. Locals had interacted with the stony landscape of the Burren through the ages and now this interaction could potentially be linked with the tourist infrastructure that had made Clare a renowned destination for travellers including Shannon Airport and Bunratty Castle. Mannion also felt the nature of tourism had shifted from Irish Americans looking for 'packages' towards a more globalised traveller who wished to experience nature first hand. Therefore the Interpretative Centre needed to be closer to the source. A sensitive siting of the interpretive centre would facilitate new forms of eco-tourism, as the 'backpacker' type of traveller would make their own way through the Burren unless a tourist trail was provided for them.

Peace (2005 p. 498) has outlined an ideological dichotomy between 'supporters' and 'the opposition'. The supporters' camp brought together the 'institutional pillars of conservative, petit bourgeois mentality…wedded to a conservative capitalist dogma' (ibid). And yet this view hardly characterises young indigenous entrepreneurs such as Mannion whose own life is as intertwined with the landscape as any who took part in the debate. So it would appear that something less ideological and more socially complex occurred during the Mullaghmore dispute. Ultimately, the landscape at Mullaghmore was recognised as a fragile and distinctive setting which would be best left in its pristine state. In April 2005 new plans to manage the Burren National Park were unveiled under the auspices of the EU backed 'Burren Life Project' which aims to

> "develop the region under a sustainable framework in order to conserve the habitats and species designated under the EU Habitats Directive and to empower farmers to adopt land management practices to achieve a favourable conservation status for the Burren" (*Irish Times* April 4 2005).

In addition, Clare County Council and Shannon Development announced their 'Burrenbeo' plan which would improve signage throughout the area, improve infrastructure and visitor management at eight 'viewing points' in the area alongside increased development of driving routs to more 'robust' destinations (ibid).

This integrated response was welcomed by the spokespersons of both camps. Local TD and Junior Minister Tony Killeen of Fianna Fáil welcomed the announcement as 'the most significant development in tourism related initiatives to take place in the Burren' (ibid) since the dispute began. Meanwhile, the Burren Action Group's spokesperson Professor Emer Colleran also welcomed the initiative stating that 'it was long overdue … and is to be welcomed as long as the proposals are open to debate and involve all of the stakeholders in the community' (ibid).

Conclusion

Both the Mullaghmore and Minnesota disputes can be analysed to provide better understandings of the critical features of regional conservation disputes. While these campaigns can be located within the context of the economic and political control over the land and natural resources (Lewicki et al 2003 p. 116) and the relationship between property rights and the implementation of policy (McGrath 1996 p. 25), ultimately the disputes have been characterised by competing sets of deterministic territorial frames which led to them being protracted. In each case local citizens have had to respond to policy initiatives which lacked local knowledge and provide alternatives which could be integrated into local lifestyles and hinterlands.

In other words, sustainable development would appear to require a degree of local consultation and input in order to realise any desired sustainability through conservation. In both cases local experts were required to assess the extent to which local ecosystems could absorb heritage park development infrastructure. In fact local experts such as Professor Colleran were performing a plethora of services in their voluntary capacities as environmental advocates. In Professor Colleran's case these services included ecological impact assessment, the auditing of ecosystems, proposing viable alternatives to established heritage plans and stewarding of local conservation efforts. This was in addition to maintaining a campaign with social, political and legal ramifications while performing her duties as a professor of chemistry and director of an academic research centre. As in many local disputes such commitment to environmental protection defines a form of public service which affords advocates such as Emer Colleran with an enduring respect from the public which most politicians can only dream of.

However, the success of individual or groups of advocates and volunteers should not come at the price of a complete withdrawal or abdication of state or local authority responsibility for regulatory discourse capacities in cases of conservation or heritage. Perhaps these are in a dualistic role for both the Environmental Protection Agency and watchdog groups such as An Taisce in future heritage disputes through the introduction of extensive public consultation processes before, during and after the implementation of heritage policy initiatives.

This open ended dialogue should be readily achieved in a pluralist society and include:

> practical deliberation between and among environmentalists, developers, farmers, industrialists and officials from distinct, perhaps competing, subdivisions of government parties who are conventionally thought to be antagonists (Sabel et al 2005 p. 117).

By achieving this degree of extensive consultation by recognising the significance of competing discourses a more comprehensive and sustainable form of conservation could be achieved. By recognising that nature is only a resource when it is afforded stringent protection throughout any development or amenity phase future heritage regulation may serve to transform attitudes while conserving environmental goods and creating an innovative form of policy discourse which embraces grassroots and economic interests. The Mullaghmore also dispute serves as a reminder of the valuable contribution of environmental advocates to issues of heritage which have a complexity about them which go beyond matters of economy and development.

Chapter Nine

Anti-Incinerator: GSE and NIA

Introduction

The onset of the accelerated growth that became synonymous with the 'Celtic Tiger' economy in the 1990s had many repercussions across the regions. One result was a series of discursive contests which emerged as a consequence of local opposition to the development of the state's regional waste management plans. We can locate these waste disputes within a wider dynamic which envelops the multilayered regulatory frameworks of the European Union, the Irish state and local authorities. The critical circumstance which gave rise to these local contests was the lack of any pre-existing waste-management infrastructure or policy at the onset of affluence and inherent consumerism in Ireland (Fagan 2003 p. 68). As consumption increased so did the state's waste crisis as an ongoing over-reliance on landfill, at rates of over 90%, became unmanageable.

The primary reasons for this waste-management logjam were twofold. On the one hand European Commission (EC) regulations compelled the state to introduce changes to their waste-management strategy that embraced the EU's waste-management hierarchy which prioritised reduction, reuse and recycling and placed landfill as the least favoured option. On the other hand, local communities were protesting about the location of new landfills or 'superdumps' in their areas at a time when many regional landfills were beginning to reach capacity. While localised responses to waste management issues have been dismissed by adversaries as emanating from a NIMBYist or 'not in my backyard' approach, the emergence of a grassroots response to the waste crisis has also been acknowledged as part of 'a networked governance' (Fagan 2003 p. 69) in response to the inadequate or under utilisation of the communication and partnership models contained in existing state waste regulations.

The emergence of a national network of opposition to the infrastructural waste projects of the state occurred in the second phase of environmental campaigning in Ireland (Leonard 2005 p. 111). This extension of local campaigns from their inception and focus into a national network addressing a range of issues can be acknowledged as a type of 'ideological development' (Szasz 1994) synonymous with anti-toxics and anti-incinerator campaigns worldwide. The broad spectrum of issues which were embraced by Irish anti-incinerator groups included health risks, democratic deficit and the growth of a movement from local campaigning extending the NIMBY or local focus of a campaign and embracing national and global issues (Leonard 2005). This emergent mobilisation of second phase environmental activism drew on the resources, political opportunity structures and framing processes of first phase anti-multinational groups. The achievement of the campaigners in delaying the implementation of infrastructure has been acknowledged although licences for some regional incinerators were granted in late 2005.

Background

The last decade of the twentieth century saw a dramatic increase in community challenges to the infrastructural projects of the state. Environmental and community groups focused on many issues with Waste Management projects and roads coming to the fore as the primary objects of campaign activism. These campaigns corresponded with a number of events which shaped Irish society in the 1990s. Without doubt, the two major events of this decade of change were the Peace Process in Northern Ireland and the emergence of an affluent, consumption-driven society which became characterised as 'the Celtic Tiger' (O'Hearn 1999). As the economic experience accelerated growth a waste-management crisis ensued. The establishment of the Environmental Protection Agency (EPA) in 1992 was an attempt to deal with the state's previous regulatory failure in the light of the increased responsibilities which followed on from the increase in environmental directives emanating from the European Commission (EC). While the EPA was criticised by some commentators for prioritising growth of environmental protection a waste management framework was put in place by the agency to deal with the regulatory and infrastructural deficit surrounding waste solutions nationwide. This regulatory framework for waste included the following initiatives:

- Waste Management Act
- 1998   Waste Policy Statement: Changing Our Ways
- 2000   Millennium Report
- 2001   Regional Waste Management Plans (Leonard 2005)

The regulatory framework embraced the concept of ecological modernisation (EM) whereby the best available technologies would be applied to the processes of pollution reduction and prevention with costs and even profits factored into the equation. A system of Integrated Pollution Control (IPC) was introduced to facilitate the promotion of eco-modern techniques and expertise throughout the industrial sector. Local communities were also to be included in the new waste management regime with municipal and domestic recycling schemes being introduced alongside the new regulatory framework. This 'top down' approach to the introduction of a regulatory waste framework experienced two main setbacks: a series of 'bottom-up' campaigns of resistance from communities opposed to the siting of superdumps or incinerators in their vicinities together with a continued prioritisation of economic growth and industrialisation by the state and the Industrial Development Authority (IDA).

The continuation of the state's emphasis in the imperative of economic growth over environmental protection caused many to question the new regulatory regimes being introduced. In addition, the lack of public consultation with communities over the introduction of proposed projects such as incinerators caused many activists to become concerned at the growing democratic deficit surrounding the state's neo-corporatist model. While this model of social partnership brought the state, trades unions and industry together autonomous middle class professionals were growing increasingly alienated by the siting of unwanted infrastructural projects in their communities (Leonard 2005).

While often characterised as 'NIMBY' or 'Not in My Backyard' forms of local resistance many of the community campaigns which emerged in the 1990s would move 'beyond NIMBY' (Szasz 1994) into a wider network of environmental resistance which had links to anti-war and anti-globalisation networks. Furthermore, the 1990s brought opportunities for Irish grassroots environmentalism which had not previously existed and which emerged from the increased levels of education and expertise now found throughout Irish society as the brain-drain phenomena of mass emigration was reversed. This led to increased resources for communities such as:

- Returned emigrants with experience of campaigns abroad.
- Increased networks, both domestic and global, due to internet technologies.
- Increased hostility from the state due to a series of social and political 'scandals'.
- Wider understanding of environmental issues due to media and education.
- The cultural phenomenon of environmental activism resulting from pop-culture concerns with Greenpeace, the Rainforest, World Hunger and Global Warming.
- The increased autonomy of the new middle class in Ireland who became 'floating voters' and were less restricted by family ties to maintain political parties.
- International advocacy researchers who had globalised their activities to campaign against trans-national corporations (TNCs). These experts were available in person or on-line to communities to provide a scientific response to technocrats of the state or industry.

In this regard, many campaigns could not be strictly perceived as NIMBYist due to their ability to construct wider networks via the internet. The creation of knowledge-flows across the globe meant fewer campaigns could be isolated by the authorities or portrayed as acting merely out of self interest. Over time, environmental campaigners would emerge from their activist base in attempts to influence the political landscape either locally or nationally. Two such campaigns were undertaken in Galway and Meath by anti-incinerator activists in the aftermath of the state's introduction of its regional waste plans in late 1999.

Galway for a Safe Environment (GSE)

The state's regional waste plans included three options: landfill, which was the destination for over 90% of the country's waste, recycling and incineration. The inclusion of plans for an incinerator at certain named locations in and around Galway city caused local middle class professionals to instigate a campaign of opposition to what was initially the siting of the plant but which would emerge into an anti-incineration campaign with extended links regionally and globally while attempting to influence the 2002 General Election (Leonard 2005). GSE opened up three main frames as part of their campaign:

- Highlighting health risks.
- Emerging from NIMBYism.
- Highlighting democratic deficit (ibid).

These three frames sometimes merged into each other as GSE's leadership attempted to politicise their campaign by moving 'beyond NIMBY' (Szasz 1994) and single issue activism into a political entity which could mobilise dissent amongst the public while accessing the political structures of the mainstream parties in government and opposition. The initial phase of their campaign gave rise to a series of protests, marches and media appearances which allowed GSE to highlight the issue of health risks posed by incinerator emissions. GSE's health links frame provided many protest links frames and also provided many potent images for the anti-incinerator activists to manipulate in order to create issue salience amongst the public. All aspects of community politics were integrated into GSE's anti-incinerator ménage, including exploiting anti-abortion sentiment still prevalent after recent debates. GSE prioritised the image of dioxins in baby's milk as one of their main health risk concerns.

Furthermore, GSE outlined the damage caused to European agricultural processes when exposed to incineration to exploit another cultural frame based on existing mistrust of toxic multinationals in rural areas. In doing so, GSE were able to extend their cultural frame to embrace rural environmental sentiment while also preventing a rural/urban divide, something which would have benefited their opponents. This strategy resulted from the prior experience of one GSE committee member Aine Suttle, who had experience of anti-incinerator campaigns in Canada. Her links to the international anti-toxics campaigner, Dr. Paul Connett, would provide GSE with a vast resource of scientific data which provided the basis of their health links frame. In fact, GSE were able to provide a great deal of information on incineration to the public, local politicians and media sources, to the extent that the interest driven data came to shape the debate with the state and industry being forced into a reactive stance. At the height of their campaign GSE were holding major public meetings debating the issue live on the evening news while their petition against incineration received 22,000 signatures in a city of only 70,000 (the city of Galway has an approximate population of 200,000 in total).

This mobilisation of support was also reflected in the extent to which GSE influenced local councillors who went on to reject the regional waste plan. Many councillors stated that GSE's campaign had influenced their decision while many reported an upsurge in voter concern on the issue. The state's response to this rejection of their waste policy was to rescind the decision-making powers of all regional councils on waste management issues, a move which provided GSE with the political opportunity of extending their democratic deficit frame. For GSE and their supporters the state's initial approach to pushing through incineration without consultation or referring to any potential health risks in the regional plan was one example of a lack of accountability or transparency on the issue. However, the removal of the councillor' powers allowed GSE to politicise their campaign by attempting to gain wider access to the political structures on a national level. The opportunity for that strategy presented itself through the 2002 General Election.

As the dynamic of the political opportunity structure surrounding the anti-incinerator campaign continued to shift GSE were able to extend their democratic deficit frame gaining further leverage during the general election campaign in the spring of 2002. Having decided against running their own candidate in order to facilitate supportive political figures from the mainstream GSE began to merge their three main frames into an anti-Fianna Fáil offensive. This emergence from a single issue protest into a wider involvement in national politics saw GSE achieve their most significant level of political access while also contributing to an eventual trailing off of their campaign in the aftermath of the election due to activist fatigue. While Fianna Fáil had targeted three seats in Galway West, GSE created strategic alliances with one government party candidate, Noel Grealish of the PDs and one opposition party candidate, Niall O Brolcháin of the Greens. Both were first time candidates who had offered high profile support to GSE throughout their anti-incinerator protest (Leonard 2005).

One of GSE's most decisive strategies was their plan to have all parties remove any mention of support for incineration from their election manifestos. This strategy afforded GSE significant access to the policy formation process at a point when the parties were most vulnerable to eco-populist sentiment in the pre-election period. Due to a range of variables such as the vagaries of proportional representation, external and internal party rivalries and the clientelist nature of the Irish political system GSE were able to gain increased leverage during the election campaign resulting in all parties, except Fianna Fáil, removing incineration from their waste management manifestos. Indeed, parties went on to clarify their anti-incineration credentials in the hope of maximising support from the eco-populist lobby. GSE also maintained their emphasis on the health-risks frame with the support of international anti-incinerator spokesperson, Dr. Paul

Connett, who made a series of high profile public appearances in the run up to the election. As GSE's frames began to overlap the scientific expertise of Dr. Connett was utilised to reinforce the prevailing anti-Fianna Fáil sentiment as he called on Environment Minister Noel Dempsey to resign claiming the government had 'rejected democracy' by ignoring GSE's campaign (Leonard 2005 p 164). Both Connett and GSE were able to present an alternative waste plan which prioritised the 'zero-waste' process, emphasising re-use, reduction and recycling.

However, GSE's attempts to influence the 2002 General Election had mixed results for both their own campaign and their political allies. In the run up to the vote in Galway-West GSE had set out their position regarding support for the Greens and the PDs in order to have a link to either potential coalition in the post-election phase. This strategy, however, alienated many Labour and Fine Gael supporters who had been active throughout GSE's campaign. Furthermore, it created a degree of friction within GSE itself as its committee was made up of people of various political beliefs from eco-feminists to radical republicans. It also put some distance between GSE and high profile political figures such as Labour's TD, Michael D. Higgins and local councillor, Catherine Connolly, who would go on to become Mayor of Galway in 2004. Both of these figures had been very supportive of GSE's campaign and would have expected a stronger endorsement from GSE.

Ultimately, it was the PD's Noel Grealish who benefited most from GSE's campaign as he took the third seat from Fianna Fáil in a surprise result. Local media reports attributed the PD's ability to attract a 'green' vote in Galway-West as a factor in their success citing their candidates' stance on incineration as significant (Leonard 2005 p 175).

In the final analysis, the return of the Fianna Fáil/PD coalition to power spelled an effective defeat for GSE's attempt to politicise their campaign. As the demands of striking a deal on a programme for government would come to prevent the PDs maintaining their anti-incinerator stance GSE's campaign lost momentum and the campaign was effectively co-opted by the local Green party as key members withdrew due to campaign fatigue. Essentially, GSE's key alliances had proved to be no more than a 'perceived' opportunity (Tarrow 1998) rather than the key leverage which would lead to their campaign influencing policy at a national level. Nonetheless, while municipal incinerators for Cork and Meath were announced in November 2005 any such plans for Galway have been delayed, with Fianna Fáil keeping one eye on the potential populist backlash in a future election.

Meath: No Incineration Alliance (NIA)

At the same time as GSE were having their initial meetings concerned citizens in County Meath formed the No Incineration Alliance (NIA) in November, 2000. The Leinster Regional Waste Plan (LRWP) contained provisions for an incinerator at Duleek, Co. Meath. The NIA was established in order to raise awareness around the issue through advocacy research and submissions, the first of which was lodged to Meath county council in March 2001. When the council granted planning permission for the incinerator despite over 5,000 objections the NIA appealed. The NIA's committee had taken the decision early in their campaign to use the legal process in order to challenge plans for an incinerator.

The NIA also gained national prominence alongside anti-incinerator campaigns in Cork and Galway for their public demonstrations and marches but found that an outbreak of 'foot and mouth' disease hampered their mobilisation during the spring and summer of 2001 (*Socialist Worker* May 2001). While the NIA was Drogheda based, Duleek was primarily a rural area. The concerns of local residents were heightened by Indaver's appealing of the conditions set out in their planning permission which stipulated that waste for the Duleek Plant would only be taken from the North East Region (www.Indaver.ie August 29 2001).

In the summer of 2002 the NIA's Eric Martin attempted to take out an injunction to prevent An Bord Pleanála from convening an oral hearing on the Duleek plant (ibid). Martin would later take a High Court challenge against Indaver on behalf of the NIA. However, neither strategy proved to be successful. Martin was faced with a legal bill of €200,000 as a result of Justice Smyth's ruling; an outcome which demonstrates the risks taken by community activists who, when acting as named individuals on behalf of their community and environment, can be found liable for huge legal bills. These costs were awarded against Martin despite statements by government Ministers such as Michael McDowell and Dick Roche claiming they would oppose incineration in their own Leinster constituencies; an indication of the geo-political and populist spatial planning that surrounded the citing of incinerators around the country.

The NIA framed their submission to the 2002 oral hearing around health risks to people living in the vicinity of the plant. The NIA utilised existing data from communities affected by incinerators around Europe and the United States. As Duleek was within the designated heritage site surrounding the Boyne Valley the NIA extended their framing process to include a detailed frame which highlighted the ecological risks posed by the plant. By taking this strategic route the NIA were able to go 'beyond NIMBY' (Szasz 1994) by encompassing ecocentric concerns. In addition the NIA's ecological frame enabled the mobilisation of consensus amongst the region's tourism and agricultural interests. The NIA were also able to mobilise rural sentiment through this frame galvanising their populist campaign by presenting their case as one of rural community versus urban technocrats and polluters, particularly as waste from Dublin was earmarked for the Duleek plant.

The site at Duleek was deemed 'fundamentally inappropriate' (NIA Oct 2002) for a development such as an incinerator. The site was zoned for agricultural purposes and the NIA highlighted the risks posed by the ingestion of dioxins through the food chain as had been demonstrated in European cases. Furthermore, the NIA argued that Ireland's 'green' image as a producer of dioxin free foods would suffer as a result of the development making the plans economically unviable. The NIA set out their ecology frame in the appeal by highlighting risks posed to the area's wetlands and areas of conservation:

- visual intrusion
- impact on Tourism and Heritage
- impact on ground water
- traffic impact
- property devaluation
- failure to consider alternative sites (NIA October 2002)

The first three points were derived from the NIA's ecology frame while the second encompassed more traditional, localised concerns for a NIMBY group. However, the NIA were able to emerge from any accusations of NIMBYism by extending their framing process to include wider concerns such as tourism, heritage and agriculture while maintaining an essentially localised core which drew on rural sentiment. However, much like the rural campaigners of the Womanagh Valley in Cork during the 1980s (Peace 1994), the NIA's rural populist frame did not translate well during the oral hearing process despite their establishment of cultural action frames. Another approach, undertaken as part of the appeal was outlining of the inadequacies in the Environmental Impact Statement (EIS) particularly in an area of fragile wetlands such as the Boyne Valley. The NIA raised the essential issue of contamination of the water table and underlying aquafier. The NIA combined ecocentric and anthropocentric concerns on this issue detailing both the risk of ecological degradation as well as the risk posed by contamination of the local drinking water supply.

The NIA's framing process also involved applying the EU's own waste hierarchy, which placed incineration and landfill last, against the plans for an incinerator. According to the activists the state's waste plans contravened the EU's waste hierarchy by promoting incineration over recycling. The NIA were also able to demonstrate the problems posed by the lack of planning for waste separation which would increase the toxicity of any subsequent emissions from the proposed plant. The NIA extended this institutional, regulatory frame by also highlighting the fact that incineration contravened the UN's own principle of sustainable development due to the contribution of emissions made to greenhouse gasses and ozone depletion. The costs of incineration also ran counter to the goals of sustainability.

One interesting strategic plank of the NIA's campaign was their decision to run a candidate in the 2002 General Election. Unlike GSE, who attempted to influence the election externally, the NIA put forward the Independent Anti-Incineration candidate, Pat O'Brien. However, much like GSE, O'Brien's campaign effectively took on the mantel of being anti-Fianna Fáil. O'Brien also highlighted the growing concerns of Fianna Fáil backbenchers on the issue as eco-populist protest votes cut into Fianna Fáil majorities in some constituencies. O'Brien accompanied a Green party delegation to Environment Commissioner, Margot Walstrom's office in Brussels to make a complaint about the government's waste plans. As Meath lacked a Green party candidate the path was clear for the NIA to put O'Brien's name forward whereas the Green's Dan Boyle in Cork and Niall O'Brolcháin in Galway had been closely connected with local anti-incinerator campaign in those constituencies.

The last decade also gave rise to a series of environmentally related issues which contributed to a wider mobilisation of community-based campaigns. While these grassroots responses were varied in size and duration they came in an era where public affluence, expertise and disenchantment with the establishment combined to create a prevailing sense of ecopopulist dissent across the country. There were many factors which surrounded this response ranging from institutional initiatives through to enhanced communications due to the onset of the internet. For its part the state placed a priority on changing public attitudes towards environmental issues through the introduction of the EPA in 1992. Although the EPA has been criticised by some commentators for its pro-industry leanings (Taylor 2001) its presence on the national scene provided a focus for environmental regulation and disputes which may not have been addressed were it not in existence. Furthermore, the external pressure placed on the state due to EU environmental directives provided ecological issues with a degree of exposure which they otherwise might not have been afforded.

The Irish Green Party made gains during this period, emerging from An Chomtarlas Glás into a party with representatives in both the Dail and the EU Parliament. Nevertheless, this emergence has sometimes led the party away from the grassroots as the leadership at times attempted to justify its presence to potential coalition partners. The most notable exceptions to this can be seen in the election of representatives such as Cork TD, Dan Boyle, who was integrally involved with CHASE in the campaign against incineration in Cork Harbour. However, despite the depth of feeling which similar campaigns aroused in Cork and Meath the Greens were unable to further capitalise on anti-incinerator sentiment in the 2002 General election.

The local elections of 2004 were a different matter and here the Greens experienced a national upsurge in their vote gaining council seats nationally. However, while the Greens doubled their number of local authority seats, reaching nearly 15% in affluent Dublin suburbs such as Malahide and Lucan, their share of the vote was less than 1% in rural constituencies such as Mid Roscommon, Tuam in Galway and the Glenties in Co. Donegal. The Greens also suffered the setback of losing two MEPs in the European election (Kavanagh 2004, p 81).

The Green party's failure to gain a foothold in rural Galway occurred despite using opposition to the state's plans to site a 'superdump' in the east of the county. A campaign of opposition emerged to contest the landfill which had links to GSE the city-based anti-incinerator campaign. GSE's committee were concerned from their inception in 2001 that the state would attempt to play rural and urban campaigns off each other, a strategy their members had witnessed in North American campaigns (Leonard 2005). These concerns led to the formation of the Galway Safe Waste Alliance (GSWA) which was comprised of GSE together with anti-landfill groups from rural areas such as Ballinasloe, New Inn and Newbridge. The GSWA provided Galway City and County councils with a joint submission on the Connacht Waste Plan (CWP) in 2002. The submission put forward their case for rejecting the CWP as well as providing an alternative plan. The GSWA framed their rejection of the state's regional waste plan around a series of issues dealing with landfill in the following manner:

- Rejection on environmental and economic grounds of the transportation of toxic ash from a city based incinerator to a landfill in east county Galway as this was contrary to the EU Proximity Principle.
- Lack of updated site selection for CWP and lack of regard for health risks posed by landfill.
- Increased road traffic in rural areas.
- Insufficient attention to archaeological and heritage sites in the area.
- An underestimation of people's willingness to recycle (GSWA submission 2002).

The GSWA's Alternative Plan included the framing of their position around the EU's own environmental principles of sustainability in waste management with emphasis on The Proximity Principle which emphasised that communities should deal with their own waste locally and that toxic waste shouldn't be transported to other destinations for treatment. The GSWA used the institutional frame to present a viable alternative. Their links with 'Zero-Waste' advocate, Dr. Paul Connett, provided the Group with valuable information on alternative waste management processes which had been introduced in Australia and Canada. Elements of the GSWA's campaign included court cases, lobbying public representatives along with the submissions and petitions against the CWP.

However, perhaps the GSWA's greatest legacy is the partnership the group created across the urban and rural divide, an indication of the potential for cooperation and increased networking amongst environmental groups. This community-based campaign was built from existing grassroots networks in the county, drawing support from disparate groups such as the 'Tidy Towns' committee in Newbridge to international figures such as Dr. Connett. The Galway Safe Waste Alliance also took on the mantle of local advocacy researchers, taking part in a visit to a 'model' landfill in Swindon, England, which was organised by Galway County Council. According to the group, this visit 'failed dismally' to diminish local concerns about municipal landfilling 'realising our worst fears and further convincing us that we will not accept a dump' (Newbridge Action Committee October 1999). The Newbridge based 'Safe Waste' activists maintained a website which included details of the GSWA's major events while also providing information on alternatives such as recycling.

Other anti-landfill groups emerged in this period in Kerry, Cork, Clare and Longford. These groups voiced their opposition to Ireland's 93% reliance on landfill as its primary waste option, a figure which was second only to Russia (O'Sullivan 2000 p 21). Most of these campaigns involved local individuals taking a legal action against the local authority on behalf of the community, an indictment of the authorities' approach to consensus building and cooperation, two principles contained in the regional waste plans. Many of the legal actions led to the temporary or permanent closure of dumps in these vicinities exacerbating the national waste crisis. Local campaigners framed their challenges around issues such as nuisance factors, agricultural impacts and breaches of existing legislation. Threats to tourism and heritage were also prominent in many anti-landfill actions. The case taken by residents against Clare County Council over the proposed dump in Doora, near Ennis, led to a 23 day hearing where the campaigners highlighted environmental impacts rather than focusing solely on anthropocentric issues such as property prices, while the action taken against the Carrowbrowne dump outside Galway City highlighted breaches of the planning laws (ibid).

Many of these events took place against a backdrop of the dramatic changes which occurred in Ireland in recent years. A book by the *Irish Times* Environmental Editor, Frank McDonald and James Nix, *Chaos at the crossroads*, details the major issues which surfaced in the decades either side of the Millennium. The issues highlighted incorporate a diverse range of problems associated with accelerated growth such as urban sprawl, uneven development, one-off rural housing and the conservation of heritage. Located at the core of these off-shoots of the boom economy is competing understandings of sustainable development. Sustainability is defined by the beholder and can be re-interpreted by state officials, technocrats, community activists or environmentalists. This has led to policy anomalies such as the introduction of the plastic bag levy in 2002 which visibly reduced pollution levels across the roadways of the countryside; while the state was threatened with a series of legal actions from the European Commission for non-compliance with 128 Directives. These actions involved failure to comply with legislation involving the protection of wildlife and nature, pollution, waste and sewage treatment (McDonald and Nix 2005 p 12).

The problems of sprawl, one-off housing and property values have confounded spatial planners and set the state at odds with An Taisce. The nature of the one-off rural housing debate set populist rural sentiment at odds with the 'official environmentalism' (Tovey 1992 b) of An Taisce. As the debate about property rights and visual amenity became keenly contested throughout 2004 and 2005, An Taisce's opposition to building in scenic areas at An Bord Pleanála hearings led to calls from local authority officials that the body's proscribed status should be de-listed (MacDonald and Nix p 115). The government's concern at its poor electoral performance in some rural areas during the 2004 local elections led to a rethink on legislation that would proscribe building in sensitive areas, an example of the strength of rural sentiment during the political opportunity posed by the onset of elections.

While property location and values continued to be controversial topics in both rural and urban areas the government's expansive National Development Plan (NDP) has created a further controversy regarding the extensive road building projects which were at the heart of the state's vision of the built future.

Conclusion

The major campaigns against incineration in Ireland that have occurred in a variety of locations including those at Galway, Meath and Cork are studied in this book. Other anti-incineration campaigns have taken place in Poolbeg, County Dublin, in County Clare and in Wexford. While many of these protests were undertaken at the sites proposed for incinerators the campaigns extended beyond their initial single issue dispelling the notion of anti-incinerator campaigns as being merely NIMBYist in focus. The campaigns in Galway and Meath differed in their tactical approaches. One of the main areas of distinction was the use of ecological expertise on the aqua-life and plant life of the Boyne Valley, which NIA used to create a heritage frame. This allowed their protest to move beyond the single issue of being simply anti-incinerator and falling into the NIMBY trap. Another strategic area where NIA and GSE differed was on taking legal action. GSE considered this option but took the decision to gain leverage from the political opportunity of the 2002 general election. NIA took the legal hearing route in the form of a case taken by environmental advocate Eric Martin. The judicial review of An Bord Pleanála's decision to grant a licence for an incinerator at the Duleek site places the ecology of the Boyne Valley and specifically the limestone reserve and aquafier at the centre of its opposition. By linking heritage and health frames NIA presented an extensive set of arguments against the incinerator planned for their area despite the outcome of the hearing.

GSE's campaign was influenced by the more politicised members of its committee who took the view that any campaign against incineration should exploit political opportunities such as the 2002 general election to challenge the coalition government and Fianna Fáil specifically. However, the reversals suffered by the 'Soldiers of Destiny' in the 2004 local elections demonstrate the leverage that campaigns can achieve at the local level. The anti-incinerator campaigns in Galway and elsewhere have also led to the mobilisation of a community-based environmentalism which has forged networks nationally and internationally. One of these campaigns, Cork Harbour for A Safe Environment will be examined in the next chapter.

Chapter Ten

CHASE: Cork Harbour for a Safe Environment
Anti-Incineration

Introduction

The area surrounding Cork Harbour has long been a site of contestation regarding environmental disputes. As the second most populated city in the Republic of Ireland Cork has experienced uneven bursts of planned development in between decades of neglect. The perceived imposition of industrial projects in residential or scenic areas has exacerbated the sense of grievance held by many in Cork in relation to state or multinational activities. In the aftermath of keenly contested disputes involving the Raybestos Manhattan plant and dump in Ovens and Merrill Dow's factory in the Womanagh Valley during the 1970s and 1980s environmental networks were embedded in the local community.

The political opportunity for further environmental campaigns emerged in the wake of the announcement of the state's regional waste plans in 1999. The inclusion of a provision for municipal and industrial incinerators in Cork Harbour led to the development of a campaign of opposition that grew from a local response by Ringaskiddy residents through to the emergence of Cork Harbour for A Safe Environment (CHASE). The campaigners embarked on a considerable drive against the state's plans for incineration which would eventually lead to CHASE offering support for the Green's successful candidate in the 2002 general election. In addition, the CHASE campaign established a comprehensive set of issues with which they framed their objections, aided by the expertise of Dr. Mary O'Leary, who became the campaign's spokesperson. This evolution from a concerned residents group to a campaign of national significance demonstrates that CHASE is one of the leading advocacy groups of recent years.

With the onset of rapid development, the constraints faced by the state regarding the problems of dealing with industrial and municipal waste became the political opportunity for the Cork campaigners. Moreover, the existence of similar campaigns such as GSE and NIA created the potential for a national anti-incinerator network to emerge from what might have been dismissed as NIMBYist disputes.

Background

In August 2001 the Ringaskiddy and District Residents Association (RDRA) released a document called "Ringaskiddy – A Living Community not a Toxic Dump". This document charts the development of the area from the 1970s as the state and local authorities invested heavily in the infrastructure necessary to attract heavy industry to Cork Harbour. Multinationals such as Pfizer and Beechams were drawn to the area by the state's attractive investment packages. The process involved a phase of accelerated development which led to the loss of large tracts of the rural hinterland, transforming Ringaskiddy into a built-up, industrialised zone with little regard for complementary planning. Although this process was completed over two decades the local community remained rooted in its rural origins and displayed elements of rural fundamentalism during the many campaigns against multinationals that occurred in the 1970s and 1980s.

While there are obvious economic benefits emanating from this transformative process the costs in regard to health risks and increased pollution combined with the loss of local hinterlands have had an effect locally. The feel of village life of Ringaskiddy was lost and localised practices in the areas of agriculture and fishing were impacted significantly. The area has also seen local infrastructure and social capital eroded while visually 'emission stacks and exhaust plumes dominate the skyline' (RDRA 2001 p. 20). For the residents 'community' is determined by 'common place and common purpose' (ibid). The imposition of an industrial zone on their area, together with the lack of enforced pollution contracts, was seen as a threat to the future of that community. Seen in this context, Indaver's plans to build two incinerators east of Ringaskiddy were described as 'ludicrous' (ibid). The Ringaskiddy community felt that it had conceded enough in the name of development and growth. By establishing a community protection frame the RDRA were drawing on aspects of rural fundamentalism to establish a basis for their opposition that was rooted in the local environment.

The residents' second frame was built around the health threats posed by incineration. By utilising the latest available material on these threats the RDRA set out the risks faced by those living near incinerators, including concerns about the affects on respiratory and immune systems as well as heart disease and reproductive deformations. These affects stem from the pollutants in incineration emissions, many of which are non-degradable. As well as airborne inhalation these pollutants can be ingested through local food produce grown in contaminated soil. The RDRA sourced this material from the latest studies by the University of Essex. The residents also used material from other scientific sources such as The Lancet Medical Journal report on students in Belgium, who were shown to have a high level of pollutants and dioxins in their systems, having grown up near incinerators. One suggestion drawn from the report put forward by the Irish scientists who reviewed the Belgian study was that it would be wise 'to embrace better technology in dealing with waste than burning' (RDRA 2001 p. 6).

Considering these health affects the residents went on to question the siting of two incinerators in the Ringaskiddy area. By using the Environmental Impact Statement (EIS) prepared by Indaver for an incinerator in County Meath, which placed significance on the fact that the Meath site had a low density population, the residents asked why two incinerators should be acceptable in a heavily populated area such as theirs. They also argued that any emissions would fall in a line that encompassed many other factories thereby exposing their workforce to the potential affects and risks posed by such pollution. These facts would counter the economic arguments put forward by Indaver in favour of the plants. The residents concluded that any attempt to introduce incineration in the area would be 'irresponsible' (ibid).

In regard to monitoring pollution the group argued that a trust deficit existed between locals and either industry or state monitors who were felt to be tacitly compliant in promoting pro-industry findings. The fact that there were no plans for waste separation meant that all manner of waste such as plastics, carcasses, hospital and industrial waste would be burnt with domestic waste, releasing hazardous dioxins into the atmosphere. This enforced postponement of state policy by community campaigners represented what has been described as going 'beyond NIMBY' (Szasz 1994) into a post-NIMBY national coalition of community-based environmentalism.

Cork Harbour for a Safe Environment (CHASE)

In November 2001 the Irish subsidiary of the Belgian Incineration Company, Indaver, applied for planning permission to build a Hazardous Waste Incinerator at Ringaskiddy in County Cork. The local community, which had been mobilised in previous environmental campaigns such as the opposition to Raybestos Manhattan in the 1970s, prepared for yet another campaign. By the summer of 2001 the Ringaskiddy and District Residents Association (RDRA) began to mobilise a campaign of resistance to the proposed incinerator. The RDRA produced a statement entitled 'Enough is Enough' which set out their arguments against the siting of incinerators in the area.

Beck (1995) has characterised the onset of 'risk society' whereby politics has been reinvested through a process driven by the recognition of the risks posed to society by scientific and technological change. One aspect of risk society which has become a feature of Irish life in the post 'Celtic Tiger' era of economic growth, and the subsequent increase in consumption, has been seen in the onset of a waste management crisis. This waste crisis has had implications for communities and policy makers alike as the once unspoilt landscape of the Irish countryside became blighted with legal and more latterly, illegal, dumps and the state's over-reliance on landfilling as its primary waste management pollution became untenable. This crisis was shaped by pressure from two fronts, the EU's environmental directives and waste hierarchy from above, in addition to community campaigns against waste management infrastructural projects from below (Leonard 2005).

The state's response to this external pressure was the introduction of a series of regional waste plans towards the end of 1999. Euphemistically referred to in the literature as 'thermal treatment plants' this option for regional incinerators provided further political opportunities for environmental campaigners who wished to oppose the state's waste policies. While this opposition has been characterised as 'parochial, subjective and emotional' (Wynne 1996 p. 62) or 'ruled by selfish NIMBYism' (Davies 2004 p. 86) recent studies have demonstrated that environmental campaigners who have targeted the state's plans for regional incineration have been innovative, articulate and politically astute in the way they mobilised resources and exploited political opportunities (Leonard 2005). Crucially, community campaigners against incineration in Ireland have been able to forge links with key experts in the areas of science and politics while in some cases maintaining the tried and tested legal challenge route as a strategic manoeuvre to support their campaigns. Essentially, anti-incinerator campaigns in the Irish case have mobilised communities and experts against the state's waste policy by exploiting the combination of rural sentiment and democratic deficit that has surfaced in Ireland in the recent post-scandal tribunal era.

Within the democratic deficit context of the Irish waste management crisis lies the core issue of public participation. Policy frameworks are shaped by technocrats and consultants hired by the state. These unattached figures provide one form of expertise on issues such as incineration which can result in outcomes derived more from social tensions emerging from the technocratic process of favouring economic growth and technological methods in the face of public uncertainty or opposition (Fisher 1997 p. 184).

Existing social resistance to technocracy can be exploited by 'advocacy researchers' (ibid) who mobilise communities against infrastructural projects such as incinerators. In the Irish case this contest between technocratic and advocacy experts became a prominent feature of local challenges to the state's regional waste policies in areas such as Galway (Galway for A Safe Environment), Meath (No Incinerator Alliance) and Cork (Cork Harbour for a Safe Environment) amongst many others (Leonard 2005). These campaigns represented a culmination of three decades of environmental protest in Ireland and campaigns such as those mentioned above mobilised their communities in innovative ways through the use of computer and internet technologies, influencing election campaigns and combining ecological and health-risk issues to such an extent that by 2005 no incinerator had yet been built in Ireland.

The Cork Harbour residents outlined in a document the risk from the ash residue which must be landfilled. According to their document, filtering and transportation process increased the risk of airborne pollution. In addition, no landfill site for such toxic ash existed in Ireland. Local concerns about dump sites from toxic plants dated back to the campaign against Raybestos Manhattan in the 1970s so the group asked where Indaver planned to locate such a site. According to the residents the two incinerators proposed for Ringaskiddy would produce 34,000 tonnes of ash residue creating a considerable secondary issue around the provision of a landfill for this fly-ash which few communities would be likely to want in their vicinity.

Further concerns were expressed regarding the extension of any landfill in order to facilitate an intake of toxic waste from across the country. Plans for an all-Ireland toxic incinerator and dump had been previously put forward by the state and the Northern Ireland office for a site in Derry in the 1980s (Allen 1992) and the RDRA feared a similar plan was possible in Ringaskiddy. Concerns were also raised by the residents regarding the capacity of the plant and its subsequent affect on road transport in the area during construction and operation (RDRA 2001 p. 11). The group put forward a series of conclusions on the issue including the following criticisms of Indaver's plans:

- inconsistencies between the criteria for site selection between the Co. Meath site and that proposed for Ringaskiddy.
- emissions risk to local population
- risks to existing industry in the area
- risk posed by toxic ash (ibid)

The residents concluded that Indaver were not interested in solving Ireland's waste crisis and that incineration would not provide a solution as it created too many external problems. They cited the fact that both the EU and the US-EPA were moving away from incineration in their own waste hierarchies.

By the autumn of 2001 a new organisation, Cork Harbour for a Safe Environment, had been established broadening the extent of anti-incinerator mobilisation and enveloping the often radicalised Cork Harbour area. This mobilisation of existing residents and anti-toxics campaigners under the umbrella of CHASE provided the basis for a united front against both Indaver and the state over plans for incineration in the area. In order to reinforce this extensive mobilisation CHASE framed their arguments around the health-risks posed by dioxins. The provision of expertly sourced data about the health risks provided anti-incinerator groups with their most potent image and engendered a good deal of public empathy and support. CHASE also outlined an economic frame stating that incineration would be expensive while competing with the more sustainable process of recycling. In order to appeal to the widest support base possible CHASE argued that cancer rates near Belgian incinerators were noticeably higher over a three mile radius. The group noted that any plant located in Ringaskiddy could potentially affect outlying areas such as Cobh, Monkstown and Carrigaline, heavily populated areas where concerns over health risks had often been raised in relation to Cork Harbour's many toxic industries. CHASE also put forward arguments outlining actions

179

taken by the Belgian government to reduce reliance on incineration as well as the EU's ban on the use of fly-ash in building materials on landfills, highlighting the potential problem of fly-ash disposal (CHASE 2001 p. 2).

CHASE was determined from an early stage to frame their campaigns around a wider community response that extended beyond local communities such as Ringaskiddy and Carrigaline. This framing process focused on certain issues to facilitate the clarity and saliency of the campaign.

The primary frames of CHASE's campaign were as follows:

- Community wide opposition to the state's plans for 2 incinerators in the Cork Harbour area.
- Further opposition to all seven of the incinerators proposed nationally in the state's regional waste plans.
- The highlighting of the health, environmental and economic implications of incinerators.
- The promotion of public debate on the waste issue together with the provision of safer non-incineration alternatives such as recycling (ibid).

CHASE also opened up a democratic deficit frame claiming that the Minister for the Environment had 'forced through' legislation for the seven regional waste plans (ibid). The group's campaign was extended into the realm of electoral politics in the spring of 2002 when CHASE exploited the political opportunity which arose from that year's general election. CHASE targeted the Fianna Fáil party which was the party of Environment Minister Noel Dempsey, author of the regional waste plan. A campaign of local press statements condemning Fianna Fáil for their pro-incineration waste policy was undertaken in the Cork press. In addition CHASE activists held a protest at the launch of the Fianna Fáil election manifesto at Government Buildings. The protestors were joined by anti-incineration campaigners from across the country and held up placards condemning the government's "Buy and Burn" waste management policies (CHASE 2002 p. 1).

CHASE chairman, Sean Cronin, highlighted Fianna Fáil's solitary stance on incineration:

> We are calling on Fianna Fáil to read the writing on the wall. Fianna Fáil are now isolated as the only political party allowing incineration as part of its environment policy with the PDs and Fine Gael rejecting incineration in the last few weeks due to the swelling tide of public opinion (ibid).

CHASE was still concerned about plans in the PDs manifesto to implement a form of incineration, known as the Herhof Refuse Derived process, in certain Dublin local authority regions. CHASE attempted to highlight the potential instability in the coalition over the incineration issue focusing on the PDs' commitment in their election manifesto stating that no incinerators would be built in Ireland (PD election manifesto April 2002).

Individual PD candidates became unlikely allies for anti-incinerator groups in locations such as Cork, Dublin and Galway. In Dublin Justice Minister, Michael McDowell, argued against incineration while in Galway rural County Councillor Noel Grealish, who had appeared at anti-incineration rallies, won a surprise seat for the PDs with support from Galway for a Safe Environment (GSE). While the PDs may have wished to hold their own against their coalition allies by playing a populist card on this issue, the demands of forming a government after the election led to a diminishing of interest from the PDs both locally and nationally. Furthermore, it could be said that local anti-burn groups who courted support from a party who were part of the government that introduced the policy initially were somewhat naïve in a political sense (Leonard 2005). CHASE also provided details of discussions they had undertaken with various Fianna Fáil TDs opposed to incineration. According to CHASE, these anti-incinerator TDs constituted a majority of the parliamentary party indicating that there was no real support for incineration outside of the Cabinet.
(CHASE 2002 p.1).

CHASE also opened up a democratic deficit frame after the FF/PD coalition was returned to power. One of the plans forwarded by incoming Environment Minister, Martin Cullen, was a proposal to fast-track waste-management and infrastructural projects directly to An Bord Pleanála thereby removing an individual's or communities's rights to oppose or appeal planning permission for projects such as dumps or incinerators. The opposition and/or appeal strategy had long been used with degrees of success by environmental campaigners who cited objections based on the threat of health risks or ecological degradation. In itself, the lodging of appeals usually served as an important statement of intent by fledgling movements or campaigners while also serving as an initial mobilisation strategy which notified both the authorities and local community about the issue itself.

Echoing many environmental groups across the nation CHASE Chairperson, Sean Cronin, said that 'Minister Cullen's fast-tracking proposals were anti-democratic and anti-community responsibility' (CHASE 2003 p. 1). Invoking the fact that the regional waste plans called for increased community input Mr. Cronin outlined the ambivalence in the Minister's position on this issue: 'He either believes in community participation or he does not and this measure would indicate strongly that he does not' (ibid). CHASE was also keen to highlight the undemocratic and unsustainable nature of the Minister's regional waste policy claiming that his rejection of zero waste went against the democratic issue of public choice and participation in local decision making. The Minister had rejected those who favoured a 'zero-waste' approach to waste management as 'short sighted and dangerous to their communities'. Zero-waste was a process that prioritised the reduction, reuse and recycling approach to waste, an option which was then at the 'most favoured' apex of the EU's waste hierarchy.

CHASE was also quick to point out that incineration and recycling were competing processes, as one approach took waste away from the other, making the Minister's plans to introduce them together both uneconomic and unsustainable. Furthermore,

CHASE learned that incineration needs to generate increased amounts of waste to make profits for the private sector rendering waste-reduction plans as problematic. CHASE outlined the 'Zero Waste Plan for the UK' forwarded by Greenpeace as an ideal alternative to introduce in Ireland, removing the need for an expensive technology such as incineration. The Zero Waste study detailed the feasibility of this approach presenting figures for required state funding and policy initiatives in order to make the plan work. CHASE called on the Irish Government to accept this approach as a safe and sustainable alternative while simultaneously decrying the state's waste plans as 'medieval solutions' i.e. burying or burning our household rubbish. CHASE also outlined the fact that many UK local authorities had adopted zero waste as a target, as had many major corporations such as Honda, NEC and Hewlett Packard (ibid).

CHASE continued their campaign by participating in the oral hearing held by An Bord Pleanála at the Neptune Stadium in Cork in September 2003. While oral hearings were a common feature in Irish environmental disputes the 'rural discourse' of early anti-multinational campaigns was often lost in the formal legal arena (Peace 1997). However, CHASE was able to emerge from existing rural sentiment by using scientific experts, such as Dr. Gasten Tusscher, to demonstrate the universal nature of the health risks posed by the dioxins found in incineration emissions. By extending their health risks frame in this manner CHASE was able to contest the arguments put forward by the state while also highlighting the health affects which would be faced by all in the Cork Harbour vicinity if the incinerations came into operation.

According to Dr. Tusscher a series of world-wide problems with the dioxins, furans and PCBs that are contained in incineration emissions have been recorded. Health affects resulting from the ingestion of these toxins have included high mortality rates, diminished IQ levels and higher instances of respiratory problems. Italian studies outlined high instances of foetal disruption and liver damage after accidents at the Seveso incinerator (CHASE 2003 b p. 1). Chase was able to forge alliances with local politicians who shared their concerns complementing the health experts such as Dr. Tusscher and providing a broader front for their anti-incinerator campaign. One such politician was the Fine Gael TD, David Stanton, who told the oral hearing that he saw no need for a national waste incinerator. Deputy Stanton praised businesses in the Cork Harbour area for their successful attempts at controlling production line waste and he argued that an incinerator would disrupt this process. Accordingly, he called on Bord Pleanála to refuse permission for the plant (ibid). By opening up their network circuits to mainstream politicians such as Deputy Stanton CHASE was able to extend their framing profile to incorporate common sense, pro-business arguments based on economic principles, which located their campaign within the sustainable principles set out by the EU as well as the state's own National Hazardous Waste Management Plan.

One significant political ally for CHASE was the Green Party candidate, Dan Boyle, who successfully contested the 2002 general election in Cork South Central. Boyle actively participated in their protests against incineration and benefited from the support of CHASE activists and sympathisers during his election campaign. As a councillor Boyle had lodged an objection on behalf of the Green Party against the Ringaskiddy incinerator. This objection presented several arguments against the proposed plant, including the problems of toxins, transport, proximity of housing and the fact that incineration undermines recycling (Green Party January 3 2002). The Green Party stated that they would put waste management to the fore of any negotiations for government in any post electoral discussions.

Boyle also questioned the role of the incinerator company, Indaver, who had claimed that the arguments put forward by CHASE were misleading. Boyle claimed he had made representations to Indaver on behalf of his constituents but that he had not received any reply from them (Green Party January 13 2002). Boyle claimed that Indaver was attempting to misrepresent CHASE's stance on the issue as part of a wider contestation of expertise between an advocacy campaign and the corporate sector. Furthermore, Boyle questioned plans to bring the Health and Safety Authority (HSA) into the planning process for the incinerator. Boyle also stated that the incineration issue was too great a concern to the public to be presided over by an underfueled HSA (ibid). During the election campaign Boyle returned to the subject of incineration claiming that Indaver's highly paid for Public Relations was unable to present their side of the issue as clearly as a citizen's group such as CHASE, whose validity was based on higher concerns (ibid).

Boyle had been expected to have to fight for his seat, with former mayor Deirdre Clune (FG) and disabilities campaigner Kathy Sinnott contesting the final seat. However, Boyle received 4,956 first preferences and outpolled candidates from both Fianna Fáil and Fine Gael as the Greens benefited from an electoral surge, rising from two parliamentary seats to six nationally. Boyle would continue to support CHASE after the election but the fact that the Fianna Fáil/PD coalition was returned to power meant that the issue of incineration still loomed over Ringaskiddy.

Throughout 2003 CHASE continued their campaign using their political and scientific alliances to open up a new front which would lead to an oral hearing on the issue. In their submission to the hearing, Campaign chairperson Mary O'Leary set out the group's objection to the granting of a licence for the Ringaskiddy waste incinerator. CHASE also took the opportunity to criticise the EPA's absence from the hearing as the group's submission was delivered. The Cork activists also raised concerns about the lack of transparency in the licensing process, arguing that the EPA presided over events as both 'judge and jury'. In addition, the campaign highlighted the fact that the EPA was able to exonerate itself from any responsibility for its own decisions due to changes in the EPA charter (O'Leary 2003). These issues were seized upon by CHASE to highlight the accountability deficit surrounding the EPA's remit, as the lack of public accountability caused poor policy planning and implementation.

CHASE again took the opportunity to set out their main concerns such as the fact that neither the EPA nor Indaver had addressed concerns raised by both CHASE and the EPA themselves over issues such as the treatment and disposal of contaminated sludge from the incinerator (ibid). For Cork environmentalists the lack of clarity from Indaver in the treatment of sludge called into question any other issues of toxicity surrounding the incinerator such as emissions. The campaign was able to highlight mistakes in the categories of hazardous waste which the company would be dealing with at the plant that allowed them to call into question all of the statistics being put forward about toxicity levels. CHASE also raised concerns about evidence of Belgian emission levels being breeched on several occasions by the company (ibid).

Another concern raised by CHASE was the lack of personnel with previous experience of running an incinerator, something CHASE claims was stated by Indaver themselves on separate occasions (ibid). In regard to the state's national policy on waste, CHASE demonstrated that waste prevention was the primary objective of the National Hazardous Waste Management Plan rather than incineration and therefore Indaver's claim to be in line with the state policy was inaccurate (ibid).

The group set out six main objections to the plant in their submission. These were:

- Risk to public safety.
- Lack of confidence in the company.
- Contamination of the harbour.
- Terms of the Draft Licence
- Classification of waste.
- The health issue.

We can examine the core arguments relating to these objections and so build a better understanding of CHASE's framing process. Each aspect of the objections allowed the campaigners to develop their main frames surrounding each transparency, health risks and the raising of doubts about both Indaver and the EPA in the public's minds. Together these frames provided the campaign activists with the resources to construct a cultural narrative which merged with existing public concerns about risk society, democratic deficit and the state's carte-blanche approach towards facilitating multinationals (O'Leary 2003 p. 3). The campaigners developed the objections put forward in their submission to the hearing from these main frames. We can examine the objections in more detail to gain further insights into CHASE's framing narrative.

Risks to Public Safety

The Cork campaign raised concerns about the problems surrounding the technology of incineration which, they claimed, was 'problematic and prone to fires' (ibid). The group relied on the expertise of senior chemical engineers to contest Indaver's own expertise on incineration technology. Another concern was the nature of the waste being accepted into the incinerator which relied on customer statements regarding its suitability and safety for incineration. Any mistakes could have a devastating affect on the Cork Harbour area according to the activists. CHASE attempted to contrast the professionalism of the community's response to these concerns with what they perceived to be a less than forthright approach to the issue from Indaver or the EPA (ibid).

The anti-incinerator activists highlighted the refusal of the Chief Planning Inspector at the An Bord Pleanála hearing who stated that he could not guarantee that there was no risk to public safety from the plant. CHASE also raised the question of whether the EPA were duty-bound to accept information on health risks from sources other than the applicant company in order to maintain the EPA's stated core values of 'integrity, independence and professionalism' (ibid).

Lack of confidence

One of CHASE's main framing tactics was to create a lack of confidence in Indaver and the EPA's handling of the licensing system. The activists were aware that they could provide scientific expertise which would counter Indaver's own data.

The group were able to draw on the long-standing mistrust and resentment of toxic multinationals which had emerged during the first phase of environmental campaigning in Ireland in the pre-boom decades of the 1970s and 1980s (Leonard 2005). One of the approaches taken by the campaigners to build on the resource of existing mistrust of both multinationals and the state in the Cork Harbour area was to point out weakness in the licensing process such as the EPA's reliance on data from Indaver alone as well as the lack of qualified or experienced staff for the proposed site. CHASE were also able to play on people's existing concerns about 'risk society' (Beck 1992) in relation to dioxins, toxic ash and the threat of flooding at the plant.

Terms of the Draft Licence

CHASE were quick to highlight some of their concerns about the terms of the licence such as the fact that the EPA required Indaver to build a second municipal incinerator without gaining planning permission for a domestic waste plant. This condition was included despite the fact the Cork County Council had refused planning permission to Indaver and had rejected a material convention of the County Development Plan (CDP) or planning permission for the plant. The terms of the licence also went against the Cork Area Strategy Plan (CASP) which called for the rejuvenation of Cork Harbour as a civic amenity following on from the clean-up of 'dirty industries' in the area (CHASE 2003 p. 6). The group were also able to extend their 'democratic deficit' frame by highlighting the manner in which the licensing terms ignored the wishes of democratically elected councillors in the area.

Health

CHASE extended their health affects frame by outlining the Health Research Bureau's (HRB) report on the affects of incineration on human health which sets out the problems that arose from the lack of adequate risk assessments for waste facilities in Ireland (ibid). They also raised concerns about Indaver's reclassification of what they considered to be hazardous waste as well as detailing the 100 meter high toxic ash mountains which come from European incinerators (ibid).

The recommendations of An Bord Pleanála's senior planning inspector, Philip Jones, provided a detailed breakdown of the factors which militated against the granting of a licence for the plant. The senior inspector's report refused planning permission on the following grounds:

- The inadequate Environmental Impact Statement (EIS).
- An incinerator would go against prevention targets in the National Waste Management Plan.
- Lack of a hazardous waste landfill site.
- An incinerator ran counter to the Cork Waste Management Plan.
- The site was zoned for enterprise and industry.
- The plant was contrary to Cork County Council's objective for stand alone industries in the area.
- The plant was inappropriate to the development of Cork Harbour.
- The plant would be visually obtrusive.
- The scale of the development was unsuitable to the site.
- Proximity to high density housing in the area.
- Excessive traffic.
- Existing congestion in the area.
- The road network in the area was deficient.
- Risk to public safety (*Irish Times* 17 January 2004).

By the following January An Bord Pleanála decided to reject the report, overturning the findings of its own senior inspector, Mr. Philip Jones, who had also presided over the oral hearing. CHASE chairperson Dr. Mary O'Leary stated that

> we are completely shocked by this decision. The case we put forward at the oral hearing was extremely strong...the question must be asked that if, in light of all this and against the inspector's recommendation, a project is allowed to proceed – what is the value of

having a planning process at all? (CHASE Press Release 16 Jan 2004).

CHASE returned to the mobilisation of the local community to reinforce their campaign after this setback. As over 30,000 people had lodged objections to the plant public opinion was running high after the An Bord Pleanála decision. The group also responded to the planning reversal by re-establishing their framing process in a document entitled 'Comments on proposed incinerator in Ringaskiddy'. This document set out several main frames which were significant at that point of the campaign. These frames built on the campaign linking health affects and democratic deficit with concerns about the planning process.

Democratic Process Failed

CHASE's concern with the disregard shown to local and national development plans was heightened in the wake of the overturning of An Bord Pleanála's Inspector's report and the fact that the second incinerator was exempt from planning laws. This overruling the democratic process allowed CHASE to extend their democratic deficit frame.

Health Affects

CHASE were able to extend their health affects frame beyond its initial concern about dioxins due to the exclusion of health issues from the planning process, the lack of health monitoring and the lack of further research into potential health affects arising from the plant.

Unsuitability of location

The group opened up a framing angle around the location of the plant mobilising grievances about the special positioning of toxic incinerators in an area affected by flooding and erosion, with an inadequate road infrastructure, in proximity to the densely populated and industrialised area. CHASE also highlighted what was seen as 'unreliable' advice from the Health and Safety Authority to the Planning Authority.

Deficiency of the Waste Licence

The Cork activists opened up a discursive frame which set out to erode public confidence in the waste licensing process. Here CHASE could utilise existing concerns about democratic accountability and risk society to challenge the licensing system. According to the campaigners the waste licence facilitated increased risks from larger amounts of waste to be burned in an expensive process which made no provision for any clean-ups in the aftermath of potential problems at the site. Further concerns were raised about unqualified staff, the inadequate Environmental Impact Statement and the lack of health risk assessments.

Lack of adherence to major policies

The democratic deficit frame was extended beyond the local planning processes to incorporate the disregard shown for major policy frameworks such as the EU Waste Management hierarchy which places incineration at the bottom of the list alongside landfilling, the National Hazardous Waste Management Plan, the Kyoto Protocol and rulings by the World Health Organisation, according to CHASE.
(CHASE: Comment on Waste Incinerator, 2004).

In March of 2004 the Ringaskiddy and District residents' association along with eleven harbour residents lodged an application to the High Court for a judicial review of An Bord Pleanála's decision. The High Court appeal was adjourned on four separate occasions and in October 2004 no judge was available to hear the case as the authorities procrastinated over their response to the challenge. CHASE held a protest outside the Dáil that same month along with other anti-incinerator groups from across the country. A letter of protest was handed in to Environment Minister Dick Roche as the campaign maintained a public profile throughout delays surrounding the High Court hearing.

A second oral hearing into the licence for the Ringaskiddy plant took place between the 14 February and March 1 2005. CHASE was joined by groups such as the Cork Environmental Alliance (CEA), the Ringaskiddy Residence Association and An Taisce at the hearing which was held at the Cork Great Southern Hotel. The presentation put forward by CHASE focused on five main issues drawn from the discursive action frames established during the campaign:

- Lack of a monitoring body for health affects
- Objections of An Bord Pleanála's Inspector due to risks to public safety
- Concerns about the integrity of the oral hearing process
- Concerns about the incinerator company
- Lack of planning permission for a second incinerator at the site (CHASE press release 14 February 2005).

The oral hearing also received presentations from chemical engineers who claimed that inadequate separation of waste could lead to explosions in the incinerator, a problem which would be increased due to the lack of experienced staff at the plant. Further concerns were raised about the absence of the EPA's Board of Directors from the hearing despite repeated calls by the objectors for them to attend, as the EPA board had the ultimate decision making powers regarding any decisions over waste licence. The board's absence did however strengthen CHASE's framing of the integrity of process issue and allowed the group to further decry the EPA's behaviour throughout the dispute.

CHASE exploited the political opportunity which emerged from their integrity frame by extending this position into a critique of Enterprise and Employment Minister Michael Martin who was TD for the Ringaskiddy area. His absence from the hearing was also criticised by the group who claimed 'the silence from Minister Martin is deafening' (CHASE press release March 2005). Minister Martin had gone on record as opposing the incinerator but the activists were in no mood to let any government representative off the hook: 'The absence of the Minister from the EPA Oral Hearing at this late stage, day twelve, is an indication of the lack of concern the Fianna Fáil minister has for his Constituents' (ibid). The extension of the integrity frame into a wider critique of the government was demonstrated in press releases from April and June 2005 that criticised the government's attempts to introduce a National Infrastructure Board that would fast-track major infrastructural projects and free up the planning process. CHASE contrasted this with the state's lack of haste in establishing departmental responsibility for health risk monitoring.

According to CHASE members of the community who objected to infrastructural projects due to health or environmental concerns were 'key stakeholders' in the process. Their removal from the planning process would be a loss to society which valued transparency, according to the group. For the Cork campaign the National Infrastructural Board (NIB) represented a 'further erosion of democracy' (CHASE press releases April and June 2005).

However, on 25 November 2005 the EPA announced its decision to grant a waste licence to Indaver Ireland to operate a 100,000 tonne municipal waste incinerator at Ringaskiddy. CHASE announced their anger at the move but claimed it came as 'no surprise' due to previous decisions of the EPA. According to the campaigners the EPA 'had not fulfilled their legal obligations and have exposed the public to unnecessary harm' (CHASE press release 25 November 2005). The subsequent explosion at an oil storage depot in Hemel Hempstead in the UK, which shrouded parts of London in a toxic fog, was seized upon by CHASE as an example of what could happen at the Ringaskiddy plant.

The Cork Environmental Alliance (CEA) were critical of what they saw as the EPA's 'manipulation' of the waste licence issue accusing the agency of issuing their most controversial 'bad news' announcements 'during periods of least media attention' in August or at Christmas (*Ireland from Below* November 2005). CHASE chairperson Mary O'Leary, summed up the emotive response of anti-incinerator campaigners in the area: 'the last time Cork was burning we could blame the Black and Tans. This time the burning is just a bit more refined' (ibid). For their part Indaver Ireland was just as apprehensive about the campaigners who opposed them. Their managing director, John Ahern, claimed he was 'terrified' of the Cork campaigners 'who had given the company a tough time' (ibid). Ahern also claimed he felt that previously existing sentiment which had built up from the asbestos plant controversy in the 1970s led to the strength of opposition the company had encountered and that the company and CHASE 'should have met more often' (ibid).

Conclusion

The campaign against incineration in Cork can be located within the overall context of a series of ongoing campaigns by residents in Cork Harbour and its environs stretching back to the Raybestos Manhatten dispute in the 1970s. Essentially, Cork Harbour has been a site of disaffected protest by local citizens who carried concerns about the environmental and health risks posed by the state backed industrial sector through what has been identified as the two phases of environmental protest in Ireland. The Cork environmental protests occurred throughout both of these stages which included first phase anti-multinational campaigns which had a radical left influence and second phase anti-infrastructural protests which were influenced by the anti-globalisation movement. In the first phase the state's pre-economic growth concern for multinational-led development at almost any cost forced many communities to view the consequences of a toxic industry locating in their area. In the second phase, the post-boom era, the state's attempts to introduce waste management and roads infrastructure in the wake of hyper-consumption resulted in campaigns of opposition from local communities concerned about the environmental and health risks posed by waste technologies or urban sprawl (Leonard 2005 p. 45). While CHASE undertook a series of strategies to highlight their concerns about the health affects posed by incineration they were unable to prevent the announcement that licences for two incinerators for the area would be granted.

The reason for this setback is complex and has its basis in the state's planned development of the Cork Harbour region which dates back to the late 1960s. As Ireland's manufacturing sector declined in the wake of globalisation the imperative to develop Cork Harbour as a hub for US chemical and pharmaceutical industries increased. One of the core infrastructural projects required to make this form of regional development work is an industrial incinerator which can cope with the massive outflow of toxic waste produced by chemical industries. By opposing both the industrial and municipal incinerators planned for Cork Harbour CHASE found their campaign targeting the state's industrial development plan for the region in addition to the state's waste management plans. While leverage in relation to political structures may have been achieved through events such as the onset of elections or highlighting local grievances the battle for Cork Harbour was one which the state could not afford to lose. Ultimately, while CHASE vowed to continue their campaign in light of the granting of the licence for an incinerator in the area strategically their campaign may need to be reassessed with a focus on emissions monitoring replacing the goal of preventing incinerators in the long term.

Chapter Eleven

Resources

The Rossport Five –"Shell to Sea"

Introduction: Resources

In a recent review of a text the 'quest for environmental justice' Christopher Rootes highlights what he calls a 'characteristically incisive' contribution from American eco-activist Chris Foreman who argues that 'environmental justice is less about disparity of risk than about community empowerment' (Rootes "Environmental Politics" Vol. 15 No 1 2006 p.138). However, this bold statement is qualified by the claim that communities are more likely to respond to the threat of 'serious risk' to their area in order to maintain their common interest over any other environmental issue.

Looking further back in our own history we know that rural or peasant society had many occasions to strike out in common cause as has been noted by Michael Pellion who has noted the significance of the 'land wars' of the 19th century as a key determinant of social change in that era. Pellion locates the Land League within the context of a rural social movement that attempted to address not only economic change but also less tangible issues such as 'insecurity' and 'resentment' (Pellion 1982 p. 60). The rise of the Land League represented a resistance campaign of collective action by the farmers (ibid) which drew on tactics such as boycotting, ambush and even assassination. And yet the League was primarily a rural tenants' movement organised around the rentier class rather than labourers who were seeking recognition within the existing system of rural political economy.

The Land League succeeded in mobilising rural dissent in Irish society and nowhere is this sentiment more deeply felt than in County Mayo, home of Michael Davitt. From the Land League Irish farmers gained rates and tenure rights long before the foundation of the Irish state. Other social phenomena such as the rise of the cooperative movement alongside the 'meitheal system' of pooled labour share their origins with collective mobilisation of the farmers of the West of Ireland with a link between Davitt's movement that can be traced through subsequent groups such as Muintir na Tire, the Irish Farmers Association (IFA) and the 'Save the West' campaign of the 1960s and 1970s. With the commencement of the laying of a gas pipeline through the heartland of the Erris coastline in North Mayo the underlying psyche which has its roots in prior rural collective action was resurrected. The resulting 'Shell to Sea' campaign has witnessed the mobilisation of rural sentiment in addition to something far more 'visceral' in the words of Mark Garavan the campaign's spokesperson. While the attempt to lay the pipeline represented an invasion of space for many locals this trespassing on a space that is seen as 'sacred' by some including the Rossport 5's Micheál O'Seighin who has noted the 'continuum' between those who agitated through the Land League in the past and the wider community who feel threatened by the gas pipeline project today.

Background

The debate about natural resources ignited with a vengeance in the aftermath of the announcement that Shell were to build a gas pipeline from the Corrib field 80 kilometres offshore through the townlands of County Mayo in 2001. Five local men were imprisoned for 94 days as a result of their campaign against the pipeline which widened the mobilisation of support for the men and their families from around the nation and beyond. The campaign also saw the re-awakening of some of the rhetoric of the past as the spirit of the 19th century nationalist leader Michael Davitt was evoked at rallies across the country. The story of the 'Rossport 5' as they came to be known and who were Michael O Seighinn, Vincent McGrath, Phillip McGrath, Brendan Philbin and Will Corduff caught the nation's imagination as their 'Shell to Sea' campaign mobilised mass support at protests and rallies across Ireland.

However, to fully explore this campaign we must first examine the sell-off of the natural resources which occurred over the previous forty years as successive governments attempted to lure in multinationals through a series of contentious deals. These deals were highlighted in a rousing speech given by left wing TD Michael D. Higgins to a 'Shell to Sea' rally in Galway in August 2005:

> "I'm glad we're having a seminar on this issue, it's badly needed in this country. I was involved in the Resource Protection Campaign in 1973. At that time, Energy Minister Justin Keating, signed away the licences for bounty-payment. Then the state had the right to participate in decision making about resources. The people must be allowed to have ownership and maintain controls over the companies doing the drilling. Our resources are finite so the state should be involved. In 1977 Keating lost his seat and Jack Lynch's Fianna Fail government came in on a populist wave of support. Now, Keating was criticised by us but now the people got people like Ray Burke. There is now an absence of moral courage. I hear people speaking of Michael Davitt well the people of the left said that our resources shouldn't be taken from us.
>
> The five men in jail are a reflection on law and morality because they wanted to protect their families. The injunction is flawed because the state hadn't given permission for the pipeline. These men have contempt for an injunction that is based on a lie. The government should ask for the injunction to be lifted. Minister, it's not your gas. You will have to buy it from the company; I suppose we poor peasants should be on our knees and carry the multinationals. Every aspect of this deal stinks! It should face a tribunal of inquiry. This project should be examined in all its aspects. Shell speak of

their projects in Africa where the poorest companies have their resources taken from them by colonising multinationals. Here in Ireland Davitt's heart was broken. He said 'the end will come – but the people will be gone'. There is a need for a change of consciousness. We must show solidarity for the men and their magnificent families. They have but one small demand – that the gas is cleaned at sea.

There is something ugly happening in Ireland when people now have affluence and land. Some of our politicians have behaved outrageously. This should not be about personalities; we should oppose the culture of greed. They have sold off our resources, our gas, our fisheries. They're not ours anymore. This is the culture of greed they voted for. I support these men and their families. I demand their release and this entire story must go before a Tribunal and I'm speaking as President of the Labour party one of whose founders was Michael Davitt." (Michael D. Higgins, TD, August 2005)

The campaign of the Resource Protection Group (RPG) was involved in disputes about mineral resources in the 1970s and 1980s. This left wing group which included a young Michael D. Higgins as one of its spokespersons was critical of the Labour party Industry and Commerce Minister Justin Keating's plans to develop oil and gas resources. Under Minister Keating's terms set out in 1975 the state would retain a 50% stake in any development of our off shore resources without having to play exploration costs. Keating was influenced by the Norwegian government's state oil company Statoil and hoped to launch a partnership with the multinational sector (Connolly and Lynch 2005 p. 9). This partnership was heavily criticised by the Resource Protection Group who maintained an ideologically driven opposition to any involvement by the multinational sector in the resources of the state which they claimed ultimately belong to the people of Ireland.

However, the Irish electorate were less concerned about resources at that time and in 1977 elected Jack Lynch's Fianna

Fáil government on a populist ticket that included plans to develop all available resources to stimulate economic growth. Keating's successor Des O'Malley established the Irish National Petroleum Corporation (INPC) in response to the global oil crisis which had seen a dramatic rise in the cost of petrol. By 1985 Labour energy minister Dick Spring reduced state dividends and participation in off shore explorations (ibid). However, by 1987 Fianna Fáil was returned to power and Ray Burke became energy minister. Burke has been criticised for the manner in which he drew off the new conditions for drilling licences which were seen as being too favourable to the industries (Cambell December 2002). Sinn Fein TD Martin Ferris claimed Burke 'was responsible for the rape of our natural resources' (ibid). SIPTU's Joe O'Toole has claimed that under the new terms established by Burke the inclusion of on-shore pipelines was critical to the commercial success of any off-shore find (ibid). It was the issue of the on-shore pipelines running alongside the homes of the Rossport Five which would ultimately ignite that controversy.

In 1986 the Corrib gas field was discovered off the Mayo coast. It was the second largest in the country after the Kinsale field which was the subject of some controversy in the 1970s. In 2001 primary applicants Enterprise Oil in conjunction with Statoil and Marathon applied to the Department of Marine and Natural Resources for a lease to develop the Corrib Field at an estimated cost of $400 million. Marine Minister Frank Fahey claimed the news was 'most opportune' due to the decline in the Kinsale Field which had provided much of Ireland's indigenous gas supply (Shell to Sea January 16 2001).

Planning permission for a processing plant at a 400 acre site at Ballinaboy was granted in August 2001 while a petroleum line was agreed in November of that year. At the same time the government announced new compulsory purchase orders for inland pipelines that allowed private land to be occupied over the objections of the owners (Connolly & Lynch 2005 p. 14). Here the state was facilitating land occupation directly and whereas past disputes such as Tynagh mines were characterised as exploiting people's ignorance of their rights now the state was actively consorting with industry against local landowners through their law-muting capacity. Clearly the state had hoped that local opposition could be stymied when faced with the law making capacity of the state. By March 2002 an amendment to the Gas Act allowed commercial industries entry to private lands under the new compulsory acquisition rights (ibid).

By February of 2002 An Bord Pleanála's oral hearing against the planning permission for the onshore terminal commenced. An Bord Pleanála's senior planning inspector, Kevin Moore, concluded that the site was inadequate claiming that Rossport was 'the wrong site' from the perspective of 'strategic planning...government policy on regional development...minimising environmental impacts and sustainable development' (ibid).

Enterprise Ireland (EEI) responded to these findings by announcing it would delay the laying of the offshore pipeline in order to address the concerns of An Bord Pleanála (RTE News July 2002). That autumn local residents in Rossport, along with environmentalists and political figures, announced that they would be 'renewing their opposition to the terminal' (corribsos.com 23 Oct 2002). Having put their case to the oral hearing the objectors made the decision to extend their campaign. Plans were made to make a submission to a second oral hearing in November when An Bord Pleanála reviewed EEI's re-appraisal of the safety and suitability concerns raised previously. The Rossport objectors had already opened up a network of 'political circuits' (Tilly 2004) which embraced local farming and fishing groups as well as local politicians such as the Independent TD Jerry Crowley. However, other local groups such as the Council of the West had called for support to be shown for the gas pipeline. The Rossport objectors also found support from Sinn Fein who criticised the Taoiseach for meeting the President of Shell Oil in October as TD Caoimhghin O'Caoláin queried whether the meeting had any bearing on the proposed critical infrastructure Bill particularly in light of Shell's 'special treatment' on royalties (Shell to Sea October 14 2002), criticism which the Taoiseach denied.

On the 27th of November the English television station Channel 4 ran a news item which questioned the plans for an onshore pipeline and terminal in County Mayo. The report claimed that locals had faced pressure to sign over their property and that the deal with the Royal Dutch Shell company was 'unprecedented in Europe' (The *Irish Examiner* November 27 2002). Records were produced in the report which raised allegations of political interference and pressure being brought to bear on Mayo County Council's planning committee while it was also revealed that Fianna Fáil received donations from two of the companies involved in the Corrib Field operation. The Channel 4 report was critical of the manner in which Ireland's national resources were being given away without any revenue making its way back to the Irish taxpayer with the Corrib deal giving a poorer return than similar deals signed in Nigeria (ibid). In December the connection between Ireland and Nigeria was strengthened by the appearance in Ireland of Dr. Owens Wiwa, brother of the murdered author and anti-oil industry activist Ken Saro Wiwa, who backed the campaign against Shell. The campaign had an international context which ran from Norway to Nigeria and the Rossport campaigners were able to exploit this.

The campaign had a major success in April 2003 when An Bord Pleanála upheld its inspector's decisions due to the pollution risk to local rivers. EEI expressed their disappointment at the decision and stated that the whole project for the Corrib Field gas supply would be reconsidered. The holding of a second oral hearing by An Bord Pleanála was in itself unprecedented and the hearing was the second longest in the board's history (Shell to Sea: Project timeline). The Taoiseach, Bertie Ahern, met with senior Shell executives to reassure them but confirmed that the project would have to go through the national planning process.

Undoubtedly, state and multinational frustration at the delays caused by community objectors to planning hearings contributed to plans for a National Infrastructure Board (NIB) which would fast track major projects such as the Corrib Field through over objections of local campaigners. EEI responded to the upholding of the ruling by submitting a new planning application to Mayo County Council for an onshore gas terminal which included plans to resource large tracts of peat land from the area around the site. By this time EEI had changed their name to Shell E&P Ireland.

The complexity of the debate about developing resources was characterised at this point by the concerns about the project expressed by former government advisor TK Whitaker who had a holiday home in nearby Bangor (*The Guardian* May 29 2004). Mr. Whitaker was seen by many as the architect of Ireland's economic success dating from his period as senior civil servant in the Sean Lemass Fianna Fáil government of the 1950s and 1960s. The Lemass/Whitaker plan for multinational led development through direct foreign investment was credited with establishing the foundation and patterns of Irish economic rejuvenation. It was most telling that this renowned figure, with a background in state facilitated multinational-led growth, was expressing concerns about a project such as the Corrib Field. While Lemass was often quoted with stating that 'a rising tide lifts all boats' in regard to his economic policies perhaps the tide had turned against local communities as the state and their multinational partners placed profits over people, environment and resources.

The Corrib Field project became an issue in the 2004 European elections. Sinn Fein's candidate for the Connacht/North West constituency called for a full investigation of Shell in Ireland (Sinn Fein press release 23 April 2004). He accused Shell of inconsistencies about the extent of their reserves. Sinn Fein stated that while they were not opposed to developing the country's national resources they wanted any development to benefit the Irish people (ibid). However, despite these concerns Mayo County Council granted planning permission for the onshore terminal on the 30 April 2004. Although the permission was dependent on seventy five conditions imposed due to environmental concerns Shell stated they would be appealing many of these. Local campaigners were appalled particularly in the wake of serious landslides in the peat-bog areas around the proposed site during heavy storms in the previous winter (*The Guardian* May 29 2004). The objectors announced that they would appeal the decision. However, in October 2004 An Bord Pleanála granted Shell planning permission for the gas terminal at Ballinaboy. While Shell made plans for the immediate commencement of work at the site campaigners disgusted by the decision assessed their options. Events in 2005 would see the issue explode onto the national scene.

Framing the Argument: 'Shell to Sea'

The 'Shell to Sea' campaign was able to draw on the expertise of Mayo academic Dr Mark Garavan a lecturer in the Castlebar campus of the Galway-Mayo Institute of Technology. Garavan's own PhD thesis *The Patterns of Irish Environmentalism* focused on the mobilisation of environmental disputes in Ireland so he was in an ideal position to offer his advice on mobilisation. However, the Shell to Sea campaign extended its framing process to embrace a much wider discourse than previous Irish environmental campaigners had allowed for including a near militant exposal of 'defence of space' sentiment combined with a strong expression of cultural nationalism as the rhetoric of Mayo nationalist Michael Davitt emerged alongside the traditional rallying cry of 'The West's Awake'.

The main frames of the Shell to Sea campaign emerged around this combination of local populism and a wider expression of cultural nationalism alongside traditional campaign focus points such as health and safety concerns:

- The dangers and risk posed by the pipeline.
- Local duty to defend families and property.
- The unsavoury behaviour of Shell and the government.
- The misrepresentation of facts on the issue.
- The prioritisation of corporate profits over local concerns.

The Risk frame highlighted the dangers posed by the onshore gas pipeline which was planned to run alongside the homes of many families in Rossport. Minister Noel Dempsey confirmed in a written reply in the Dáil to Deputy Michael Ring that such a pipeline would be unparalleled in Ireland, Europe or elsewhere. The rated pressure of the pipeline would exceed that used by An Bord Gas nearly five times while the gas that would be transported through the pipeline with unrefined oil and water could cause blockages and be risk prone with obstructions occurring far from the gas field where they could be treated (Shell to Sea website June 05). A further concern raised by the Mayo campaigners was the lack of any material benefit for the local community that was bearing the brunt of these risks as all of the gas would be piped through the county into larger cities such as Galway and Dublin. In this way the campaigners were able to extend their risk frame by increasing the sense of 'shared grievance' (Klandermans 1988) surrounding local identity, sense of place and sense of exploitation which was running high throughout the county. For the Shell to Sea campaigners this approach would have the double negative affect of having all profits repatriated to Shell while the chance to develop the west's gas supply would also be lost to the country's sprawling urban area.

Shell attempted to serve their state-backed Compulsory Acquisition Orders (CAOs) on locals in the Rossport area in January 2005. By March the company had applied to the High Court for restraining orders against six local landowners: Phillip McGrath, Brendan Philbin, Willie Corduff, Monica Muller and Brid McGarry. Subsequently shell began excavating peat from the proposed refinery site around nearby Ballinaboy. Amid chaotic scenes diggers began to sink into the bog while heavy vehicles crashed on the inadequate roads surrounding the area. Locals were unable to get past heavy machinery on the one narrow road into the area. As Shell planned for 70 truck movements a day for three months confrontations became inevitable. Local residents turned for help to a sympathetic local TD, the Independent Jerry Crowley, who claimed that the 'people of Erris who have been compelled to have the Corrib gas upstream pipeline adjacent to their homes are scared out of their minds' (Connolly & Lynch 2005 p. 43).

The High Court Action taken against the Rossport residents restrained the named defendants from refusing to allow pipe-laying on their lands. The landowners had been summoned to the High Court on four separate occasions at great personal cost. The landowners had sought evidence of the CAOs in due course before they would allow entry to their lands. This evidence was held back for up to two and a half years (Shell to Sea website 10 June 05). A further attempt to gain entry to the lands at Rossport was followed by the summoning of five local men to the High Court. The men, Willie Corduff, Michael O'Seighin, Phillip McGrath, Brendan Philbin and Vincent McGrath were all charged with breaching the interim order of the court after the men confirmed to Justice Joseph Finnegan that they could not abide by the terms of the Court Order (Lynch 2005 p 45). In a statement to the court Michael O'Seighin summed up the men's position:

> The farms form the basis of the identity of the people. Monetary compensation cannot compensate for undermining the social identity of the people.

The five were jailed for contempt of court despite, as O'Seighin would state from prison, the fact that the constitution under Articles 40 and 43 demand that the State protect the fundamental rights and property of every citizen (Shell to Sea website 5 July 2005). With their incarceration the Rossport 5 would become the news story of the summer. Most papers held daily updates of the campaign and the men and their families took on celebrity status. As the men were taken away to prison local supporters surrounded the men's land to prevent Shell from gaining access. The campaign took on a new momentum.

Shell to Sea : *The West's Awake*

The imprisoning of the 'Rossport 5', as they became known, changed the minds of many locals who had previously favoured the terminal. The Shell to Sea campaign began to mobilise on a wider level as picketing, rallies and placarding were extensively stepped up. The significant alliances which the families had forged took up the campaign as key figures such as Dr. Mark Garavan of the GMIT, Padhraig Harrigan of SIPTU and Jerry Crowley TD organised the committee.

Another mobilisation strategy of the campaign following the men's imprisonment was the placing of pickets on Shell or Statoil petrol stations around the country. In addition, a series of rallies were held nationwide that drew thousands of ordinary people who wished to express their concern about the imprisoning of the five men. Shell's terminals were also the target of organised blockades by environmentally minded 'ecowarriors' such as the 'Cork Pagans', while ecological societies from the University sector were also prominent at many of the campaign's events. This wider support base gave rise to a mobilisation of support unparalleled in previous environmental campaigns. Support for the Rossport 5 came from all levels of Irish society including the Labour Party, Sinn Fein, The Greens, local TDs Jerry Crowley (Ind.) and Michael Ring (Fine Gael), left-wing political groups, SIPTU, the Irish Cattle and Sheep Farmer's Association, the Gluanteacht anti-globalisation network, Louth and Sligo County Council as well as activists such as Robert Ballagh and musicians such as Christy Moor (Shell to Sea Website: Who's Who). This cross section of support allowed Shell to Sea to extend their framing process to incorporate a much wider remit as oppositional politics and cultural discourse were embraced.

This progression from a single issue 'backyard' dispute into an extensive form of ecopopulist dissent corresponds broadly with 'the transition from NIMBY to ecopopulism' (Szasz 1994) which environmental campaigners had been attempting over the various campaigns of the last four decades. The fulcrum of this evolution was, undoubtedly, the imprisonment of the five men. However, while similar fates have been meted out to protestors in recent years it must be said that the Rossport 5's eloquent statements in defence of their actions during their 94 days in Mountjoy jail won a great deal of public support for their cause.

Even though the men were fully committed to their cause they were shocked at their treatment claiming that they were only seeking justice:

> We were put in prison for protecting ourselves. They said we broke the law but we only broke an injunction that shouldn't have been there. We never did any harm. We were just trying to protect our families and rather than listen to us they put us into prison for 94 days.
>
> *(Phillip McGrath, in interview with Rory Hearne November 2005).*

While the camp at Rossport continued to attract sympathisers and grassroots activists from around the country and abroad the Shell to Sea protests continued with events occurring at an almost daily rate. On the 22 of July a National Day of Protest was called against Shell and Statoil. While localised picketing was opposed organised pickets occurred at stations in Wexford, Galway, Kilkenny, Athlone and Wicklow in one day. A national petition was organised as thousands put their signature or e-mailed in messages of support to the Shell to Sea website. This website www.corribsos.com provided the campaign with a powerful tool in the highly computer-literate Ireland of 2005. Grassroots bloggers and activist websites such as 'indymedia' and Ireland from Below gave prominence to the campaign and links between protestors across the globe were established via the internet. It could be said that this new communication technology provided the links to environmental circuits which were lacking before the late 1990's. Internet technologies opened up possibilities for environmental campaigners such as Shell to Sea that also facilitated their ability, not just to gain media coverage but to shape the news and influence the public perception of the debate.

Such power is unwieldy unless applied well and Shell to Sea ran a compelling campaign. The Shell to Sea website was a mobilising resource in itself providing updates and messages from the men and their families. Moreover, it set out a series of strategies which activists would support, such as suggesting participation through:

1. Inviting activists to Rossport and the Mayo Solidarity Camp to learn more about the issue.
2. Supporting the Shell to Sea All-Ireland speaking tour
3. Financial donation and Fundraising
4. Contacting the Media, Letters to the Press
5. Getting Unions, community groups, religious groups, etc, to support the campaigns.
6. Poster and Flyer distribution, with posters ready for downloading from the Shell to Sea website
7. Organising meetings, protests and blockades and boycotting Shell and Statoil
8. Signing or distributing the Shell to Sea petition which was also online and could be downloaded
9. Asking radio stations to play some of the songs written and recorded for the campaign such as "The Rossport 5 song". A DVD was also distributed by the campaigners.
10. Contacting government ministers including the Taoiseach with e-mail addresses being provided.
11. Contacting the Norwegian ambassador or government directly with e-mail addresses supplied (Shell to Sea website).

The provision of this array of campaign strategies on the Shell to Sea site allowed the campaign to circumvent established media outlets and provided the widest range of involvement for the public from petition signing to the organisation of blockades. By mobilising their campaign in this extensive manner Shell to Sea became a resource in itself as the centrepiece to a burgeoning grassroots eco-movement which encompassed locals, environmentalists, students and political activists in a manner not witnessed since the Carnsore anti-nuclear protests.

One response from the state to the controversy was the announcement of a safety review of the Corrib gas pipeline by Natural Resources Minister Noel Dempsey. The minister stated that officials had inspected Shell's onshore site and that in his opinion a serious breach of the consents given to Shell had occurred. In the hope of resolving the dispute the Minister ordered the dismantling of the length of gas pipeline that had already been assembled at the site. In August Shell announced that it would lay off 128 workers at the site. Minister Dempsey's initiative included the establishment of a technical group to monitor the Corrib gas project which included senior civil servants, geographers, engineers and legal experts (*Irish Times* July 05 2005). As the men completed their first month in prison, Shell were coming under increased pressure to lift their injunction to allow the men to go free, particularly in the wake of the breach of its technical consents (ibid). Legal attempts were made to free the men due to the fact that Ministerial consent had been given for preparatory work only, rather than the construction and installation at the site. Opposition leaders also called for the men's release. Shell to Sea spokesperson Mark Garavan cautiously welcomed the Minister's intervention although the campaign noted the timing of the announcement on the eve of a major rally in support of the men and in the week of their latest court hearing (ibid).

The end of July saw a significant upsurge in campaign activity. The National Rally in Dublin attracted over 2,000 people including Sin Fein leader, Gerry Adams. Pickets were arranged in diverse locations such as the Norwegian embassy in Brussels and the McGill Summer School in Donegal where Minister Dempsey was confronted by Shell to Sea protesters. Over 1,000 people picketed outside Shell petrol stations that month, some of them organised by Sinn Fein. However, the campaign was beginning to cause political fallout for figures outside the government. In particular, Fine Gael leader and Mayoman, Enda Kenny, was coming in for criticism about his lack of support for the Rossport men and their families. Kenny was constrained by the fear of being accused of pandering to local populism for electoral gain rather than focusing on the development potential of the Corrib Field, particularly in an unemployment black spot such as County Mayo.

While the government parties also faced their dilemma the situation for the leader of the Opposition was more complex.

Kenny was roundly criticised for sitting on the fence on the issue, particularly by Independent TD Jerry Crowley who had become an effective spokesperson for the Shell to Sea campaign. Mr. Kenny's plight was compounded by the longstanding support given to Shell to Sea by Mayo Fine Gael TD Michael Ring. Both Ring and Cowley were also critical of Mayo County Council for not backing the Rossport men, stating that the council had voted against gold mining at Croagh Patrick in the past despite the threat of legal action from the developer in that case (*Irish Times* 20 July 2005).

In early August the wives of the five men staged a sit-in at the Council's offices in Castlebar. The sit-in, which lasted six hours, came after Caitlin O Seighin, Mary Corduff, Aggie Philbin and the two Maureen McGraths, together with local landowner and objector Brid McGarry had made appeals on behalf of the Rossport 5 for the Council to hold an emergency meeting on the issue. As consultations went on the women were joined by family members, friends and musicians, as well as by Shell to Sea spokesperson Mark Garavan and TD Jerry Crowley. In the interim an emergency meeting was agreed. While the protesters were pleased with the outcome they again criticised Enda Kenny for not clarifying his position on the issue (*Irish Times* August 4 2005). This outcome was tempered by the news that the Minister was allowing Shell to proceed with its pipeline only days after ordering the pipes to be dismantled. The jailed men issued a statement from prison condemning the announcement while Jerry Crowley called for the Minister's resignation, claiming that Shell had not responded to the Minister's request for clarification on Shell's obligations. Local Fianna Fáil councillors in Mayo also condemned the Minister's decision. Mark Garavan criticised the announcement and claimed that the government's valuation of the project was wrong, stating that '35, at most, will be employed here on the Corrib Field when construction is complete' (*Irish Times* August 3 2005).

Further criticism of the state's policies was highlighted in a local news feature on the issue by an American energy regulator. All concerned parties including the protestors, industry and the political sector were constrained by the lack of 'uniform safety requirements for gas pipelines', a policy which was 'at odds with international practice' (*Western People* August 9 2005). The article contrasted safety regulators in the United States for gas pipelines that emanated from two government agencies including an Office of Pipeline Safety with what was called 'a frightening lapse' (ibid) in the Irish regulatory framework. Pipelines in the United States are also protected by a 'certificate of public convenience and necessity' (ibid) words which would have a ring of irony to the imprisoned Rossport men. Public enquiries and written submissions were an integral part of the licensing system in the United States. As the men spent their 50th day in jail they must have found such regulatory discrepancies to be very questionable.

While Shell negotiated with Mayo County Council on the issue the men offered to engage in dialogue with Shell if the Court injunction against them was lifted. Andy Pyle, Shell Ireland's chief executive, claimed the injunction was a matter for the courts but welcomed the men's statement nonetheless. Shell claimed it would be open to legal challenges if it relinquished the injunction, something which was rejected by many including Labour Party leader Pat Rabbitte. As Shell continued to negotiate with Mayo County Council their chief executive, Andy Pyle insisted that the company 'had to preserve its legal position' (*Irish Times* 20 August 2005). One strategic response of the men in prison was their claim that Shell's refusal to lift the injunction was preventing them from preparing their case for the full hearing on the issue and that as Shell had suspended work on the site the injunction now made no sense. The men accused Shell of not being interested in dialogue and said that they were obliged to defend their families as the state had refused to do so. According to Mark Garavan Shell 'were more interested in their strategy than the law' (*Irish Times* 21 Aug 05). The men accused Shell of 'vindictiveness' (ibid) for not withdrawing the injunction claiming that they could not impede work at the site while it was non-operational. Councillors and Community groups from Mayo called for the injunction to be released while

Labour Leader Pat Rabbitte stated that the continued imprisonment of the men was 'bordering on becoming a national disgrace' (*Irish Times* 31 Aug 2005).

The summer ended with a series of events organised by the Shell to Sea campaigns. Protests were held outside the corporate tent hosted by Fianna Fáil at the Galway Races while blockades and picketing continued in Galway, Cork and Dublin. At this stage Shell to Sea had established links with many environmental groups around Europe and participated in events such as 'EcoTopics' in Moldova and the Glastonbury Festival in the UK. Another significant development in the extension of the campaign was the pressure which was brought to bear on Statoil and the Norwegian government. Pickets were held at Norwegian embassies and in September 2005 family members and Shell to Sea supporters went to Norway where they met with representatives of Statoil and the government while supporters picketed the Norwegian embassy in Dublin. Shell to Sea were seen to make the point that the Norwegian tax payer would benefit from 36% of any revenue from the Corrib Field while the Irish taxpayer would receive no benefits at all. The protestors were also keen to exploit the political opportunity which arose from the Norwegian general election campaign that was underway at the time. A further extension of the campaign's international frame was the links created with the Nigerian resource activists including the brother of Ken Saro-Wiwa, Dr. Owens Wiwa, who joined the march to the Dail in support of the Rossport 5. The march coincided with the men's appearance at the High Court as they approached 94 days in prison.

On the 30th of September 2005 High Court President Mr Justice Finnegan freed the Rossport 5 to cheers from their families and supporters. Justice Finnegan stated that the injunction 'no longer served any useful purpose'. Council for the men, John Rogers SC, asked the court to also remove the order of committal claiming it to be 'coercive' and that the men should not face further sanction in the future. However, while the men offered an apology for breaking the court order they refused to give an undertaking on any future activities. In a further development

Justice Finnegan indicated to Shell's council, Patrick Hanratty, that he wanted the company to address its breach of the Minister's licences but that he would not deal with that issue while the men languished in prison (*Irish Times* Saturday October 2 2005).

As the men walked free with their jubilant supporters they vowed that their campaign would go on. The issue was set to continue the following month as Shell stated its intention to pursue the matter of a permanent injunction against the men and any other objectors to the pipeline. The safety review established by Minister Dempsey was also scheduled for that month. The Minister announced plans to appoint a mediator to negotiate with both parties (*Irish Times* October 1 2005). The men made a triumphant appearance at the Shell to Sea rally in Dublin alongside supportive politicians and Dr. Wiwa. As they returned to Mayo traditional bonfires lit the way along their route back to Rossport. According to Micheál O'Seighin the men's victory showed that 'Irish people expect a higher state of democracy and they expect more of their Government in relation to people's safety and welfare' (ibid). The men also indicated their willingness to return to prison if necessary.

Prominent campaign supporters such as TDs Jerry Crowley and Michael Ring indicated that the extension of the campaign into Norway during their general election had played a significant part in building the momentum that led to the men's release. The newly elected administration was believed to have instigated the meeting between senior Statoil executives and Minister Dempsey the week before the men's release in the wake of the visit of Shell to Sea and Jerry Crowley to Norway. Dr. Crowley said that his meetings with Statoil and the Norwegian authorities revealed that 'they did not know what was happening and were shocked by it' (*Sunday Business Post* 2 October 2005). Dr. Crowley felt that the men would have remained in prison but for his Norwegian trip and subsequent intervention. He said Shell to Sea supporters had met to work out the best way to get the men released. As the Norwegian government owned 71% of Statoil it was decided to bring the campaign to Oslo. Crowley was able to plan the trip with the help of Norwegian journalists and trade unionists whom he had developed links with during the campaign. They supplied Shell to Sea with valuable details, contacts and lists of who to meet during their time in Oslo, maximising the impact of their mission. They were able to get national exposure on Norwegian television as a result at a time when Dublin City Council were threatening to prosecute anyone who put up posters advertising Shell to Sea's Dublin rally. The most significant meetings during their trip were with Norwegian Oil and Energy Minister Thorid Widvey and Senior Vice President of Statoil Helga Hattested who would meet with Noel Dempsey a week after the Shell to Sea mission (*Mayo News* 4 October 2005).

While the men celebrated with families and supporters they continued to plan the next phase of their campaign. They insisted that Minister Dempsey should participate in any talks between the families and Shell claiming that 'the state cannot remain neutral in this' (*Irish Times* October 3 2005). The men thanked the public who had supported them with up to 150 cards while they were in prison. They were particularly grateful to Jerry Crowley but poured scorn on Fine Gael's Enda Kenny, stating they told him he had 'let them down' when they met (ibid). The men won further support from the public for their eloquence and resolve on their release including the manner in which they highlighted conditions facing the inner city youth who were their prison mates in Mountjoy. The men claimed they got no special treatment in prison but were well treated by their fellow prisoners.

In October one of the men, Micheál O'Seighin, attended the Minister's Safety review where Minister Dempsey outlined a 'post hoc' justification of the government's strategy for the terminal. The men were critical of the hearing stating that it was 'an attempt to retrospectively suggest that consultation had occurred' (*Irish Times* Oct 13 05). Members of the Shell to Sea campaign and the other members of the Rossport 5 did not attend due to the constraints of the outstanding injunction. The review heard evidence that some of the initial objections to the project may not have been forwarded to the Minister's technical advisory group (ibid). Other evidence at the review included a submission from a retired US Naval engineer who stated that a pipeline explosion would devastate everything within 250 yards of the pipeline releasing 'the equivalent of 3,500 tonnes of TNT. The absence of many of the Shell to Sea campaigners at the hearing was compensated for by the submissions of expert allies like the naval engineer David Aldridge as well as supportive groups such as the Erris Inishowen Fisherman's Association and An Taisce.

At the High Court the Mayo men accused the Minister of 'using the mediation process as a ploy' (*Irish Times* Oct 25 2005). There had been no contact between the Rossport 5 and the Minister since their release from prison. The men stated that the Minister had helped Shell to lift their injunction to 'take the spotlight off the serious safety issues we were highlighting' (ibid). The Shell to Sea campaign continued throughout this period with the five men making appearances at rallies and meetings across the country. The Solidarity Camp at Rossport continued to be a fulcrum of activity while up to 16,000 people had signed the petition organised by Shell to Sea. 31 of the 34 landowners affected by the acquisition orders for the pipeline had taken the side of the men by that stage of the campaign (ibid). However, supporters of the gas project produced a list of over 40 organisations and Councillors who were in favour of the project for economic reasons. This group, The Pro-Erris Gas Group, claimed to have strong backing for their proposal to postpone the dismantling of the pipeline with the allocated money for the dismantling work being spent on community projects in the area. Their claim of community support was weakened in light of reports by some organisations from the area, listed as supporters of the pro-gas group, who claimed that they were not consulted nor were they supporters of the Rossport 5 (*Western People* October 26 2005).

Further claims of misrepresentation on the issue emerged in the aftermath of a survey conducted by Shell as part of the company's communication programme (*Irish Times* Nov. 17,

2005). The survey which was criticised by Shell to Sea due to its coinciding with the state's mediation process involved selected participants being paid €50 to participate in recorded meetings. Some participants felt misled about the nature of these meetings claiming that they had thought they were food surveys or political debates (ibid). While there may have been some degree of miscommunication around this survey Shell to Sea were able to portray the multinational as attempting to manipulate the local community on the issue extending their framing of Shell as a ruthless multinational and to incorporate allegations of 'underhand tactics' (ibid).

November also saw the release of a report on the Corrib gas issue by the Centre for Public Inquiry (CPI). The report claimed that An Bord Pleanála was subjected to 'external pressure' on the issue, a claim it denied (*Irish Times* Nov 24 05). The report's executive summary put forward a number of findings. These included criticism of the state's handling of resources and royalties, its regulatory framework surrounding the introduction of the Compulsory Acquisition Orders (CAOs) and the gas pipeline, the location of the pipeline and terminal and the supervision of work carried out at the site. The report was also critical of the access provided for Shell executives to senior politicians, including the Taoiseach (Connolly and Lynch 2005). The Centre for Public Inquiry (CPI) would also become the centre of a political row due to accusations made by Justice Minister Michael McDowell about the alleged activities of the Centre's Executive Director, Frank Connolly. An independent report released in conjunction with the CPI's findings claimed that the onshore pipeline could rupture causing 'high fatalities' (Kuprewicz 2005 p. 6). The Corrib pipeline was irregular 'due to its operational pressure, lack of historical data in the system evaluation, proximity to people and dwellings and deficiencies in the demonstration of maximum pipeline pressure' (ibid). While Shell to Sea welcomed the CPI report the subsequent political row surrounding the Centre threw a cloud over its findings, further demonstrating the degree of complexity and political intrigue which surrounded this issue.

The government's own safety review's preliminary findings recommended limiting the gas pressure for the pipeline, while Shell rejected the accusation that hydrogen sulphide or 'sour gas', which had similar qualities to cyanide, would be released or corrode the pipeline (*Irish Times* Dec 27 05). The Company claimed that it would be 'unlikely' that concentrations of the toxic substance would reach dangerous levels at the site. Shell to Sea acknowledged the report but their website promised a major escalation in their campaign of opposition including requests for 'gifts' such as night-vision goggles and bolt-cutters for cutting fencing (ibid). Shell to Sea also announced that a major rally was planned for the spring of 2006 to coincide with attempts by Shell to recommence work at the site (ibid). A roadshow was organised with the intention of building the Rossport Solidarity Camp by holding meetings at various points around the country. This series of meetings was organised to facilitate the mobilisation of the second phase of Shell to Sea's campaign promoting the Solidarity Camp for people who wished to participate in the protest and who would be able to provide logistical expertise. While the camp was originally a spontaneous demonstration of support for the Rossport 5, Shell to Sea were prepared to extend their campaign into a much broader project of activism that could extend out to embrace the anti-globalisation grassroots movements with which it had opened up links. This intent can be seen from the following posting on the Shell to Sea website:

> This is a major opportunity to defeat an environmentally hazardous development and the struggle thus far has already been an inspiration to many people around the country. Victory will have a significant radicalising affect, not just on a remote corner of Mayo, but across the island (corribsos.com).

Academic activists were following on an established thread which had been defined by Professor Blacklith during the Carnsore Point protest and were carried on very effectively by prominent figures such as Professor Emer Colleran at Mullaghmore.

Conclusion

While the dispute at Rossport was initially about Shell's onshore pipeline being located near a number of local homes, it has long since moved away from that single issue and has come to represent a range of concerns and responses. These responses have come to mean different things to those involved while attempts to comprehend the events at Rossport can be seen to be almost as intrusive as Shell's pipeline. While many in North Mayo harbour fears about the imposition of the pipeline this fear does not always extend to a full understanding of whether the pipeline is safe or not, nor what economic benefits it may or may not bring. According to Mark Garavan many locals 'simply do not want it'. The pipeline represents an unwelcome intrusion into their land and community. It is this very sense of place that the Shell to Sea campaigners wish to protect and the threat posed by outsiders has reawakened a determined resistance in the North Mayo community that has its roots in Davitt's Land League identity born of the past with little concern for notions of 'progress'.

A higher standard has been set in North Mayo, one that values family and community. This form of moral framing has a subconscious element to it which has been instinctively unleashed in many Irish disputes over time. A subsequent sacrifice to defend the blood lines rooted in the hinterlands has been witnessed over many centuries in Irish history including the execution of the leaders of 1916 or the H Block hunger strikers in the early 1980s. The Rossport men's near one hundred days in prison and the traumatic effect this injustice had on family and neighbours can be understood from this perspective. This trenchant stance has been acknowledged by Shell who have appointed local spokespersons to try and comprehend the depth of feeling directed against them. Alternative routes for the pipeline have been suggested to try to meet peoples' concerns. Shell have also apologised for any 'mistakes' they had made during the dispute, and hinted that alternative routes frot he pipeline may be considered in the wake of the Advantica report on the pipeline (*Irish Times* May 5 2006). However this once localised campaign has caught the imagination of the Irish public and with networks extending from Norway to Nigeria. Coming from such a position, the Shell to Sea campaign may just be beginning.

Chapter Twelve

Anti-Roads Campaigns
Glen of the Downs, Carrickmines and Tara/Skryne

Introduction

Campaigns against the development of major motorways through environmentally sensitive areas have long been a feature of environmental movements across the developed world. This form of anti-infrastructural protest gained prevalence in the late 1980s and 1990s when Earth First began a series of protests around Europe. The most famous of these occurred at the Newbury by-pass and at Twyford Downs. The direct action of anti-roads protesters attracted a radical element to the environmental cause that were willing to take extreme measures, such as chaining and tunnelling, to prevent construction continuing. Earth First's international mobilisation of local, single-issue anti-roads campaigners turned the NIMBYist nature of roads protests on its head. Where once local voices struggled to be heard Earth First's experience in radical action provided a number of experienced and committed activists for an issue that could be ignited anywhere that roads developments were being undertaken. Borrowing the idea of a defence camp from the Greenham Common anti-nuclear protestors the anti-roads protests laid the foundations for the anti-globalisation protests of today, linking committed activists across Europe and North America in a common cause which combined opposition to growth economics with ecological concepts. The campaigners used internet technologies to link global groups around local issues and set the tone for eco-activism in subsequent years.

In time, the focus on the Irish state's increased road building capacity has led to three main anti-roads protests. These occurred at the Glen of the Downs in County Wicklow, Carrickmines in County Dublin and at Tara/Hill of Skryne in

County Meath. All three protests emerged at a time when the state was attempting to develop the commuter hub around Dublin city. The case of Tara/Hill of Skryne would lead to a heated debate about the manner in which heritage is dealt with in an age of rapid growth as the ancient site of Tara came under threat from the state's Critical Infrastructural Bill. This Bill which was introduced in the wake of a series of environmental campaigns has been seen by many as an attempt to stymie such collective responses in the future.

Background

Glen of the Downs

As the construction of this burgeoning roads network began to encroach on sites of archaeological importance a network of campaigns began to emerge to contest these developments. One of the first of the protests occurred at the Glen of the Downs in County Wicklow. This campaign was influenced by the Twyford Downs protest in the UK, a dispute that established a strategic framework for roads protests which provided some of the impetus for Irish campaigners. Emerging from radical groupings such as the Animal Liberation Front (ALF) and the Hunt Saboteurs the UK anti-roads groups used a form of militant direct action that was not previously associated with eco-protests (Garner 2000 p 146). The most notable tactical innovation of the UK roads protestors was their use of direct action by what came to be known as 'eco-warriors'. These were groups of committed activists who occupied sites to halt progress after building had commenced. Amongst the tactics employed by the eco-warriors in both the UK and Ireland were 'lock ons' or the chaining of protestors to mechanical equipment or trees. Protestors built camps in tunnels or trees making further construction work or arrests difficult. This tactic provided the media with an event to focus on in a way that oral hearings never could.

The Glen of the Downs dispute emerged in the aftermath of the relocation of thousands of people from Dublin to the outlying counties of Wicklow, Kildare, Meath and Wexford. As these new commuters became ensnared in notorious bottlenecks around the perimeter of the capital the National Development Plan (NDP) presented planners with a series of options to improve traffic flows with rezoning, leading to the doubling of the population of commuter belt villages within half a decade (McDonald and Nix 2005 p. 60). With rezoning proving to be a controversial issue in many of the planning tribunal's local resistance to roads building was rising. However, the tactics of the 'eco-warriors' together with the satirical depiction of some of these campaigners in the tabloids meant that potential alliances between activists and local communities were not easily established. One account of the eco-warriors camp at the Glen of the Downs illustrated the gulf which existed between the conditions endured by activists in contrast with the occasional visit by a sympathetic councillor:

> "Conditions at the Glen of the Downs in Wicklow where the eco-warriors have staked their ground are miserable, tough and unforgiving. Around 30 people are living permanently on site in specially built tree houses... The rain is unrelenting and there is nowhere to shelter... It is hard to believe anyone can live in these conditions... The warriors are annoyed that some people have called them dirty. To wash with hot water they would sometimes be invited by locals to use their showers... There are no toilet facilities so they use a hole which has been dug in the ground... you are in darkness most of the time" (*The Examiner* 1999).

While the eco-warriors' plight was bad the occasional unrest and court appearances of activists kept the Glen of the Downs protest in the news; it would ironically be the courts that ended the protest as the activists were threatened with imprisonment if they breached undertakings not to occupy lands at the Wicklow site. As the eco-warriors' protest petered out the €85 million dual carriageway through the Wicklow hills was completed.

While this initial instance of anti-roads activism was unsuccessful the stance of the eco-warriors did lead to the establishment of a number of links with the subsequent campaigns and initiatives while a cultural challenge to the dominant way of life was initiated. Though many found the 'deep green' alternative lifestyle of the eco-warriors too extreme, student groups and environmental protection groups were enthused by the Glen of the Downs campaign as environmentally sustainable existence became a feature of many young professionals' lives.

The onset of internet technologies during the 1990s led to the establishment of websites dedicated to providing a resource for activists and researchers. Among the most prominent of these was *Ireland from Below* established by the academic and activist Laurence Cox and the writer Robert Allen with others. This website provided a forum for the establishment of links between the myriad campaigns and societies which were agitating for the environment. The website has recently been re-established with input from environmental writers such as Robert Allen. As an alternative culture emerged links between new age practitioners, feminists, ecologists and political radicals lead to a series of initiatives, conferences and workshops on grassroots approaches to building a new modernity at the turn of the millennium. These linkages provided an activist base for many campaigns in the first half decade of the new century including the anti-war alliance, the Rossport 5 dispute and the second major anti-roads protest at Carrickmines Castle in County Kildare.

The Carrickmines dispute gave rise to a combination of environmental and heritage protection frames as a new wave of academic activists came to the fore linking professional expertise regarding local archaeology and heritage with an articulate defence of community and landscape.

Carrickmines

Plans for an interchange for the M50 at Carrickmines were included as part of the south-eastern motorway development and led to an extensive archaeological excavation around the site of the 13th century castle in the area. Evidence of significant artefacts was found by an international team of experts after a two year investigation led to an occupation by a group of concerned activists who had been involved in the roads campaign. This group, which came to be known as the 'Carrickminders', had two main strategies to prevent the M50 development. The established method of taking a legal action was the first. However, the second strategy drew upon approaches undertaken by the eco-warriors a decade earlier as the Carrickminders attempted to prevent the development by occupying the site of the ancient castle. The legal frame established by the roads protesters utilised the National Monuments Act as a vehicle to prevent further works at the site. The Carrickminders also challenged Duchas, the national heritage agency and Dunlaoghre-Rathdown Council in relation to the archaeological licence for the excavation (*Irish Examiner* 17 February 2002). The group's spokesperson Ruadhri McEoin had staged a month long sit-in at the site and claimed that sections of the castle's wall had been dismantled by workers at the site contravening the Monuments Act.

The Carrickminders had forged alliances with both the National Museum and local Green Party TD, Ciaran Cuffe, with both giving their support to the group's legal challenge. The extension of the dispute into one which set the National Museum at odds with the state's heritage agency provided the protestors with the weight of one official environmental entity while the Green Party's support was more pronounced due to that party's electoral successes in the 2002 General Election. Another political figure to lend his support was local Fianna Fail Councillor Barry Andrews, who complained about the wall removal to the Gardai. The fact that land deals around the site came under investigation during the Flood Tribunal into corruption added to the sense of crisis surrounding the roads project.

Ultimately, the National Roads Authority (NRA) announced that the dispute had led to costs for the South-Eastern motorway running into an extra €10 million with the project being delayed by over a year (RTE News January 6 2004). Transport Minister

Seamus Brennan reacted to this overrun by welcoming the High Court's dismissal of the protestors' legal action while the NRA called for the reform of the state's heritage laws to prevent similar actions in the future (ibid). A European Commission report on the dispute criticised the lack of any attempt to find an alternative route for the motorway, the role of Duchas in favouring the development over its remit to protect heritage and the lack of a proper concern for archaeological sites (McDonald and Nix 2005 pp 157, 158).

For their part the Carrickminders submitted an alternative plan for the motorway as well as the development of a heritage park at the Carrickmines site. Environment Minister Martin Cullen's response to the dispute was to amend the legislation for the preservation of national monuments providing increased ministerial powers in similar cases to allow for demolition of sites to facilitate infrastructural projects. Both the Carrickminders and their political and academic allies were appalled at this outcome claiming it would allow developers to bulldoze sites of heritage for expedience and profit.

Tara / Hill of Skryne

The contentious subject of the destruction of an ancient heritage site to facilitate a roads network again emerged as a result of plans to build a dramatically imposing tolled intersection for the M3 motorway near the ancient heritage site at the Hill of Tara in conjunction with an extension of the M2 motorway at the nearby Hill of Skryne in County Meath. Both of these developments had parallels with the roads disputes in the Glen of the Downs and Carrickmines Castle as like Wicklow and rural County Dublin, Meath had become a primary location on the extensive commuter belt surrounding the capital. As property prices in Dublin city continued to rise significantly land prices in rural areas of Leinster surrounding the capital also came to a premium. With the government now emboldened by the amended National Monuments Act of 2004 conservationists were astounded by the news that the ancient Celtic site at the Hill of Tara was threatened by a roads development. This news came in the wake of four decades of destruction of the country's monuments and ancient hill forts in an era when the east coast's rural way of life was giving way to an aggressive agri-business sector alongside an increase in urban sprawl.

While successive governments had prioritised rural development the need to conserve sites of scenic beauty on heritage value contributed to a debate on the right of rural families to build houses in the countryside. While concerns about 'bungalow-blight' emerged during the first phase of environmentalism in the 1970s and 1980s rural communities that had witnessed a traumatic demographic haemorrhaging throughout their history remained defensive of their surrounding hinterlands. By 1999 the National Spatial Strategy had identified that 15,000, one-off houses were built in that year alone accounting for up to one third of the state's housing output (IPC 2003). As the issue's salience increased through extensive media coverage of disputed planning applications calls were made to limit planning permission in scenic areas. This response represented another incarnation of the contest between official and populist environmentalism (Tovey 1992 b) with the planning lobby and heritage groups such as An Taisce at odds with local communities who were the key stakeholders in the disputed regions.

Rural communities were alarmed to find that policy-makers considered the extent of rural housing development to be unsuitable (McDonald and Nix 2005 p 112). With housing prices soaring in urban centres many urban dwellers were seeking to build in rural areas, a trend exacerbated by the influx of returning migrants who had left the country during the 1980s. An additional component to the debate was the increase in land value at a time when domestic agriculture was beginning to decline making selling land for housing developments an attractive proposition. As rural housing increased the additional infrastructure such as roads, electricity and water necessary for burgeoning communities, served to increase both the extent of ecological and visual degredation and costs to the state for the provision of services. As most employers, such as the

multinationals, tended to locate near urban centres commuting and the inherent loss of social capital became a further concern.
One of the main areas for antagonism identified by the Irish Planning Institute (IPI) was the inconsistencies contained within the planning process across the country and within local authority regions (IPC 2005). An inconsistent planning culture was exacerbated by the clientelist political system whereby local councillors supported individual cases to attract electoral support. The uneven nature of the clientelist brokerage system had increased the sense of frustration experienced by unsuccessful applicants for planning permission and furthered the onset of rural hostility which many felt precipitated a backlash against the government coalition parties at the 2004 local elections.

Despite the announcement of guidelines on rural one-off housing in March of that year the issue had also given rise to a series of attacks on the heritage watchdog, An Taisce, a group that became the focus of some unsettled councillors' wrath in the run up to the local elections. The fact that An Taisce was singled out for criticism provides an indication of the confused and emotive nature of the one-off housing debate particularly in light of evidence which demonstrates that the heritage group was involved in appeals in less than 1% of cases (McDonald and Nix 2005 p 14). Ultimately, there has been a growing recognition of the need for landscape and heritage protection in areas of scenic beauty across the country. While urban planning has become regulated a system of environmental assessment has been called for to prevent further abuses of the planning process in relation to inappropriate developments.

The 'Save Tara' campaigners framed their arguments around a number of issues. The primary frame of the campaign was based on the heritage value of the area with the mobilisation of international and national academic support to testify for the area's near-sacred significance. One gathering of academics to protest at the Tara site brought together Professors of history, Celtic Studies, archaeology and anthropology from Europe and North America to petition the government to reroute the motorway. Further support for the campaign was offered from the *Sunday Tribune* newspaper which featured a series of articles on the issue. The academic/heritage frame established an understanding of the international importance of the site which contained artefacts that could reveal layers of information from prehistoric times through to the Middle Ages. The campaigners were able to engage with political allies such as the former Taoiseach, John Bruton, who had represented Fine Gael in Meath as a TD. Mr. Bruton called for the rerouting of the M3 away from the 'globally unique' site calling it a 'sacred space' (McDonald and Nix p. 188). The combination of academic experts and political allies was strengthened by the emergence of the 'Artists for Tara' group which provided the campaign with high profile supporters such as the actor Stuart Townsend who arrived from Hollywood to offer his help (http/www.showbiz ireland.ie 11 October 2004).

Townsend referred to the plan as 'a travesty' and was praised by protest organiser Vincent Salafia for raising the profile of the protest. According to Salafia the support of celebrities afforded the campaign greater media attention and would allow incoming Environment Minister Dick Roche "a chance to understand what is at stake here at Tara" (http/www.breakingnews.ie 10 October 2004). Another tactic which emerged from the academic heritage frame was a submission to the Joint Committee of the Oireachtas on Environment by two professors of archaeology from NUI Galway, Joe Fenwick and Conor Newman. These academics framed their arguments by linking economics and heritage claiming the valuation by the NRA of €20 million to have an archaeological resolution was considerably undervalued (McDonald and Nix 2005 p 189). An alternative route east of Skryne and nearer to Dublin was put forward by the academics.

The political opportunity afforded by the Meath by-election in 2005 was seized on by the campaigners with the local Fianna Fail candidate who supported the M3 being defeated. Environment Minister Dick Roche announced further excavations and enhanced landscaping along the proposed route as well as limiting commercial developments in the area.

However the fact that the M3 was allowed to go ahead despite the cultural arguments of the campaigners was decried as 'an act of vandalism' by concerned archaeological spokespersons (ibid).

The Tara campaigners also took a High Court challenge to the M3 route through their spokesperson Vincent Salafia. Part of this legal action involved the extension of the heritage frame which involved depictions of the site as an area of national, archaeological and mythical/spiritual significance. Salafia was intent on promoting the heritage angle to prevent other issues such as NIMBYism, property values or alternative routs emerging as competing frames during the dispute. Another spokesperson, Muireann Ni Bhrolchain, was also keen to promote the heritage as the pivotal issue in the dispute giving it primacy over secondary concerns about the role of the state agencies or the future of transport in the area (Allen 2006 p. 11).

As in Carrickmines and the Glen of the Downs the Skryne Valley was part of the commuter belt around Dublin which the state and private developers had earmarked as an area of potential developments that could address the insatiable demands of property buyers priced out of the capital and its environs. While some form of decentralisation had been mooted to alleviate the demand for living space throughout the Pale, no real attempt had been made to allow people to live and work in rural areas across the country. The Tara campaigners' tactical approach of promoting heritage conservation rather than attempting to address urban sprawl was visionary in this context, as solutions to the housing, transport and amenities needs of commuters have escaped many in the planning and political sections. On the other hand, a heritage discourse had succeeded in previous environmental disputes, most notably at Mullaghmore.

The strategic direction of the Tara campaigners was one of protecting the Hill of Tara from both road developments and the enforced archaeological digs which were a requirement of such developments. The whole of the Skryne Valley was part of an area of national heritage that needed to be protected from inappropriate developments. The campaigners produced arguments for alternative transport plans, that were railway rather than road based, for the area claiming much of the line was still in existence (Allen 2006 p. 12). Their legal challenge alleges that the state was in breach of its 'constitutional duty to protect the heritage of Ireland' (ibid). Their campaign had heightened understandings of relevant issues as they had extended it into the political sphere through the Meath by-election in 2005 by interaction with local councils and at government level.

The campaign had also gained considerable coverage in the media. In an interesting parallel with the 'No Nukes' protests at Carnsore nearly forty years previously, a musical tour helped to raise awareness about the issue. The 'Magentic Music Tour: Tunes for Tara' had spread the word across Ireland and the Continent while the campaign's cultural frame had embraced the support of Ireland's burgeoning New Age community (ibid). The cultural frame's most notable contribution was the 'Artists for Tara' group which was led by the renowned Celtic artist Jim Fitzpatrick, designer of many famous Thin Lizzy album covers amongst other notable works. The establishment of an extensive cultural frame has reinforced the heritage based arguments of the 'Save Tara' campaigners.

Conclusion

The introduction of the 2004 National Monuments Act placed major constraints on conservationists who planned to challenge infrastructural projects of the state which impinged upon heritage sites around the country. From the state's perspective the Act, like the Infrastructure Bill which was introduced subsequently, provided an opportunity to circumvent the incidents of protest that delayed projects and contributed to escalating costs. These costs came in the wake of the state's investment of over €6.8 billion alongside the €12 billion contributed for roads by the private sector (MacDonald and Nix 2005 p. 286). This combination of state and private funding for roads, when combined with the ideologically charged adversarial approach to environmentalism taken by the neo-liberal Fianna Fáil and Progressive Democrat coalition, created the conditions whereby the ethical considerations appropriate for a heritage site such as the Hill of Tara were reduced to no more than an economic afterthought. The rejection of the High Court challenge by environmentalist Vincent Salafia in March 2006 can be placed within that wider ideological context of the unified rejection by industry and the state of any moral, ethical, legal or environmental consideration of heritage sites as having a universal significance that went beyond the infrastructural needs of one generation.

Furthermore, the weight of the High Court ruling has implications for all environmental activists. The findings of Mr. Justice Smyth criticised the timing of Vincent Salafia's challenge and rejected his argument that the challenge was delayed due to Salafia's involvement in the Carrickmines protest. Therefore the findings in this case charge environmental activists with a responsibility to match the agendas of those who wish to cause environmental degredation or harm to heritage sites, rather than acknowledging the voluntary contribution of concerned members of civil society who wish to raise objections to infrastructural projects. And while the significant financial overrun that had come to characterise roads projects in the Republic benefit no one, many of these problems were caused by the lack of available land rather than by the relatively small number of environmental protests involving roads projects. For instance, there were no environmental protests surrounding the construction of the Dublin Port Tunnel and yet its costs practically doubled from €220 million to €580 million (MacDonald and Nix 2005 p. 289).

While the state and its industrial partners should provide a value for money roads infrastructure for the tax payer, the state is also charged with maintaining a concern for the country's heritage and the well being of its citizens. Yet the current climate has produced an atmosphere where personalised hostility is directed at advocates such as Vincent Salafia whose expertise was pronounced at the High Court to be *locus standi* or not entitled to a hearing. Salafia was portrayed as a solitary, arrogant protestor intent on delaying critical infrastructure, in one media report of the High Court Action which characterised his actions as 'almost pathologically vexatious' (*Daily Mail* March 2 2006). The fact that Salafia was one member of a campaign which united locals, Irish and international academics and gained support from celebrities, demonstrates the extent to which a significant number of the population shares Salafia's concerns.

If the weight of the system is turned on advocates the constraints on environmental activism become too great and a sector of civil society, already excluded by the existing structures of social partnership, becomes increasingly alienated. This form of neo-corporatist exclusion by the state and industrial interests is alien to the core tenets of a pluralist society where the contribution of elements from civil society is recognised as a significant layer in the structural composition of life in a democracy.

Chapter Thirteen

Conclusion

Outcomes: The Consequences of Environmental Activism

Throughout this examination of collective responses to environmental threats a number of framing processes, strategies and types of campaign have been identified. But what are the consequences and outcomes of the various environmental campaigns witnessed n Ireland since the Carnsore point protests? Without doubt, the Irish environmental movement has made an impact on Irish society. We can examine the impact of grassroots campaigners more effectively by applying the six most beneficial outcomes of environmental activism as identified by Freudenburg and Steinsapir in 1992. The six beneficial outcomes can be summarised as follows:

1) Increased community control over public health.

2) The introduction of eco-efficient processes by the corporate sector.

3) Increased regulation or elimination of toxins from the production processes.

4) The establishment of wider support networks for communities that were once isolated.

5) Increased environmental and heritage awareness amongst the wider community.

6) The expansion of civic participation in environmental decision making.

So then how can we apply these six outcomes to the Irish environmental movement? In the first instance we can see that a number of potentially harmful projects have been delayed or abandoned due to environmental campaigns. We can include the nuclear power station planned for Carnsore as well as multi-national industrial plants such as Raybestos Manhattan's asbestos plant and dump in the 1980s in addition to the more recent campaigns against incinerators or the Shell pipeline in Mayo in this category. And while these industries and their state sponsors have decried the abandonment or delay of such projects all of the campaigns covered in this book have increased civic awareness of environmental, health or heritage issues. The Mullaghmore dispute and the more recent anti-roads protests have led to substantial national and international debates about how we perceive and conserve heritage sites in an age of accelerated development. Furthermore, each of these campaigns have contributed to the awakening of local knowledge and concern about hinterlands allowing for an augmentation of community derived 'social capital' that politicians and commentators have come to value so highly.

Politically, successive environmental campaigns have strengthened the responses of civil society from the grassroots up, bolstering pluralistic discourses at a time when that aspect of democracy has come under threat from a variety of sources including an increasingly technocratic state and a body-politic damaged by a series of planning related scandals. Environmental social movements have benefited mainstream politics in Ireland as witnessed by the rise of the Green party in local, national and European elections over the last decade. One distinctive outcome of environmental conflict has been the establishment of the Environmental Protection Agency (EPA) in 1992. The EPA was originally criticised for its location of a regulatory framework within the context of the state's industrial development policies (Taylor 2001) but the agency has come into its own over time and is now a leading component of institutional environmentalism in Ireland spanning a range of ecological, educational and regulatory responses. However, some distance remains between the EPA and many grassroots campaigns and the bridging of this gap remains an outstanding issue for all levels of environmentalism in the Irish case.

Table 2	Campaign	Outcomes					
	Political	Social	Cultural	Legal	Institutional	Economic	Scientific
No Nukes Carnsore Point	Policy Abandoned	Inter-group Networking	Issue Salience Unions & Environmentalists United	Moral and Legal issues debated	Nuclear Energy option abandoned	Energy policies altered	Nuclear arguments abandoned
Anti-Toxics Anti-Multinational Cork	State emphasis on TNC led development maintained	Increased Networking	Divergence between unions & Environmentalists	Legal actions, Legal threats against campaigners	IDA policy on TNC development maintained	State policies on TNC development maintained	Interest-led debates on toxics begin
Anti-mining,Tynagh, Donegal, Croagh Patrick	State resources sold off	DUC and Carnsore Campaigners networking	Rural defence of space campaigns	Compulsory purchase laws enacted	State resource agencies established	Resources sold off	Debates about Uranium and Cyanide
Heritage Mullaghmore	State policy on interpretive centre defeated	Successful challenge to state policy	Raising of awareness about heritage	EU Legal option utilised by campaigners	OPW challenged Policy abandoned An Taisce's source	Tourism policy altered	Increased understanding of ecological issues

Anti-Incinerator GSE & NIA	Regional waste management policy delayed	Mobilisation & Networking of Anti-Incinerator groups	Increased participation by Community Groups	Legal Challenges against Incinerator Licences	EPA and An Bord Pleanála hearings	Waste plans shift towards recycling	Increased understanding of dioxins and waste flows
Anti-Incinerator CHASE	Contestation of Regional Waste policy	Re-emergence of Cork Environmental campaigns	Increased Community participation in Chase Campaign	Legal challenges by CHASE	An Bord Pleanála hearings	Waste plans for Cork pivotal to State	Increased understanding of wider issues relating to incineration
Resources Shell to sea	Developing campaigns of resistance	Emergence of rural Political Movement	Wider rural sentiment Articulated	Imprisonment of Rossport Five	State backs down on pipeline	Gas resources held by multinational	Debates about Resources
Glen of the Downs, Carrickmines Tara/Skryne Anti-Roads	Direct Action Campaign against infrastructural projects	Mobilisation of New wave of Environmental movement	Debates about development and heritage	Legal challenges against routing of motorways	Roads Authority developing Nationwide Roads Network	Emphasis on private transport despite energy crisis	Ecological and Energy issues raised

Our understanding of 'successful' outcomes for movements has been shaped by Gamson (1975) and Burstein et al (1995) who have identified that 'realisation' and 'influence on policy' (state action) are the key factors in campaign impact assessment. These concepts have been further developed by Amenta and Caren (2004 p. 463) who have perceived the distinctions inherent between actual achievement of stated goals and the achievement of certain 'advantages for constituents'. Inevitably, movement success has therefore become synonymous with state acknowledgement and response to movement grievance. However, the subsequent achievement of aspects of a campaign's aims has also been recognised as a long term result of collective action particularly when outcomes result from 'unintended consequences' (Amenta and Caren 2004 p. 463). Changes to policy or adoption of movement aims as part of state policy can be part of this process. The formation of Irish environmental policy could be viewed as emerging in a dualistic response to bottom-up grassroots agitation on the one hand in addition to 'top down' EU legislation on the other. In the Irish case its populist political make-up lends itself to the attainment of some leverage for movements particularly at local level. However, the economic imperative of the state still dominates at policy level despite the occasional opening up of political opportunities at times of elections (Leonard 2005).

At the same time the overall achievements of environmental movements have benefited all in Irish society rather than just campaign participants. On the other hand some negative consequences of environmental activism can be witnessed in the increasingly technocratic approach to infrastructural disputes. They have led to policy responses such as the Critical Infrastructure Bill which may constrain future collective action on environmental issues. It remains to be seen as to whether single-issue candidates from movements or advocates running for the Green Party will achieve enough political power to influence policy decisions in future governments.

The Cultural Outcomes of the Environmental Movement

Without doubt, environmentalism has made an impact on our

lives. As Dunlap and Riley (1992) have claimed 'history will surely record the environmental movement as among the few that significantly changed our society'. In the Irish case the environmental movement stands alongside other new left movements such as feminism and civil rights as the main political issues of recent decades. At a time when core values have faded for mainstream parties primarily concerned with maintaining economic growth it has been the new social movements of environmentalism, feminism and civil rights that have shaped a coherent response to a society that was in transition.

There has been little attention paid to the cultural consequences of environmental movements. Where social movement literature has examined this (Hart 1996), (Earl 2004) three main areas of cultural impact have been identified. These are (i) the social-psychological, (ii) cultural production and (iii) collective community or world views (Earl 2004 pp.511-518). The literature on social-psychological impacts and the works on cultural production examined have tended to focus on changes to values and beliefs arising from movement activity. The third area has examined the 'creation of new collective identities' (ibid) or subcultures where the very praxis of participation has a transformative affect on people's lives.

Many social groups have come to understand themselves through the transformative process of collective action and in the Irish case we have seen the manner in which local identities are strengthened by collective resistance to perceived threats from outsiders. This form of collective identity transformation demonstrates the interactive relationship between local communities, emergent movements and their hinterlands. Moreover local identities are strengthened when communities respond collectively in defence of their territory. This form of social-psychological bonding may lead to a period of intensive transformation of local identities that may last for generations. The projection of a collective 'us' versus a sometimes less than tangible but threatening 'them' becomes a significant component in the context of social-psychological collective identity building in areas where both the community and their environment are threatened.

As this study has demonstrated the process of establishing potent cultural, moral and social frames lies at the heart of any successful cultural transformation (or re-awakening) of local sentiment during the course of environmental disputes. Wider cultural references such as the anti-nuclear concerts by Bruce Springsteen and Crosby, Stills and Nash were replicated in the Irish case. Over the decades since Carnsore Point one participant, Christy Moore, has become the embodiment of cultural integrity from his work with Moving Hearts through to his solo work.

The emergence of celebrity advocates has become a feature of Irish Social Movements. U2 front man, Bono and his wife Ali Hewson have been involved in campaigns such as Drop the Debt and Adi Roche's Chernobyl Children's Project. While Bono's advocacy alongside Bob Geldof has become a feature of global advocacy on a range of issues from debt reduction to AIDs prevention, the work of Ali Hewson and Adi Roche as advocates for children of the devastated Chernobyl region presents a two-fold cultural frame (i) aiding the children who have suffered from the aftermath of the Chernobyl nuclear plant meltdown in addition to (ii) presenting a very humane and moral representation of the dangers of nuclear power.

This form of advocacy comes at a time when many actors ranging from environmentalist J. F. Lovelock, author of the Gia Hypothesis, to the Irish state agency Forfas have argued about the need to embrace nuclear power as an environmentally friendly alternative to fossil fuels. Essentially the dichotomy between institutionalised initiatives aimed at sustaining economically-driven growth and cultural responses to the risks created by such policies has become a feature of the politics of the new millennium. The cultural consequences of movement activity are often impacted on in a wider manner by the involvement of celebrity advocates in an era when much emphasis is placed on the role of celebrities in shaping culture.

In many cases the emergence of an environmental issue only gains public attention due to depictions in popular culture. The anti-nuclear movement benefited from the film *Silkwood*, which featured the 'whistle blowing' story and tragic death of Karen Silkwood while more latterly sinister films such as *Erin Brockovich* have presented a similar tale of an anti-toxics legal advocate. Szasz (1994) has examined the emergence of toxics as an issue from the 1970s onwards with the chemical spills or illegally dumped and leaking chemical drums becoming a staple item on the evening news, in television action dramas, documentaries and even cartoons. In many ways, anti-industrial or environmentally friendly framing has become a cultural signifier of the times; part of a persuasive symbiotic process that has led to even the most heavily polluting industries attempting to re-brand themselves as eco-friendly dolphin lovers.

And while this may have led to a co-option of green issues within a politically correct cultural milieu alongside other new left movements the cultural persuasiveness of this form of environmentally charged cultural capital makes the heavy handed attempts to impose infrastructural projects on Irish communities all the harder to understand particularly at a time when An Taoiseach, Bertie Ahern, is calling for increased community based public participation (*Irish Times* 15 April 2006). Ultimately, this study of Irish environmental movements has highlighted the significance of the 'discursive opportunity structure' (Gamson 2004 p. 249) surrounding community responses to environmental risks. As with the concept of 'political opportunity structure' discursive structures are not fixed but have a 'variable element' (ibid) where cultural framing becomes a primary source of discursive capital with discursive opportunity structures becoming the 'playing field in which framing contests occur' (ibid).

The Political and Cultural consequences of Irish Environmental Campaigns

We can apply this understanding of a discursive opportunity structure to the Irish environmental campaigns covered in this study in order to examine the consequences of this form of collective action. We can apply understandings of the types of protest, tactics, framing processes and outcomes to the different campaigns that have formed a part of the Irish environmental movements. A series of frames have been used by these movements including political, cultural, social, legal, institutional, economic, scientific and moral. Invariably the discursive framing patterns presented in cases of Irish environmental activism have emerged from a populist context.

Kitching (1989) examines populism from the perspective of developing societies and makes the distinction between populism and neo-populism. While both are presented as critiques of industrialisation and mass-production in favour of small and localised entities 'populism' is defined as being based primarily in a social and ethical critique, whereas 'neo-populism' is seen as being 'more ambitious and 'not primarily oppositional' (Kitching 1989 pp. 20, 21). The process of migration from rural to urban centres during the industrial revolution is presented as a factor in the development of populism based on rural sentiment by Kitching creating an 'anti-urban nostalgia' for the rural in elements of populism (ibid). In the Irish context a left-leaning anti-capitalism and anti-militarism informed many of what have been termed 'first-phase' environmental disputes in Ireland (Leonard 2005). This has been combined with a strong sense of identity that is grounded in rural discourse creating a strong sense of opposition to first phase, multinational projects in the 1970s and 1980s while contributing to the emergence of new middle class opposition to 2nd phase state sponsored infrastructural projects in recent decades.

The initial campaign that came to define first phase disputes was the anti-nuclear protest at Carnsore Point. Campaign leaders were able to draw on existing moral and cultural frames in the process of creating a discursive response to plans for nuclear power in Ireland. The Carnsore Point protest benefited from wider symbiotic understandings of the perils of nuclear power created by US and European anti-nuclear protestors in addition to the wider representation of the nuclear issue that were becoming part of popular culture. The linking of the Donegal uranium mining issue with the energy debates surrounding the state's plans for Carnsore brought together the anti-war and environmental camps at an early stage. However, while local populism played some role in the Tynagh mines dispute the inability of the local population to create the momentum which would go beyond the economic rationale for mining at Tynagh contributed to the horrors that followed during the mining process and the scarred, poisoned site when it was eventually abandoned. The Tynagh Mines case and the subsequent degradation that occurred at the site and across its surrounding waterways and hinterlands should serve as a reminder to those who argue that communities should comply and take whatever economic benefits accrue from such acquiescence.

The one environmental campaign that can be seen as having a successful outcome for the movement involved was that of the Burren Action Group at Mullaghmore. Through a series of legal actions combined with a comprehensive understanding of the fragility of the Burren's eco-systems the BAG campaign achieved its goal of preventing tourist infrastructure from impinging on the Burren. It also contributed to an ongoing debate about the nature of heritage, identity and development both locally and internationally. The Mullaghmore campaign provides an illustration of the significance of expertise for any environmental group that finds itself in dispute with the interests of local authorities or the state.

The importance of new middle class expertise has also been demonstrated as a key aspect of the anti-incinerator campaigns in Galway, Meath and Cork. The ability of these groups to contest the scientific data of the host industry or the state may not prevent incinerators being built in Ireland but this form of interest-led advocacy has informed concerned communities, industry and state officials about the potential risks of any incineration process that does not comply with strict processes of waste separation. In addition, the cultural importance of the reuse and recycle component of waste management has been reinforced by the anti-incineration campaigns, all of which presented recycling-led alternatives that would challenge the 'throw-away' syndrome so conspicuous in contemporary consumerism.

The debate about resources which first emerged in the 1970s and 1980s has resurfaced as part of the 'Shell to Sea' campaign. This campaign has re-invigorated the sense of community in Mayo and across rural Ireland, an identity that can be traced back to the agrarian agitation of the Land League. The territorial response of the North Mayo community to the perceived threats of the gas pipeline set to run across their lands is an instinctive one. The injustice surrounding the jailing of the 'Rossport 5' mobilised a wider response among the Irish populace which was growing angry at increased collusion between state and industrial interests at the expense of local communities.

The sense of grievance at state indifference to local or national heritage informs the anti-roads disputes. The current obsession with private car ownership over public transport has an ideological base. When combined with the destruction of heritage at Tara or Carrickmines or environmental degradation at the Glen of the Downs a new ideological response has emerged that draws on wider discursive challenges to articulate a coherent position based on a sense of environmental justice and conservation of the past.

Let us examine the consequences of environmental movement collective actions in Ireland. We can locate the campaigns covered in this study within the context of what Tovey (1992 b) has termed 'populist' environmentalism. Emerging from a wider network of anti-war and moral campaigners the anti-nuclear protestors who staged the festivals at Carnsore point achieved enough leverage to have the state abandon its nuclear energy policy. Socially a network of environmental actors was established that was all-Ireland and international in its make-up. Culturally this network provided the fledgling Irish environmental movement with a unifying issue and the anti-nuclear issue maintained its salience for campaigners and public over a number of years.

The campaign succeeded in opening a debate on a number of moral issues, many of which were covered in *A Nuclear Ireland*? With the abandonment of the nuclear energy option alternative approaches were examined by the state and in time the Irish state became a long-time opponent of the British nuclear industry. Scientifically, in the Irish case, arguments in favour of the nuclear option were abandoned until the recent energy crisis engendered a resurfacing of this exchange with prominent environmentalists such as James Lovelock suggesting nuclear power as an alternative to fossil fuels.

The anti-toxics campaigns which occurred in Cork at locations such as Ovens, Ringaskiddy or the Womanagh Valley and were written about by Adrian Peace emerged as part of the first phase of anti-multinational campaigning in pre-growth Ireland (Leonard 2005). These successive events can be analysed in the context of a number of anti-multinational campaigns in Ireland throughout the 1970s and 1980s involving multinationals such as Raybestos Manhatten, Merrill Dow, Merck Sharp and Dohme, DuPont and Beechams (see Allen and Jones 1990, Allen 2004, Leonard 2005 and Peace 1993). These campaigns can be seen as part of the 'cycles of protest' (Tarrow 1998, Snow and Benford (1992) that form part of the interconnected sense of grievance in many rural and suburban areas. Campaigns established framing processes derived from this extensive sense of grievance at the location of multinational plants that were perceived as posing a pollution risk.

One unfortunate result of the emergence of community-based campaigns against multinationals was the opening up of a divergence between community-based environmentalists and the trades unions, a gulf that had previously been bridged during the Carnsore anti-nuclear campaign. Disputes about the siting of toxic waste plants opened up the now familiar legal action or oral hearing approach for environmental campaigners and led to the establishment of the EPA in 1992. While communities gained access to expertise about toxics as a result of their campaigns the state never abandoned its policy of multinational led development. However, the onset of the 'Celtic Tiger' saw the emergence of IT-based technologies as a more popular form of multinational development with polluting industries facing constraints from the EPA on EU legislation and fines.

The issue of resources, either on or off-shore has never been satisfactorily resolved in the Irish case. The 'Shell to Sea' campaign in some ways characterises the ongoing dilemma of Irish resource management. While many European countries have developed energy policies that included resource partnerships with industry the Irish state has sold off all of the resources in the hope of making short term, small economic gains. As a result approaches to the development of mines such as Tynagh, Donegal or Croagh Patrick led to a great deal of community opposition and in the case of Tynagh mines, extensive ecological degradation. And while the type of resource has varied from mineral to uranium to off-shore gas the heavy-handed approach of the state-backed industries involved, alongside the seemingly reckless sell-off of our natural resources, led to a heightened sense of rural territorialism and a discursive process whereby communities reassessed their hinterlands when threatened by outside projects. The response of the state has been to introduce stringent laws to facilitate the compulsory acquisition of land in addition to the establishment of a series of agencies to deal with resource management, many of which seem to favour industry over local concerns.

The Mullaghmore heritage dispute provides us with the best example of a campaign that achieved a successful outcome. The campaign led to a reversal of the state's plans to build an interpretative centre in the Burren. In addition, a wider debate about economic, social and cultural aspects of tourism and heritage was entered into by the supporters and opponents of the centre. When combined with the Burren Action Group's ecological expertise and ability to utilise national and European legal frameworks as sympathetic, discursive and strategic framing patterns were established which provided the campaigners with a successful outcome. Furthermore, national and international interest in the heritage and ecology of Ireland was rekindled. However, the dispute created a dichotomy between local groups opposed to or in favour of the interpretative centre and exposed tensions between local interests that favour economic environment over such interests.

The anti-incinerator disputes in Galway, Meath and Cork had mixed results for local campaigners. In Galway no incinerator has been built at this point. However, licences for incinerators were granted for Meath and Cork in late 2005. While all three campaigns came to be involved in the 2002 general election campaign GSE engaged with a wider group of candidates from both government and opposition parties. This, in addition to the concerns of local politicians who feared an electoral backlash on the issue may have led to plans for a Connacht regional incinerator being shelved. However, the Meath and Cork plants were pivotal to the state's waste management policy which was based on a combination of incineration, landfilling and recycling.

While recycling levels achieved in Galway would make incineration unviable the multinational sector was demanding thermal treatment for industrial waste. The sites at Meath and Cork were adjacent to major urban centres thus creating the momentum for the granting of licences in these areas. While GSE forged political links NIA in Meath and CHASE in Cork took the legal route, a tactic that diminishes any sense of community based sentiment in the context of any subsequent oral hearing (Peace 1993). However, all three anti-incinerator campaigns as well as those in Clare and Dublin have raised awareness about the issue of dioxins.

The introduction of incinerators as part of the state's waste management plans is linked to the wider consumer society which produces waste flows that have led to the exportation of Irish waste to destinations in Asia. These moral issues must be addressed as part of any comprehensive solution to the issue of waste management in the future.

The 'Shell to Sea' campaign has raised the complex issue of a community response to an infrastructural project based on both a sense of grievance about the intrusion of the project in the area and fears about the safety of the gas pipeline. The response of the North Mayo community has emerged from a historically derived sense of place which has been articulated as part of a wider discursive framing process that links cultural nationalism with community based environmentalism. Politically the issue can be traced back to the long standing state policy of selling off resources while facilitating land acquisitions by partners. Local political response has been mixed with Independent TD, Jerry Crowley, supporting the 'Shell to Sea' campaign while mainstream councillors and TDs were ambivalent or chose to favour on-shore development. From a populist perspective the rural or agrarian politics of the Land League has been rekindled while the 'Shell to Sea' campaign has developed an international support network from Ireland to Norway and Nigeria.

The initial phase of rural based community politics which was synonymous with the campaign in its early years has been extended to wider links with a new wave of direct action environmentalists who emanated from the anti-roads or anti-war alliances. The jailing of the five men who challenged the onshore pipeline in their community became the defining event of the campaign as the 'Rossport 5' and their families won a great deal of sympathy and support from the general public. Both the state and subsequently, industry have come to recognise the extent of support 'Shell to Sea' had achieved thus a mediation process was undertaken. This process, chaired by former trades unions' leader Peter Cassells, has been criticised by 'Shell to Sea' spokesperson Maura Harrington. Protestors have converged at the Rossport Solidarity Camp in the area and remain resolute in their stance. They are hopeful of a future where local voices will be heard on this issue. Their protest is part of a culture of mobilisation which has become a feature of modern society (Cox, L. 1999b).

The successive anti-roads campaigns which occurred at the Glen of the Downs, Carrickmines and Tara/Skryne had their inception in the wider anti-roads protests undertaken by Earth First in the late 1980s. This form of direct action has become a feature of the new wave of environmental activism in Ireland; one that combines opposition to growth based ecological degredation with wider issues such as opposition to the War in Iraq. However, the direct action wing of the anti-roads campaign has also extended its wider networks with second-phase anti-infrastructural campaigns including anti-incinerator groups and the 'Shell to Sea' protest. In addition, the anti-roads protestors have extended the debate about heritage in an era when even significant sites such as the Hill of Tara are coming under threat from development projects. A wider debate about the future direction of the nation in a post-growth, post-materialist phase has been embarked on in the wake of these second phase campaigns.

The ongoing fuel crisis, debates about energy alternatives ranging from wind power to nuclear energy and the moral issues of waste flows and emission tradings all remain contentious issues for the Ireland of the future. It remains to be seen whether or not this Green Nation will live up to its image as an island of unspoilt natural beauty, populated by communities rooted in the soil. The environmental campaigns which have contributed to this debate may be based on an instinctive concern for community and hinterland but they have also increased our knowledge of the issues surrounding a rapidly changing Ireland. By reconsidering a community based engagement with the landscape which characterised the past these campaigns have become a movement that may hold the key to our environmental future.

Bibliography

Advantica Consultants

(2006)
'Independent safety review of the offshore section of the proposed Corrib gas pipeline'. Loughborough: Advantica UK. Ltd.

Allen, R.   (1992)

Waste Not Want Not London: Earthscan

_____   (2004)

No Global: The People of Ireland versus the Multinationals London: Pluto

_____   (2006)

"There will always be a Tara" *Ireland from Below* Vol 2 Dublin: IFB

_____ and Jones T.

(1990)
Guests of the Nation: The People of Ireland versus the Multinationals London: Earthscan

Amente, E. and Caren, N. (2004)

"The Legislative, Organisational and Beneficiary Consequences of State: Orientated Challenges" in Snow, D. Soule, A. Kriesi, H. Blackwell companion to Social Movements London: Blackwell

Andersen, B. (1983)

Imagined Communities: Reflections on   Origins and spread of Nationalism London: Verso

Ansell, C. (2003)

"Community Embeddedness and Collaborative Governance in the San Francisco Bay Area Environment Movement" in Diani,

M. & McAdam, D. (eds) (2003)
*Social Movements & Networks:
Relational Approaches to Collective
Action* Oxford: Oxford UP

Arsensberg, C. and
Kimball, S. (1968)

Family and Community in Ireland
Harvard: Harvard University
Press

Bahro, R. (1994)

*Avoiding Social & Ecological
Disaster: The Politics of World
Transformation* Bath: Gateway

Baker, S. (1990)

*The Evolution of the Irish Ecology
Movement* in W. Rudig's *Green
Politics One* Edinburgh: Edinburgh
University Press

_____ (1998)

"The Nuclear Issue in Ireland: The
Role of the Irish Nuclear
Movement" Irish Political Studies,
Vol. 3

Beck, U. (1992)

*Ecological Politics in an Age of
Risk* London: Polity

_____ (1996)

*Risk Society: Towards a New
Modernity* London: Sage

Blackith, R. (1976)

The Power That Corrupts Dublin:
Dublin University Press

Bookchin, M. (1980)

Towards an Ecological Society
Montreal: Black Rose

_____ (1995)

Re-Enchanting Humanity London:
Cassell

Borgetta, E., Borgetta, M.
(1992)

Encyclopaedia of Sociology Vo.4,
London: Simon and Schuster

Bibliography

Boyle, D.   (2002)

          (2002)

"Greens Lodge Incinerator
Objection" Press Release, Cork:
Green Party
"Incineration Company's Claim of
Misrepresentation" Press Release,
Cork: Green Party

Bramwell, A.   (1989)

*Ecology in the 20th Century: A
History* London: Yale University
Press

BreakingNews.ie
          (2004)

"Actor joins motorway protest"
Dublin: BreakingNews.ie 10
October 2004

Burren Action Group
          (1999)

"The Burren: Alternatives
Mullaghmore Visitor Centre: A
Proposal" Burren Action Group

Burnstein, P., Einwohner, R.,
Hollander, J., (1995)

'The success of Political
Movements: A Bargaining
Perspective' in Jenkins, C. and
Klandermans, J. *The Politics of
Social Protest* Minneonapolis:
Minnesota University Press

Cable, S. & Cable, C.
          (1995)

*Environmental Problems:
Grassroots Solutions: The Politics
of Grassroots Environmental
Conflict* New York: St. Martin's
Press

Cambell, P.   (2002)

"Press conference for the campaign
for the Protection of Resources"
Dublin: CFPR

Carroll, J. and

Kelly, P.   (1980)   *A Nuclear Ireland?* Dublin:
                               Transport and General Workers
                               Union

Cassidy, F.   (1998)   "Making the Point" Dublin: *Sunday
                               Tribune*, August 1998

Castells, M.   (1983)   *The City and the Grassroots*
                               London: E. Arnold

_____   (2001)   *The Network Society* Vol. 1
                               London: Blackwell

CHASE   (2001)   Press release (Nov. 13th) "CHASE
                               to oppose Belgian Invader" Cork:
                               wwwchaseireland.org

_____   (2002)   Press release (April 26th) "Zero
                               Waste Groups tell Taoiseach to
                               Dump Incineration" Cork: CHASE

_____   (2003b)   "Incinerator will Definitely Affect
                               Health of Harbour Residents"
                               Cork: CHASE Press Release.

Chrisafis, Angelique
               (2004)   "Fear returns to idyllic bay where
                               the earth moved" London: *The
                               Guardian*, May 29. 2004

Colleran, E. (1989)   Paper given to Aquaculture
                               Conference Galway: University of
                               Galway Press

_____   (2000)   "History of the proposed Visitor
                               Centre/Gortaka Entry Point for the
                               Burren National Park"
                               http//burrenay inst 2000.html

_____   (2003)   'History of the Mullagmore
                               Conflict'
                               http://iol.ie~burrenag.hist.htm

Bibliography

Commins, P. (1986)   "Rural Social Change" from
                                       Clancy, P., Prundy, S., Lynch, K.,
                                       and O'Dowd, L (eds) *Ireland: A
                                       Sociological Perspective* Dublin:
                                       Sociological Association of Ireland

Connolly, F., Lynch, R.
        (2005)   *The Great Corrib Gas Controversy*
                                       Dublin: CPI

Cox, L.   (2006)   "Burning Issue" Review of *Politics
                                       Inflamed* by Leonard, L. *Ireland
                                       from Below*, vol. 2, 2006
        _____ (1999b)   *Structure, Routine and
                                       Transformation: Movements from
                                       Below at the End of the Century'* in
                                       Barker, C. and Tyldersley, M.
                                       (eds.) Fifth International
                                       Conference on Alternative Futures
                                       and Popular Protest. Manchester:
                                       Manchester University Press.

Cronin, M. (2000)   *Across the Lines: Travel,
                                       Language, Translation* Cork: Cork
                                       University Press

Curtin, C. (1986)   "The peasant farm and
                                       commoditisation in the West of
                                       Ireland" in N.Long et al, *The
                                       commoditisation Debate*
                                       Wageningen Agen University.

        _____ and Varley
             (1989)   *Agricultural Co-operatives and
                                       Rural Development in the West of
                                       Ireland* Eire – Ireland 24 (3)

        _____ and Shields
             (1998)
                                       "Social Order, Interpersonal
                                       Relations and disputes in a West of
                                       Ireland Community" in Tomlinson
                                       M., Varley T., McCullagh, C
                                       (1998) *Whose Law & Order?*

_____ (1984)
Kelly, M. and O'Dowd, C. (eds)

Aspects of Irish Crime and Social Control in Society Belfast Sociological Association of Ireland

_____ and Wilson, T.
(1987)

"Culture and Ideology in Ireland Galway": Galway University Press

"Ireland From Below: Social Change and Local Communities Galway": Galway University Press

_____ and Varley, T.
(1989)

Agricultural Co-operatives and Rural Development in the West of Ireland Eire-Ireland 24 (3)

_____and
Varley, T.   (1995)

"Community Action and the State" in P. Clancy, et al (eds.) *Irish Society: Sociological Perspectives* Dublin: Institute of Public Administration

Daily Mail   (2006)

Phillip Nolan "Thank God for the defeat…" Dublin: Irish Daily Mail, 2 March 2006

Dalby, Simon (1998)

The Nuclear Syndrome: Victory for the Irish Anti-Nuclear Power Movement Dublin: Dawn Train: No3 Winter 1984/1985

Davies, A
_____ (2003)

Waste Wars – public attitudes and the politics of place in Waste Management Strategies Irish Geographies Vo. 36 (1) Dublin: University College, Dublin

Davies, J.   (1962)

'Towards a theory of revolution' American Sociological Review Vol XXVII

Bibliography

Deegan, G.   (2005)   "Guarded Welcome for latest
                        initiatives to protect the Burren"
                        Dublin: *Irish Times* April 4, 2005

Della Porta, D. and Diani, M
            (1999)   *Social Movements: An Introduction*
                        London: Blackwell

Diani, M.   (2003)   "Leaders or Brokers? Positions and
                        Influence in Social Movement
                        Networks" in Diani, M. and
                        McAdam, D. *Social Movement and
                        Networks, Relational Approaches
                        to Collective Action* Oxford:
                        Oxford University Press

Doherty, P.   (2004)   "Doherty demands full
                        investigation of Shell in Ireland"
                        Dublin: Sin Fein Press Release, 23
                        April 04

Dryzek, J.   (1997)   *The Politics of the Earth:
                        Environmental Discourses* Oxford:
                        Oxford University Press

Duffy, M.   (2005)   "Norwegian mission was deciding
                        factor" Castlebar: *Mayo News* 4
                        Oct 05

Earl, J.   (2000)   "Methods, Movements and
                        Outcomes: Methodological
                        Differences in the Study of Extra-
                        Movement Outcomes" Research in
                        Social Movements, Conflict and
                        Change. London: Blackwell

_____   (2004)   "The Cultural Consequences of
                        Social Movements" in Snow, D.,
                        Soule, S., and Kriesi, H., *The
                        Blackwell Companion to Social
                        Movements.* London: Blackwell

Eckersley, R.   (1992)   *Environmentalism and Political*
                                Theory: Towards an Ecocentric
                                Approach London: University
                                College London Press

Edmondson, R. (1999)   *The Political Context of Collective*
                                Action, Argumentation &
                                Democracy London: Routledge

Eisinger, P.   (1973)   "The Conditions of Protest
                                Behaviour in American Cities"
                                American Political Science
                                Review, Vol. 67 p. 116

Fagan, H.   (2003)   "Sociological Reflections on
                                Governing West" Irish Journal of
                                Sociology Vol 12 No.1

Feehan, T.   (1991)   *Environment and Development in*
                                Ireland: Proceedings of a
                                conference held at UCD, 9-13th
                                December 1991 Dublin: The
                                University College Dublin
                                Environment Institute

Ferree, M. and Miller, F.
                (1985)   "Mobilisation and Meaning:
                                Towards an Integration of
                                Psychological and Resource
                                Perspectives on Social
                                Movements". Sociological Inquiry
                                55

Fillieule, O., Jiminez, M.
                (2003)   "The Methodology of Protest Event
                                Analysis and Media Politics of
                                Reporting Environmental Events"
                                in Rootes, C. (ed) (2003)
                                Environmental Protest in Western
                                Europe Oxford, Oxford University
                                Press

Bibliography

Fisher, F   (1999)   "Participatory expertise and the
                                           Politics of Local Knowledge: a post
                                           positive perspective" in *The
                                           Political Context of Collective
                                           Action, Argumentation and
                                           Democracy* in R. Edmondson (ed)
                                           London: Routledge

Freudenberg, N. and Steinsapir, C.
                 (1992)   "Not in Our Backyards: The
                                           Grassroots Environmental
                                           Movement" in Dunlear, R &
                                           Mertig, A. "American
                                           Environmentalism 1970 – 1990"
                                           Philadelphia

Friedman & McAdam
                 (1992)   "Meanalities, Political, Cultures
                                           and Collective Action Frames" in
                                           Morris, A., McLurg, Mueller, C.,
                                           Frontiers in Social Movement
                                           London: Yale University Press

Friel, Laura.
                 (2005)   "The Other End of the Rainbow:
                                           Gold Mining comes to Tyrone
                                           Belfast" *An Phoblact / Republican
                                           News*

Gamson, W.
                 (1975)   *The Strategy of Social Protest.*
                                           Belmont, California: Wadsworth

_____
                 (1988)   *International Social Movement
                                           Research* Vol.1 Greenwich JAI
                                           Press

_____
                 (1992)   "The   Social   Psychology   of
                                           Collective Action" in *Frontiers in
                                           Social Movement Theory* Aldon
                                           and   C.McClurgh   Mueller   (eds.)
                                           New Haven: Yale University Press

———— (1998)   "Political Discourse and Collective
                           Action" from Klandermans et al,
                           From Structure to Action
                           Greenwich: JAI Press

———— (2004)   'Discursive Opportunity Structures'
                           in Snow, D., Soule, S., Kreisi, H.
                           *The Blackwell Companion to Social
                           Movements* London: Blackwell

Garavan, M.
(2004)   *The Patterns of Irish
                           Environmentalism.* Unpublished
                           Phd Thesis, National University of
                           Ireland Galway

Garner, R.
(2000)   *Environmental Politics: Britain,
                           Europe and the Global
                           Environment* London: McMillan
                           2nd Edition

Gavin, S. O'Brádaigh, C.
(2002)   'Submission to Galway City &
                           County Councils' GSWA

Geraghty, D.   (2006)
                           "€312 project breathes life back
                           into disused Tynagh Mines site"
                           Galway Advertiser March
                           10 2006

Giddens, A.   (1984)
                           The Constitution of Society
                           Cambridge: Polity

Green, B.   (1996)   *Countryside Conservation:
                           Landscape, ecology, planning and
                           management (3rd ed)* London:
                           E&FN SPON

Grove-White, R.

Bibliography

(1993)   "Environmentalism: A New Moral
                           Discourse for Technological
                           Society" in Milton, K., (ed)
                           *Environmentalism: The View from
                           Anthropology* London: Routledge

Habermas, J.   (1972)   *Legitimation Crisis* London:
                           Routledge

Hajer, M.   (1995)
                           *The Politics of Environmental
                           Discourse:
                           Ecological Modernisation and the
                           Policy Process*
                           Oxford: Oxford University Press

Hardiman, N., (1994)   "Values and Political Partisanship"
                           in N. Hardiman and C. Whelan
                           (eds) *Values and Social Change in
                           Ireland* Dublin: Gill and McMillan

Harris, L.   (1984)   "Class, community and sexual
                           divisions in County Mayo" in
                           Curtin, C., Kelly, M., O'Dowd, L.
                           (eds) *Culture and Ideology in
                           Ireland* Galway: Galway
                           University Press

Hart, S.   (1996)   "The Cultural Dimension of Social
                           Movements: A Theoretical
                           Assessment & Literature Review"
                           Sociology of Religion 57

Haugaard, M. (1997)   *The Constitution of Power: A
                           theoretical Analysis of Power and
                           Structure.* Manchester: Manchester
                           University Press

Hearne, R   (2005)   "Whose Gas? Whose Land? Whose
                           world?" Interview with the
                           Rossport Five. *Ireland from Below*,
                           November 2005.

Hearns, O.   (2005)   "Deep division in Erris" Castlebar:
                                      Western People Oct 26 05

Inglehart, R.   (1977)   "The Silent Generation in Europe:
                                      Inter-Generational Change in Post-
                                      Industrial Societies" American
                                      Political Science Review Vol 65:
                                      pp. 991-1017

_____   (1977)   *The Silent Revolution: Changing*
                                      Values and Political Styles Among
                                      Western Public Princeton New
                                      Jersey: Princeton University Press

Irish Examiner,
                (2002)   "Mayo Gas Deal Queried" Cork:
                                      The Irish Examiner

Janicke, M   (1997)

                                      National Environmental Policies
                                      Berlin: Springer

Jenkins, J.   (1983)

                                      "Resource Mobilisation Theory"
                                      Annual Review of Sociology 9
Jones, T.   (1988)   "A Tale of Merck" Earthwatch
                                      Issue 8 Autumn 1988 Bantry:
                                      Earthwatch Ltd

Kavanagh, A. (2004)   "The 2004 local elections in the
                                      Republic of Ireland" Irish Political
                                      Studies, Vol.19, No 2 London:
                                      Routledge

Kehoe, I.   (2005)   "Norwegian government pushed
                                      for Rossport deal" Dublin: Sunday
                                      Business Post, 2 October 05.

Kelleher, C. and O'Mahony, A.
                (1984)   *Marginalisation in Irish*
                                      Agriculture Dublin: An Foras
                                      Taluntais

Kelly, O.   (2005)   "Rabbitte has plans…"Dublin:
                                      Irish Times 31 August 05

Bibliography

Keogh, E.   (2005)   "Lobby group fears a nuclear North Cork": Irish Examiner Dec. 30 2005.

Kiprewitz, R. (2005)   *The Proposed Corrib Onshore System*: *An Independent Analysis* Dublin: CPI

Kitching, G. (1989)   *Development and Underdevelopment in Historical Perspective: Populism, Nationalism and Industrialisation* London: Routledge

Kitschelt, H (1986)   "Political Opportunity Structures and Political Protest in Four Countries" British Journal of Political Science 16

Kissel, P.   (2005)   "Rossport Saga…" Castlebar: *Western People*, August 9, 2005

Klandermans, B., Kriesi, H., Tarrow, S. (eds)
                (1988)   *From Structure to Action* International Social Movement Research Vol. 1 Greenwich: JAI Press

Klandermans, B.
                (1989)   *Grievance interpretation and Success Expectations: the Social construction of Protest* Social Behaviour 4 pp. 113-25

_____ (ed)
                (1989)   *Organising for Change* International Social Movement Research Vol. 2 Greenwich: JAI Press

Koopmann, N. and
Stratham, P.   (1999)   "Political Claims Analysis: Integrating Protest Event Analysis

and Political Discourse Approaches" ICS. Leeds AC. UK

Kousis, M.   (2002)   "Environmental Impact of Tourism" from Barry, J. and Frenkland, E.G. (eds) *International Encyclopaedia of Environmental Politics* London: Routledge

Kriesi, H.   (1984)   *Die Zürcher Benegung* Frankfurt: Campus

_____   (1986)   "The Local Mobilisation of the People's Politics of the Dutch Peace Movement" unpublished Paper to the University of Amsterdam

_____   (1989)   *The Political Opportunity Structure of the Dutch Peace Movement* West European Politics 12-295, 312

_____   (1995)   "The Political Opportunity Structure of New Social Movements; Its Impact on the Mobilisation from the Politics of Social Protest" J. Jenkins and B. Klandermans: *The Politics of Social Protest* London: UCL

_____, Koopman, R., Duyvendak, JW. and Liugni, M.
        (1995)   *New Social Movements in Western Europe: A Comparative Analysis* London: Routledge

_____   (2001)   "Political Context and Opportunity" in Snow, Soule, S. and Kriesi, H. (eds) the *Blackwell Companion to Social Movements* London: Blackwell

Laffan, S., Wall, B.

Bibliography

(1988)	"Gold Frenzy Threatens the West" Earthwatch Autumn 1988 Issue 8 Bantry: Earthwatch Ltd
Leonard, L. (1999)	"Ecolaoicht Na hEireann: Irish Environmental Policy" unpublished M.Phil. Thesis: NUI Galway
_____ (2003)	*The New Technologies of Communication and Environmental Protest* Review of Postgraduate Studies Vol. 11, Galway: NUI Galway
_____ (2005)	*Politics Inflamed: GSE and the Campaign Against Incineration in Ireland.* Ecopolitics Series Volume One, Drogheda: Choice Publishing

Lewicki, R., Gray, B., Elliot, M.
(2003)   *Making Sense of Intractable Environmental Conflicts* London: Island

Low, S., Lawerence- Zúñiga, D.
(2003)   *The Anthropology of Space and Place: Locating Culture* Oxford: Blackwell

MacAdam, D. (1983)   "Tactical Innovation and the Pace of Insurgency" American Sociological Review 48: pp735-754

_____, McCarthy, J., Zald, N.
(1988)   "Social Movements" from Smelser, J. (ed) *Handbook of Sociology* London: Sage

Marcuse, H. (1991)   *One Dimensional Man* London: Bramwell

Marsden, T., Murdock, J., Lowe, P., Minton, R., Flynn, A

| | (1993) | *Constructing the Countryside* London: University College Press |

McAdam, D. (1982) *Political Process and the Development of Black Insurgency 1930 – 1970* Chicago: University of Chicago Press

_____ (1986) "Recruitment to High-Risk Activism: The Case of Freedom Summer" American Journal of Sociology 92 64-90

_____ (1988a) *Freedom Summer* New York: Oxford University Press

McCarthy, J. and Zald, N.
(1977) "Resource Mobilisation and Social Movements: A Partial Theory" American Journal of Sociology 82

_____ (1981) *Social Movements in an Organisational Society* New Brunswick NJ:

McConnell, I. (1971) *Earth Day Proclamation* New York: United Nations

McDonald, F. and Nix, T.
(2005) *Chaos at the Crossroads* Kinsale: Gandon

McGrath, B. (1995) *The Mist-Covered Mountain: Change, Conflict and Identity in Ireland's Countryside – The Case of a planned development at Mullaghmore, Co. Clare* Unpublished Masters Thesis, Galway: National University of Ireland Galway

_____ (1996) "Environmentalism and Property Rights" Irish Journal of Sociology, Vol. 6, pp 25-48

Bibliography

McNally, L., O'Brien, T.
    (2005)   "Jailed Mayo men accuse Shell..."
                        Dublin: *Irish Times*, 21 Aug 05

McWilliams, D.
    (2005)   *The Pope's Children: Ireland's*
                        New Elite Dublin: Gill & McMillan

Melucci, A. (1985)

                        "The Symbolic Challenge of
                        Contemporary Social
                        Movements" Social Research 52

Meyer, C.   (1999)

                        'Globalisation and Rising
                        Inequality in Developed Countries'.
                        Global Business and Economic
                        Review 1 (1)

Mol, A. and
Sonnefeld, D. (2000)

                        "Ecological Modernisation around
                        the World: an introduction"
                        Environmental Politics
                        Vol. 9

Morris, A., Staggenbory, S. (2004) 'Leadership in Social Movements'
                        in Snow, D. Soule, S. and Kriesi,
                        H. *The Blackwell Companion to*
                        Social Movements London:
                        Blackwell

Mueller, C. (1999)   "Protest Event Analysis"
                        Mobilization No 4 (z)

Murray, R. (2002)   *Zero Waste plan for the UK*
                        London: Greenpeace

Myers, D. and
Oliver, P.   (1999)   "Diffusion Models of Cycles of
                        Protest as a Theory of Social
                        Movements" University of
                        Wisconsin

No Incineration
Alliance   (2002)   "An Bord Pleanála Planning
                                     Appeal" Meath: NIA

Offe, C.   (1984)   *Contradictions of the Social
                                     Welfare State* London: Hutchinson

Oliver, P. and
Colleran, E.(1989)   *Interactions between Agriculture
                                     and the Environment* Dublin: An
                                     Taisce

Oliver, P., Myers, D.
             (1998)   "Diffusion Models of Cycles of
                                     Protest as a Theory of Social
                                     Movements" Montreal: Congress
                                     of the International Sociological
                                     Association

O'Doherty, C.
             (2003)   "Carrickmines dispute deepens"
                                     Cork: Irish Examiner 17 2 03

O'Hearn, D.
             (1999)   *Inside the Celtic Tiger : The Irish
                                     Economy and the Asian Model*
                                     London: Pluto

O'Leary, M.
             (2003)   "Submission by CHASE to the
                                     EPA Oral Hearing on the
                                     expanding of a Draft Licence for a
                                     toxic waste incinerator at
                                     Ringaskiddy, Co. Cork" Cork:
                                     CHASE

O'Riordan, T. (1981)   *Environmentalism* London: Pion
                                     Zedn

O'Seighin, M.
             (2005)   "Corrib gas pipeline development
                                     to date": Mayo www.corribsos.com
                                     5 July 2005.

Bibliography

O'Sullivan, J.   (2000)   "An approach to resolving the current waste crisis" Dublin: Irish Environmental and Planning Law Journal, Vol 8 No 1, pp 20-25

O'Toole, F.   (1994)   *Blackhole, Greencard: The Disappearance of Ireland* Dublin: New Ireland Books

Peace, A.   (1993)   "Environmental Protest, Bureaucratic Disclosure: The Politics of Discourse in Rural Ireland" in K. Miton (ed), (1993) *Environmentalism: The view from Anthropology*: London: Routledge

          (1997)   *A Time of Reckoning: The Politics of Discourse in Rural Ireland* London: Routledge

          (2005)   "A Sense of Place, A Place of Sense: Land and a Landscape in the West of Ireland" Journal of Anthropological Research Winter 2005 Vol 61 New Mexico: University of New Mexico University Press.

Pellion, M.   (1982)   *Contemporary Irish Society: An Introduction* Dublin: Gill & McMillan

Pepper, D.   (1993)   *Modern Environmentalism: An Introduction* London: Routledge

Phyne, J.   (1996)   "Biological Warfare: Salmon fishing, Angling Tourism and the Sea Trust Dispute in the West of Ireland" 1989-95 Irish Journal of Sociology, Vol. 6

Piven, F., Cloward, R.
          (1997)   *Poor People's Movements* New York: Panteron

RDRA   (2001)   *Ringaskiddy – A Living Community not a toxic dump (Enough is Enough):* Cork RDRA

RTE News   (2002)   "Laying of Corrib offshore pipeline delayed Report" July 2002, Dublin: www.RTE.ie

_____   (2004)   "Brennan welcomes Carrickmines ruling" Dublin: RTE 1/06/04

RPS Cains Ltd
            (1994)   "Burren National Park Visitor Centre" Environmental Impact Statement OPW: Dublin

Sabel, C., Fung, A., Karkkainen, B.
            (2005)   "Beyond Backyard Environmentalism: How Communities are Quietly Refashioning Environmental Regulation" from Dryzek, J. and Schlasberg, D. "Debating the Earth, Land and Sea"

Showbiz Ireland
            (2004)   "Townsend a Skryne Legend" www.showbizIreland.com 11 October 2004

Siggins, L.   (2005)   "Shell accused..." Dublin: *Irish Times* 17 November 2005

_____   (2005)   "Board denies..." Dublin: *Irish Times* 24 November 2005

_____   (2005)   "Shell rejects...review" Dublin: *Irish Times* December 27 2005)

_____   (2005)   "Mayo deputies dispute..."Dublin: *Irish Times*, July 20, 2005

Bibliography

_____	(2005)	"Dempsey sets up body to monitor gas project" *Irish* Times July 25, 2005.
_____	(2005)	"Pipeline to go ahead..." Dublin: *Irish Times*, August 3, 2005
_____	(2005)	"Mayo County Council to meet..." Dublin *Irish Times*, August 4, 2005
_____	(2005)	"Shell and Councillors in talks..." Dublin *Irish Times* 20 August 05
_____	(2005)	"Released men insist Minister must join talks" Dublin: *Irish Times* October 3 05
Scott, A.	(1990)	*Ideology and the New Social Movements.* London: Unwin Hyman
Scruggs, L.	(1999)	"Institutions and Environmental Performance in 17 Western Democracies" British Journal of Political Studies Cambridge: UP
Shell to Sea	(2002)	"Residents welcome gas plan delay" Press Release, www.corribsos.com
_____	(2005)	"High Court Action: Background" Mayo www.corribsos.com (10 June 5)
_____	(2005)	"The West's Awake" Website of the 'Shell to Sea' Campaign: www.corribsos.com
Smelser, N.	(1962)	*Theory of Collective Behaviour* New York: Free Press
Solomon, M.	(2002)	*Consumer Behaviour* 5th Edition London: Prentice Hall

Snow, D., Benford, R.,
(1988)   "Ideology, Frame Resonance and
Participant Mobilisation" from
Klandermans et al *From Structure
to Action* Greenwich: JAI Press

Snow, D., Soule, S.,
and Kriesi, H. (2004)   *The Blackwell Companion to Social
Movements* London: Blackwell

Storey, D.   (2001)   *Territory: The Claiming of Space*
London: Prentice Hall

Szasz, A.   (1994)   *Ecopopulism: Toxic Waste and the
Movement for Environmental
Justice* London: Minnesota Press

Taylor, G.   (2001)   *Conserving the Emerald Tiger: The
Politics of Environmental
Regulation in Ireland* Galway:
Arlen Press

Taylor, L.   (1989)   "The Mission: An Anthropological
view of an Irish religious occasion"
in Curtin, C. and Wilson, T.,
*Ireland from Below: Social Change
and Local Communities* Galway:
Galway University Press

Tarrow, S.   (1994)   *Power in Movement: Social
Movements, Collective Action and
Politics* Cambridge: Cambridge UP

_____   (1998)   *Power in Movement: Social
Movements and Contentious
Politics*: 2nd Edition Cambridge:
Cambridge UP

The *Irish Examiner*
(1999)   "Rain fails to dampen protestors'
spirits" Cork: The *Irish Examiner*
December 1999

Bibliography

Tilly, C.   (2004)   Social Movements 1768-2004
                                         London: Paradigm

Tilly, C., Tilly, L., Tilly, R.,
          (1975)   *The Rebellious Century 1830-1930*
                                         Cambridge: Harvard University
                                         Press

Tovey, H.   (1992 a)   *Rural Sociology in Ireland: A*
                                         Review Irish Journal of Sociology,
                                         Vol.2, 1992, pp 96-121 Dublin:
                                         SAI

_____   (1992 b)   "Environmentalism in Ireland"
                                         from Clancy, P., Kelly, M., Wiatr,
                                         J. and Zoltaniecki, R. (eds.) Ireland
                                         and Poland: Comparative
                                         Perspectives Dublin: UCD Press

_____   (2002)   A Review of *Escaping the Global*
                                         Village by Niamh Hourigan
                                         Dublin: Irish Journal of Sociology
_____, Share, P
          (2003)   *A Sociology of Ireland* 2nd edition,
                                         Dublin: Gill and MacMillan

Tracey, C.   (2003)   *Policy on housing in rural areas*
                                         Dublin: Irish Planning Institute

Travers, J.   (2000)   "The Evolution of Economic
                                         Policies in the Rep. of Ireland"
                                         Dublin: Forfas

Tucker, R.   (1998)   *The Marz – Engels Reader* New
                                         York: Norton

Turner, R. and Killian, L. (1990)   *Collective Behaviour* Englewood
                                         Cliffs, NJ@ Prentice Hall

Varley, T.   (1988)   "Rural Development and
                                         Combating Poverty" Galway:
                                         Social Science Research Centre

_____, Boylan, T., Cuddy, M. (eds)

<table>
<tr><td>(1991)</td><td>*Rural Crisis: Perspectives in Irish Rural Development* Galway: Centre for Development Studies, University College Galway</td></tr>
</table>

| _____ | (1991) | "Power to the People? Community Groups and Rural Revival in Ireland", from Hardiman, N. and Whelan, C. (1984) "Politics and Democratic Values", from Whelan. C. (ed) *Values and Social Change in Ireland* Dublin Gill and McMillan |

| _____ | (1991 b) | Book Review of R. Allen and T. Jones, *Guests of the Nation: The People of Ireland vs the Multinationals* Irish Journal of Sociology Vol. 1, 1991, pp. 184 – 187 |

| Walsh, E. | (2006) | 'Nuclear energy "the safest of all".' Dublin: Irish Times April 26 2006 |

| Walsh, Warland and Smith (1970) | | *Don't Burn It Here: Grassroots Challenges to Trash Incinerators* Pennsylvania: Pennsylvania University Press |

| Waste, R. | (1986) | *Community Power: Directions for Future Research* Beverly Hills CA. Sage |

| Whitty, T. | (1988) | "Jobs at any price?" Earthwatch Issue No. 8 Autumn 1988 Bantry: Earthwatch Ltd. |

| Wilson, J., | (1973) | *Introduction to Social Movements* New York: Basic Books |

Bibliography

WISE   (1978)   "Irish Anti-Nuke Show"
                             Amsterdam: WWE Bulletin July
                             1978, Vol.2

Young, T.   (1989)   *The Drama of Social Life: Essays
                             in Post-Modern Social Psychology*
                             New Brunswick NJ. Transaction

Acronyms

ALF	Animal Liberation Front
ASI	Areas of Scientific Interest
ATM	Anti-Toxics Movement
BAG	Burren Action Group
BNPSA	Burren National Park Support Association
BNFL	British Nuclear Fuel Limited
BATNEEC	Best Available Technology Not Entailing Excessive Costs
CASP	Cork Area Strategy Plan
CAP	Common Agricultural Policy
CHASE	Cork Harbour for A Safe Environment
CND	Campaign for Nuclear Disarmament
CWP	Connacht Waste Plan
CONSERVE	Council for Nuclear Safety and Energy Resource
DUC	Donegal Uranium Committee
EM	Ecological Modernisation
EEC	European Economic Community
EPA	Environmental Protection Agency
ESA	Environmentally Sensitive Area
ESB	Electricity Supply Board
ESF	European Structural Fund
FOE	Friends of the Earth
GAA	Gaelic Athletic Association
GSE	Galway for a Safe Environment
GWSA	Galway Safe Waste Alliance
Gold EIA	Gold Environmental Impact Assessment
GSE	Galway for a Safe Environment
HAS	Health and Safety Authority
HD	Habitats Directive
HRB	Health Research Bureau
IDA	Industrial Development Authority
IFA	Irish Farmers Association
IPC	Integrated Pollution Control
INPC	Irish National Petroleum Corporation
ITGWU	Irish Transport and General Workers' Union
MA	Mining Awareness

MEG	Mayo Environmental Group
NATO	North Atlantic Treaty Organisation
NDP	National Development Plan
NEB	Nuclear Energy Board
NHA	National Heritage Area
NIA	No Incinerator Alliance
NIES	Northern Ireland Electric Services
NIMBY	Not in my backyard
NGO	Non-Governmental Organisation
NRA	National Roads Authority
NSA	Nuclear Safety Association
NSC	Nuclear Safety Committee
POS	Political Opportunity Structure
RDRA	Ringaskiddy Residents and District Residents Association
RM	Resource Mobilisation
RPG	Resources Protection Group
SCM	Student Christian Movement
SESI	Solar Energy Society of Ireland
SFADCo	Shannon Free Airport Development Company
TNC	Trans National Corporation
THORP	Thermal Oxide Reprocessing Plant
USEPA	United States Environmental Protection Agency
WISE	World Antinuclear Service on Energy
WVPA	Womanagh Valley Protection Agency
WWF	World Wide Fund for Nature